DATE DUE

12:30			
12:15			
1:00			
10:41			
2:27			
10:34			
12:57			
GAYLORD			PRINTED IN U.S.A.

Owning Up

OWNING UP

Poverty, Assets, and
the American Dream

MICHELLE MILLER-ADAMS

BROOKINGS INSTITUTION PRESS
Washington, D.C.

Copyright © 2002
THE BROOKINGS INSTITUTION
1775 Massachusetts Avenue, N.W., Washington, D.C. 20036
www.brookings.edu

Library of Congress Cataloging-in-Publication data

Miller-Adams, Michelle, 1959–
   Owning up : poverty, assets, and the American dream / Michelle
Miller-Adams.
    p. cm.
Includes bibliographical references and index.
   ISBN 0-8157-0620-0 (cloth : alk. paper)—
   ISBN 0-8157-0619-7 (pbk. : alk paper)
   1. Poverty—Government policy—United States. 2. Poor—United
States—Finance, Personal. 3. Saving and investment—Government
policy—United States. 4. Economic assistance, Domestic—United States.
5. Public welfare—United States. 6. Welfare recipients—United
States—Economic conditions. 7. United States—Economic
conditions—1981–2001. I. Title.
   HC110.P6 M54 2002   2002008634
   362.5'82—dc21   CIP

9 8 7 6 5 4 3 2 1

The paper used in this publication meets minimum requirements of the
American National Standard for Information Sciences—Permanence of
Paper for Printed Library Materials: ANSI Z39.48-1992.

Typeset in Sabon

Composition by Stephen D. McDougal
Mechanicsville, Maryland

Printed by R. R. Donnelley and Sons
Harrisonburg, Virginia

To my grandparents,
Edith Dubin and Murray Miller,
who built a brighter future
for their children and grandchildren,
and to my daughter,
Eliana,
in the hope that hers
will be brighter still

Contents

Acknowledgments

When I was asked by the Ford Foundation to write a book that would introduce the idea of building assets for the poor to a broad readership, I knew that it would be critical to present the stories of real people and real places. Asset building is currently attracting attention in policy circles and academia, and *Owning Up* draws on both spheres to introduce readers to the concepts in which asset-based strategies are rooted. But the power of the approach is most evident when one examines the day-to-day existence of poor individuals and the communities in which they live. Only then does it become clear how asset-building efforts can create not just wealth, but hope.

I am deeply indebted to the individuals about whom I have written (all of whom elected to have their real names used) and the institutions and communities of which they are a part. Without the cooperation and openness of the leadership, staff, and participants in the asset-building programs I studied, this book would not have been possible: all quoted material that is not cited in an endnote comes from interviews with staff, clients, and others associated with the organizations profiled. From New York City to Kansas City, in Michigan, Iowa, and California, I have had the privilege of getting to know an exceptionally committed and generous group of people. They include: Denise Washington and the staff of Neighborhoods Incorporated of Battle Creek, including Pat Massey, Cherise Brandell, Teri Barker, and Zoe Kimmel, along with Michael Collins of the Neighborhood Reinvestment Corporation; Sandra Bradford and the staff of Wildcat Service Corporation, including Karen Shaffer, as well as Jeffrey Jablow of Origin, Inc.; Marguerite Sisson and the staff of the Institute for Social and Economic Development, especially Jason Friedman, John Else, Christine Mollenkopf-Pigsley, Jane Duax, and Angela Gravely-Smith; Lynn Jungwirth and the staff, crew, and supporters of the Watershed Research and Training Center, Cecilia Danks and Jan Mountjoy in particular, as well as Barry Shelley of the University of Massachusetts at Amherst; Regina Blackmon, George Clark, and Miguel Juarez in Kansas City, Missouri, and Dennis Boody, Kathy Kane, and Julie Riddle of Heart of America Family Services; Ray Boshara, Bob Friedman, and Brian Grossman of the Corporation for Enterprise Development, and Michael Sherraden of the Center for Social Development. All of these individuals provided invaluable insights into the creation of new asset-building instruments and the impact they can have on the lives of the poor.

The research for this book was carried out with the generous financial support of the Ford Foundation. Bernard Wasow had the foresight to include the project among a set of grants designed to enhance public understanding of asset building, and he has continued to provide advice and encouragement. Michael Conroy is the program officer who assumed responsibility for the project and saw it through with kindness and generosity. The intellectual inspiration and assistance provided by Melvin Oliver is also gratefully acknowledged. In addition, my thanks go to the editors of the volumes included in the Ford Foundation Series on Asset Building published by the Russell Sage Foundation. These volumes, as well as the conferences on which they were based, contain a wealth of information that greatly enhanced my understanding of the asset-building field.

At Brookings Institution Press, a special word of thanks to Bob Faherty and Chris Kelaher for their support throughout the publication process, to Robin DuBlanc for her excellent editorial suggestions, and to two anonymous reviewers for their comments. Research assistance by Dalene Allebaugh in the early stages of the project was immensely helpful. Vicky Stein, my friend of twenty-plus years, was a font of enthusiasm and ideas. My husband, Richard Adams, played an essential role in the completion of this project through his encouragement, critical faculties, and confidence in me. Our daughter, Eliana Marie Adams, was born just as I was finishing the revision of this manuscript. Her arrival has given me a new appreciation of the lengths to which parents will go to bequeath to their children the best future possible, and an even deeper gratitude to my parents, Rachel Galperin and Gerald Miller, for the investments they made in me every step of the way.

OWNING UP

CHAPTER ONE

Building
Assets

As the twentieth century drew to a close, the economic news in the United States could not have been better. Almost two decades had passed since the last real recession. The stock market boom, under way since the mid-1990s, was bringing new wealth not only to the upper classes but to millions in the middle class who had only recently become investors. In 2000, the poverty rate fell to its lowest level in close to thirty years, with rates for the elderly, African Americans, and female-headed households dropping to all-time lows. Unemployment, too, subsided to a thirty-year low and median household income reached a new high. Even the income gap between rich and poor, which had widened sharply between the mid-1970s and 1993, showed signs of narrowing.[1]

A troubling fact eluded most observers. Prolonged economic expansion had actually exacerbated one of the starkest divisions in American society: the distribution of assets, or family wealth.[2] A few statistics provide some insight into the magnitude of this growing divide. Between 1983 and 1998, the wealthiest 1 percent of households saw their average wealth rise by 42 percent, while the average wealth of the poorest 40 percent of households fell by 76 percent. In 1998, the top 1 percent of families owned 38 percent of the nation's total wealth and the top 20 percent held 83 percent. The bottom 40 percent of families held less than one-half of 1 percent; the average wealth of the 41 million households in this category was only $1,100.[3] This asset gap dwarfs the income disparities that are the regular focus of media attention.

What are assets and why do they matter? Assets can be defined in several ways. In a narrow sense, an asset is something that represents a monetary value for its owner—a home or car that can be sold for cash, a bank account or stock market investment, equity in a business. But the notion of assets goes beyond the tangible items that might show up on a balance sheet. The dictionary defines an asset as "any useful or valuable quality or thing, an advantage." In this sense, a list of one's assets includes not only the economic resources mentioned above but less tangible attributes like good health, work experience, a special talent, a college degree, or strong family and community ties.

This book is about assets and the difference they can make in the lives of the poor. It is also about *asset building*: a broad range of efforts to help low-income people acquire new assets and sustain or improve the quality of the assets they already possess. Four kinds of assets are addressed here. *Economic assets* are those included in traditional concepts of wealth: equity in a home or business, retirement savings, the value of an insurance policy, and a broad range of other financial and real holdings. *Human assets* encompass the education, knowledge, skills, and talents that enable individuals to support themselves and their families and that play a crucial role in national productivity. *Social assets* are those networks of trust and reciprocity that bind communities together and allow people to work collectively to improve the quality of their lives. *Natural assets* refer to the land, water, air, forests, and other natural resources that surround us and on which we depend for survival.

Whether they are economic, human, social, or natural, a central feature of assets is their staying power. Assets provide security for hard times, a buffer when things go wrong. A savings account can be drawn upon when illness strikes, home equity borrowed against when one is out of work. Well-managed land, rivers, or forests can provide a rural community with its livelihood for many generations. Tangible assets, such as money, a business, or a home, can be shared with those in need or passed from parent to child. Intangible assets, too, give future generations a head start. The children of college-educated parents are likely to go to college themselves, and a child's prospects are brighter if he or she is raised in a community where the social fabric is strong. Even very modest assets can lead to major changes: most low-income families can purchase a home with a down payment of less than $3,000, the average annual tuition at a community college is $1,500, and most new businesses in the United States are capitalized with less than $5,000.[4]

Assets have strong psychological benefits as well. Most families living in poverty find themselves focusing on the day-to-day challenge of making ends meet. If they are able to acquire assets, it becomes easier to envision and set goals for the future. People with assets are more willing to take risks such as starting a business or learning a new trade. The aim of helping people build assets is not wealth for its own sake but the advantages wealth almost always brings: stability, security, and a greater degree of self-reliance for individuals and communities.

Many people have followed an asset-building path out of poverty, including my own grandparents, who arrived in the United States in the 1920s. Like most poor immigrants, they came not just to escape harsh conditions in their homeland or simply to survive. They came to get ahead. While it turned out the streets were not paved with gold, there were opportunities for those willing to work hard. Both entrepreneurship and education had their rewards. My paternal grandfather hustled in a series of jobs, learned a trade along the way, and became a successful businessman. My maternal grandmother put her stock in education, insisting that her daughters do well in school and encouraging them to go to college. Setting their sights high and believing in the future, they built a better life for their children and grandchildren.

My grandparents understood intuitively the role assets could play in lifting them out of poverty. Today's immigrants have followed similar paths. Some open small businesses and work long hours, expecting their children to apply themselves equally hard to their studies. Some bond together in ethnic enclaves, benefiting from close networks of connections that bring them jobs and business opportunities. A similar asset-building path has been followed also by the many native-born Americans who have moved from poverty into the middle class by dint of education and hard work.

Many others have been left behind. Even with the recent decline in the poverty rate, 31 million Americans, or 11.3 percent of the population, are officially considered poor.[5] And while the most disadvantaged groups in society have seen some gains, the distribution of poverty remains far from equal. Sixteen percent of children are poor, as are 25 percent of female-headed households. Neither can the racial dimension of poverty be ignored, with poverty rates of 22 percent for blacks and 21 percent for Hispanics compared to 7.5 percent for whites. Thirty percent of black children are poor. (Present poverty figures have been called "almost meaningless" by Robert B. Reich, among others.[6] The formula under which they are calculated dates back decades and substantially underrepresents the actual needs of families. Efforts are under way by the Census Bureau to develop a more accurate measure, but progress is slow, in part because few politicians or government officials are eager to see a sudden jump in the number of families categorized as poor.)

Despite the success of welfare reform in moving people off public assistance and into jobs, many of those who have gone to work earn incomes that leave them below the poverty line and sometimes even worse off than they were on welfare. While the percentage of people in poverty has fallen, there is evidence that those who remain in this category are poorer than ever.[7] The number of homeless families seeking shelter in the nation's largest cities continued to rise throughout the economic expansion, as did requests for emergency food aid. In fact, census data show that the percentage of poor families in danger of going hungry actually increased between 1995 and 1999.[8]

Why have so many Americans failed to benefit from the unprecedented economic boom that enriched so many others? Some of those left behind are consumed with the immediate struggle for survival and simply cannot focus on the longer term. Others do not have the knowledge of new opportunities or the awareness to exploit them. Still others may have ambitious goals but lack the money or credit to overcome the barriers to achieving them. Public policy, too, has played a role. Even as the government made it possible for middle-class and wealthy Americans to build assets, it discouraged asset accumulation among the poor. The antipoverty programs developed during the 1930s and expanded in the 1960s and 1970s aimed to eradicate poverty but instead just blurred its harshest edges. Welfare payments, food stamps, and public housing subsidies helped families keep their heads above water from month to month but fell short of fundamentally changing their prospects.

Without assets, the poor struggle to survive and the cycle of poverty continues unabated. Frustrated with the meager results of past antipoverty efforts, some Americans have concluded that nothing can be done to close the gap between the haves and the have-nots—a particularly sad conclusion in the wake of unprecedented national prosperity. Yet there are plenty of reasons to reject this pessimistic view. While the poor may lack the resources that bring stability to the lives of the middle class, they share the same aspirations. Everyone wants a healthy family, economic self-sufficiency, a home in a safe neighborhood. And like their wealthier counterparts, poor people are willing and eager to make sacrifices to attain these goals. Even more encouraging is the realization that strategies to help the poor build assets do not need to be newly invented. Many programs designed for this purpose already exist. Their efforts have yielded not just impressive success stories but also broader lessons about what works. The old adage that the best way to help people is to empower them to help themselves holds much truth. The greatest promise for those living in poverty lies in approaches that enable them to acquire new assets and draw greater value from those they already possess, thereby increasing their own capabilities and those of their children. It is this emphasis on building a stake in society for oneself and coming generations that underpins the asset-building paradigm.

Assets and Poverty

Academics and practitioners began to explore the relationship between asset ownership and poverty in the 1980s as they confronted an unpleasant reality. Although a great deal of money and energy had gone into the fight against poverty for several decades, many Americans remained poor. Partly because of this, public support for traditional antipoverty programs, and the welfare system in particular, was shrinking. Poverty was still a major problem in America, but existing approaches were seen as ineffective and, increasingly, illegitimate.

In 1991, Michael Sherraden, a professor of social work, published a book called *Assets and the Poor*.[9] He argued that poor people, contrary to conventional wisdom, can and will save if they are given the opportunity to do so. He identified many of the benefits of assets in reducing poverty, noting that they improve the stability of low-income households, create an orientation toward the future, provide a cushion against risk and a head start for the next generation, and usually make it possible to acquire more assets. He also introduced the idea of a special kind of savings account for the poor in which savings would be matched by public or private funds. Like individual retirement accounts (IRAs) for the middle class, these individual development accounts (IDAs), as Sherraden called them, would be restricted to specific uses: the purchase of a home, investment in education or job training, or ownership of a small business—in short, the acquisition of assets.

Sherraden's idea, that poor people be offered a structured opportunity to save, captured the attention of many in Washington and in local communities, drawing support from across the political spectrum. Liberals welcomed the idea because it called for a new tool to help the poor, supported at least in part by public funds. Conservatives embraced the concept because it sought to reward values they had long championed, such as personal responsibility, thrift, and investment. Here was a new approach to thinking about poverty that seemed to transcend long-standing political divisions and tap into core elements of the American dream. Sherraden's research led to policy experimentation at the local and national levels that resulted in IDAs emerging as a promising new tool to help the poor acquire assets. (See chapter 6.)

Other research contributed to the growing understanding of the relationship between asset ownership and poverty. In a series of journal articles and then in their book, *Black Wealth/White Wealth*, sociologists Melvin L. Oliver and Thomas M. Shapiro examined the deep inequalities in wealth holdings between black and white Americans.[10] Coming several years after Sherraden's initial, highly optimistic work on the potential of asset ownership, Oliver and Shapiro offered a more tempered view. Their analysis found that, while the black-white income gap had narrowed thanks to the educational and occupational gains made by African Americans, the wealth gap remained. Over two-thirds of African Americans have no net financial assets, as compared to less than one-third of whites. Middle-class blacks, who earn on average 70 cents for every dollar earned by middle-class whites, possess only 15 cents for each dollar of wealth held by middle-class whites. "For the most part," Oliver and Shapiro wrote, "the economic foundation of the black middle class lacks one of the pillars that provide stability and security to middle-class whites—assets."[11] Oliver and Shapiro showed how the unequal distribution of assets by race arose in part from policies that prevented racial minorities from holding and developing assets, and they proposed remedies targeted at both African Americans specifically and the poor in general, both black and white. "Our analysis clearly suggests the need for massive redistributional policies . . . [that] take aim at the gross inequality generated by those at the very top of the wealth distribution," they conclude.[12] The authors themselves remain skeptical about the prospects for change, acknowledging that redistributional policies face almost insurmountable political barriers. Still, their work drew attention to the looming gaps in asset ownership, particularly by race, and what it means for people to live without assets.

Further insight into the issues of wealth inequality has come from economists like Edward N. Wolff. Wolff's work underscores the distinction between income and wealth, including the fact that families receiving the same income but differing in their stocks of housing and consumer durables, such as automobiles, will experience different levels of well-being. More important, Wolff notes, "is the security that wealth brings to its owners, who know that their consumption can be sustained even if income fluctuates."[13] In a series of publications, Wolff has analyzed available wealth data to reveal the tremendous disparity between the economic assets held by those at the top and those at the bottom.[14] The 1980s witnessed a particularly dramatic deterioration in wealth equality—from 1983 to 1989, the share of the top 1 percent of wealth holders rose by 3.6 percentage points, while the wealth of the bottom 40 percent showed an absolute decline. Virtually all of the absolute gains in real wealth accrued to the top 20 percent of wealth holders. The 1990s saw a broadening of stock ownership and rapid increases in the value of stock holdings, but even these trends were not powerful enough to halt the widening wealth gap. Since 1989, wealth inequality has continued to rise, although at a slower pace than during the 1980s. The racial disparities identified by Oliver and Shapiro also persist, with the mean wealth of black households in 1998 averaging less than 20 percent that of white households.

Wolff and fellow economist Robert Haveman have also calculated figures for what they call "asset poverty." (Haveman was one of the first to propose some kind of asset-based account when in 1988 he called for the creation of capital accounts for youth.)[15] Using Wolff and Haveman's most liberal definition—net worth needed to get by for three months at the poverty level—they find an asset poverty rate of 25.5 percent, or more than twice that of the current income poverty rate. This means that, depending on the measure used, between 70 and 140 million Americans are asset poor. Moreover, asset poverty is increasing, even while income poverty has decreased.[16]

The idea of asset-based development was in large part a response to the perceived inadequacies of the traditional welfare system. That system was widely seen as preventing poor people from moving into the middle class by means-testing benefits and limiting asset accumulation (for example, recipients of Aid to Families with Dependent Children, or AFDC, were prohibited from owning a car worth more than $1,500 or keeping more than $1,000 in a savings account). In some quarters, asset-based strategies have been welcomed as an alternative to the safety nets built over the years to keep poor people from falling below a certain income level. More often, such strategies are viewed as a complement to income-based policy.

To many, the problem with income-based policy is that it provides little opportunity for upward mobility. Restrictions on the accumulation of assets have made it difficult for welfare recipients to plan for the long run or invest in the future. Rather than rejecting the income-based safety net, advocates for asset-based policies hoped to relax the asset limits it had come to include and enable poor people to acquire the resources needed for greater self-sufficiency. Many of the strategies used to help the poor acquire assets build on traditional approaches to fighting poverty. These include job training, community development, and home ownership initiatives—all staples of antipoverty efforts since the 1960s. But as the stories that follow suggest, these activities are being undertaken in new ways, with greater attention to the sustainability of gains and their overall impact on asset ownership. In this sense, asset-building strategies mark not a radical break with the past but a new paradigm for thinking about poverty alleviation.

As the role of economic assets in changing the prospects of the poor came to be more widely understood, academics and practitioners began applying the same principles to noneconomic assets. It is easy to grasp the parallels between economic assets and human assets. Just as a person can increase his or her productivity by investing in physical capital, investments in human capital also yield high returns. It has long been the case that people with college degrees earn substantially more money than those without; however, the economic benefits of staying in school have increased dramatically over the past twenty years.[17] Formal education is not the only way to develop one's human assets; wage gains also accrue to workers who participate in employer-sponsored training programs or apprenticeships. As the United States strives to maintain its standing in a global economy that emphasizes human capital above raw material endowments or physical infrastructure, new skills also provide workers with greater job security and the potential for upward mobility.

Health is another area where the returns on human capital investments are high, especially for children. In recent years, a consensus has emerged that early childhood offers a particularly crucial and cost-effective window for investing in human capital. In addition to high-quality early education and literacy programs that seek to level the playing field between rich and poor children in preparation for school, preventive health care in the first years of life (and prenatal health care for poor mothers) can play a critical role in ensuring that poor children are not saddled with disabilities or poverty-related diseases that compromise their ability to learn.[18]

"There is no better way to break the intergenerational cycle of poverty and inequality than to invest in the current generation of children," write Sheldon Danziger and Jane Waldfogel. "Well-designed investments in children and adolescents today promote their future success in the labor market, family life, and social life."[19] As with economic assets, the value of human assets lies not simply in what they provide at the moment but in their future impact.

A third type of asset that has received considerable attention in recent years is social capital. Robert Putnam, author of *Bowling Alone*, explains: "Whereas physical capital refers to physical objects and human capital refers to properties of individuals, social capital refers to connections among individuals—social networks and the norms of reciprocity and trustworthiness that arise from them."[20] Think for a moment of your own community and connections. If you lose your job, are there people you can call for advice or contacts? Will a neighbor watch your house while you are away on vacation? Are you active in a parent-teacher association, a softball league, a church or synagogue? If your community is threatened with a rise in crime, a loss of jobs, or an environmental threat, will you and your neighbors work together to prevent it? All these relationships—the ongoing interactions that make up a community's social fabric—represent stores of social capital.

Unlike economic and human assets, which are generally held by individuals, social capital has both an individual and a collective dimension—or, as Putnam describes it, a private and a public face. Like economic and human assets, social capital provides individuals with a greater degree of security and well-being. People benefit from the connections they have formed, whether one is networking to find a job or relying on members of a church for support when illness strikes. Social capital, or the degree of one's connectedness to the larger society, has even been shown to have an impact on one's mental and physical health.[21] But social capital also represents an asset for the wider community. The denser the network of connections among individuals, the healthier a community will be. Jane Jacobs, the noted scholar of urban life, wrote of this phenomenon forty years ago in *The Death and Life of Great American Cities*, showing how streets are safer, children are watched over, and residents experience a higher degree of satisfaction in communities where informal contact among neighbors is high.[22] In short, people who live in an environment where the bonds of trust, cooperation, and reciprocity are strong can accomplish more than those who live in a community where those ties are weak.

Social capital is especially important for poor communities since by definition they lack economic assets. Research has shown that one of the surest routes to better-quality schools is not higher spending or lower teacher-student ratios but increased parental and community involvement.[23] Crime is lowest in neighborhoods where people know each other's names, not where there is the greatest police presence.[24] When people within a community trust each other, they are able to mobilize on behalf of their interests, keep out threats (such as a pollution-spewing factory), and bring in assets (such as a new park or shopping center). Unfortunately, many poor communities have seen their social ties weaken over the past few decades with the exodus of jobs and middle-class families from urban centers.[25] "In areas where social capital is lacking," writes Putnam, "the effects of poverty, adult unemployment, and family breakdown are magnified, making life that much worse for children and adults alike. . . . Where these reciprocity systems persist, however, they remain an important asset to poor people, an asset that is too often overlooked in popular accounts of the urban underclass."[26]

A fourth area where an asset-building approach has been applied is natural resources. Access to natural assets, such as land, water, forests, and clean air, is just as unequally distributed as access to other forms of wealth. Both renewable and nonrenewable natural resources are owned overwhelmingly by the wealthy. Low-income communities possess not only fewer assets but tend to be dumping grounds for society's wastes and environmental hazards. "The maldistribution of natural resources and environmental health is no accident," write James K. Boyce and Manuel Pastor, "but rather mirrors how wealth and power are distributed in society."[27]

Strategies for building the natural resources of poor communities include a broad range of efforts in both urban and rural settings. In many older cities, efforts are under way to clean up and redevelop polluted former industrial sites, known as brownfields. Low-income residents have taken responsibility for vacant lots on city blocks and turned them into community gardens that produce food for local consumption and sale.[28] Other communities have worked to revive local waterways and increase public access to the waterfront. In rural areas, the community-based forestry movement seeks to include those who depend on forest resources in decisions about how those resources should be used. Poor farmers are learning new techniques for increasing the productivity of their soil and are taking advantage of new marketing opportunities, such as local farmers' markets, to add value to the agricultural products they grow. The goal of these efforts is to increase the value of the natural resources already held by the poor, enable them to acquire additional assets, and reduce the level of environmental hazards to which poor communities are exposed. Just as other forms of asset building create a greater orientation toward the future, natural asset-building activities enable low-income communities to invest in the resources that surround them to achieve sustainable livelihoods and a healthier environment.[29]

Assets for the Middle Class, Welfare for the Poor

The U.S. government has long employed asset-building policies in the interests of national development. Initially, such policies were targeted toward specific groups of Americans or offered as rewards for public service. Today's asset-based policies are much more broadly based, but their benefits are enjoyed mainly by the middle class and the wealthy.

An early example of how the federal government played a crucial role in the allocation of assets is the Homestead Act (1862), designed to provide grants of public land to pioneers in the western territories. Between 400,000 and 600,000 families acquired farms, ranches, and homes this way. However, the provisions of the act were restricted to white citizens who had not belonged to the Confederacy. The Southern Homestead Act, passed four years later, extended homesteading to the former Confederate states but failed in its efforts to create a landowning class among newly freed blacks. The oft-heard promise of "forty acres and a mule" fell victim to ongoing racial prejudice and discrimination, the poor quality of the land offered, and the fact that a majority of applicants under the new law were in fact white. By far the largest beneficiaries of the land acts of the late nineteenth century were private corporate interests—namely the railroads—which received huge tracts of public land for free.

Perhaps the best-known asset-building effort in U.S. history was the GI Bill (1944), which enabled veterans of World War II to obtain college educations and buy homes. Close to 8 million veterans received vocational training under the act, over 2 million attended college, and more than 4 million purchased homes with mortgage subsidies provided by the government. The GI Bill democratized America's system of higher education and helped set off an economic boom when millions of college-trained veterans entered the workforce. It also helped spread the benefits of home ownership more widely.

The most important asset-building policies of the twenty-first century are embedded in the federal tax code and are so poorly understood by the general public that one writer has dubbed them the "hidden welfare state."[30] A substantial portion of the federal budget takes the form of tax benefits to individuals and families, with the home mortgage interest deduction and retirement savings provisions accounting for the largest shares. There has been little discussion of the impact of such policies on inequality in part because benefits delivered through the tax code are much less transparent than benefits that take the form of direct government expenditures such as welfare payments.

The mortgage interest deduction favors home buyers, who are more likely to be middle class or higher, over renters, who are more likely to be poor. Ninety-one percent of the benefits from the home mortgage interest deduction go to families earning over $50,000 (fewer than half the households in the United States), while the remaining 9 percent is shared by all families earning less than $50,000. The deduction is also tremendously expensive to taxpayers, amounting to an estimated $75 billion in fiscal year 2000.[31] Despite its high cost and regressive nature, a politically strong coalition of homeowners, builders, realtors, and lending institutions has ensured that the home mortgage interest deduction remains sacrosanct, as it was during even the most intense period of federal budget cutting in the 1980s. Anyone who has purchased a home knows that the deductibility of mortgage interest figures prominently in the calculations of what one can afford and acts as a strong incentive to buy rather than rent. But for those without the money for a down payment or without access to credit, the asset-building impact of this enormous government subsidy is nil. Housing for the poor is delivered through a completely different system: "The national government fosters home ownership among the middle classes by making the terms of private loans more attractive," writes Christopher Howard, "and it houses the poor by working with state governments to build and administer low-cost dwellings. While serving far more people, the top tier is less visible and less stigmatizing than the bottom tier of public housing projects."[32]

The federal tax code also encourages asset accumulation through provisions governing employer-sponsored retirement plans. For many years, the U.S. savings rate has been lower than the savings rates of other industrialized countries. In some years it has been negative, meaning that Americans are actually spending more than they earn. The reality today is that most Americans save money only through the structured opportunities offered by their retirement plans. The government encourages this kind of savings by allowing tax-free contributions to pension plans or IRAs. Poor people, who are more likely to be unemployed, work part-time, or be paid hourly, have limited access to employer-sponsored retirement plans. Of all retirement tax benefits, which were estimated by Michael Sherraden at $124 billion for fiscal year 2000, 67 percent go to households earning more than $100,000 a year, and 93 percent go to households earning more than $50,000 a year. (About 59 percent of all households earn less than $50,000 a year.)[33] Using a different set of data, Peter Orszag and Robert Greenstein find that two-thirds of tax benefits for pensions accrue to the top 20 percent of families, while only 2.1 percent of benefits go to the bottom 40 percent. Moreover, pension coverage rates have remained at only about 50 percent over the past three decades and are lower for part-time, Hispanic, less-educated, young, and low-income employees.[34] Forced savings through money deducted from a monthly paycheck or an IRA contribution made just before tax returns are filed enable middle-class workers to accumulate assets that can be used for retirement or borrowed against for a down payment or educational expenses. Most poor workers lack this form of security.

In short, U.S. government policy encourages people to purchase homes and save money for retirement. But the way these systems are structured and the mechanisms through which their benefits are delivered mean that it is the middle class and the wealthy that benefit the most. The poor have limited opportunities to build assets, not just because their incomes are low but also because public policy has rarely supported them in doing so.

Instead, the government has worked to construct an income-based social safety net for the poor. This endeavor is relatively recent. Throughout the nineteenth century, responsibility for caring for the poor fell to family and neighbors, religious institutions, and private charities. As the nation industrialized, the states and federal government began to support the idea of some kind of social insurance system that would make protection available as a matter of right. Before the 1930s, such assistance was limited to special groups, such as veterans, widows with children, and the families of workers injured or killed on the job. During the Great Depression, America's middle classes experienced firsthand the effects of unemployment, poverty, and even homelessness, which had long been the lot of the poor. It became clear to many that poverty was not a reflection of personal weakness but a state into which someone might fall by virtue of circumstance. It was also clear that neither the states nor private charities had sufficient resources to cope with the growing need for assistance. Out of the pain of these years came a set of policies that committed the federal government to playing a far greater role in assisting those in need.

The Social Security Act of 1935 represented the first social insurance programs on a national scale. Along with providing unemployment insurance and old-age benefits to retired workers, the act enabled the states to expand existing grants of support to widowed mothers and their children. These grants were the forerunners of AFDC, which remained the cornerstone of public efforts to assist poor families for the next sixty years. The safety net was extended in the 1960s through programs like Medicaid, Head Start, food stamps, subsidized school lunches, home energy assistance, and new public housing construction. Federal, state, and local efforts in the fields of job training and community development complemented these efforts. Spending on social welfare continued to rise during the 1970s, even after public enthusiasm for the war on poverty had begun to wane. In the 1980s, the laissez-faire ideology of the Reagan administration and ballooning of the federal budget deficit set in motion the dynamics that led to the end of the traditional welfare system. Budget cutting, a rejection of big government, and an emphasis on market-based solutions led to tighter eligibility rules, less generous benefits, and ultimately the welfare reform act of 1996 (the Personal Responsibility and Work Opportunity Reconciliation Act)—a policy change supported by a bipartisan coalition in Congress and signed into law by a Democratic president.

Since the enactment of welfare reform, the nation has seen striking declines in the welfare caseload. Nationally, the number of families receiving welfare payments fell by 52 percent between August 1996 and September 2001. State-by-state declines have varied, with smaller drops in the states with the most welfare recipients (such as California, where the rate fell by 48 percent) and larger drops in some of the southern and western states and those with aggressive welfare-to-work programs (such as Illinois, where welfare rolls were cut by 75 percent).[35] Some of the drop is due to a tightening of rules and faster action in suspending payments when such rules are violated, but much of the decline is indeed related to people leaving welfare for work as the law intended.

The apparent success of the new work rules in moving families off welfare has led to broad support for the new strategy. The public debate since welfare reform has been characterized by an emphasis on a reduced role for the federal government, greater reliance on volunteerism and private sector initiatives, and the value of tough eligibility requirements and time limits. Sometimes overlooked is the fact that much of the success in cutting welfare rolls was due to the strong economic expansion and tight job market of the late 1990s. (Indeed, the number of welfare recipients actually began declining several years before the enactment of reform.)

The problem is that many of these new workers are not finding their way out of poverty. Instead, they have swelled the ranks of the working poor—those with low-wage jobs, minimal health benefits, and not enough money to pay the bills. As journalist Jason DeParle noted in a lengthy *New York Times* series on welfare reform, "Here is the dawning surprise: [welfare reform] may end up making less of a difference in the lives of the poor, socially or economically, than much of the public imagined."[36] This dawning surprise has contributed to a policy situation that is more fluid than it has been in years. Opponents of welfare reform have had to concede that many of those once on public assistance are in fact capable of holding down full-time jobs. At the same time, those who supported welfare reform are coming to acknowledge the limits of its impact on poverty. Meanwhile, the decline in the welfare rolls left states with more cash than they needed for public assistance, making it possible for them to experiment with new strategies. As a result, state and local governments are beginning to grapple with the question of which approaches offer the greatest promise for alleviating poverty.

One of the most positive features of the 1996 welfare reform legislation is that it made it possible for states to do more to help the poor build assets. Most states have raised the limits on asset accumulation that were part of AFDC. Under Temporary Assistance for Needy Families (TANF), the system that replaced AFDC, welfare recipients can save money in an IDA without losing their eligibility for public assistance. And thirty-two states have opted to allow the use of TANF block grants to match IDA savings.[37] Michael Sherraden writes that these asset-building provisions mark "the first time in federal anti-poverty policy that asset building was no longer discouraged, and in fact could be subsidized with federal funds. . . . [They are] an important step toward establishing asset building as a policy option on equal footing with income support for welfare households."[38]

Sherraden and others point out that the shift to asset-building policies is part of a much broader trend. Since the 1970s, there has been a proliferation of new kinds of asset accounts, including retirement savings accounts such as 401(k)s, 403(b)s, IRAs, and Roth IRAs, along with educational savings accounts, college savings plans, medical savings accounts, and proposed individual accounts in Social Security. These accounts, whether public or private, typically receive substantial subsidies through the tax system. The fear among many antipoverty advocates is that the poor are not in a position to participate in or receive the benefits of such asset accounts and that the general shift in this direction may exacerbate the already gaping inequality that characterizes asset ownership in twenty-first-century America. Recent legislative changes, such as increased limits for tax-exempt contributions to IRAs and employer-based retirement plans, along with proposed capital gains tax reductions and the repeal of the estate tax, which affects only 2 percent of U.S. taxpayers, are signs that such a development may already be under way. There is no reason why asset-based approaches cannot also be used to help poor families invest in the future. Asset building can be accomplished with relatively simple policy instruments, and public policy already does it for the nonpoor. As Sherraden writes, "It should be possible, and would be more just, to do so for the poor as well."[39] Developing a new set of policies along these lines is one of the overriding challenges facing those on the front lines in the battle against poverty.

Building Assets for the Poor

The power of the asset-building approach and the range of possibilities it offers is best understood through the stories of real people and real places. This book takes you into the heart of five organizations that are at the forefront of building assets for the poor. It begins with two stories of community revitalization, one set in a small Michigan city, the other in the mountains of northern California.

Chapter 2 shows how the city of Battle Creek, Michigan, almost succumbed to the forces of deindustrialization and suburbanization that, from the 1960s on, sapped the vitality of so many towns in the Midwest and Northeast. A dwindling and increasingly poor population, threats to the city's most important industry, and deteriorating infrastructure were among the challenges facing "Cereal City" by the late 1970s. Among those responsible for Battle Creek's renaissance is an organization that has worked to revitalize the city's older neighborhoods through a combination of strategies focusing on home ownership and the creation of social capital. For most Americans, their home is their single most valuable asset. Home ownership brings families a host of material benefits, including a roof overhead, tax savings, and home equity. Ownership also provides greater protection against eviction, more personal freedom, and a stronger sense of community than rental housing. More Americans than ever own their homes, but minorities, low-income families, and single parents still lag well behind the national average. Closing the gap in home ownership is a prime target of government and nonprofit initiatives. But, as the story of Neighborhoods Incorporated of Battle Creek makes clear, such initiatives must go beyond merely increasing the rate of ownership among the poor. In many low-income neighborhoods, owner-occupied homes are badly in need of repair, while investing in them makes little economic sense because of declining property values. As these neighborhoods deteriorate, homes become assets whose value is shrinking, not growing. The impact on one woman and her family of the innovative strategies employed by Neighborhoods Incorporated shows that when home ownership initiatives are linked to education, neighborhood revitalization, and the strengthening of community ties, they can have a profound effect on low-income communities and the individuals who live in them.

Chapter 3 turns to the community of Hayfork, California, and its residents' efforts to build human and social capital in an environment replete with natural resources but economically impoverished. It was the long-running battle between timber companies and environmentalists that brought Hayfork to its knees. Nestled in a tree-lined valley in northern California's Trinity National Forest, Hayfork was a timber town until the last mill closed in 1996. By then, more than half the town's work force was unemployed, men were driving hundreds of miles to find work, and four out of five children qualified for free or low-cost school lunches. Moreover, the political and court battles of the 1980s had driven a wedge between longtime residents, impairing their ability to envision a common future or work together to achieve it. The question was whether the town itself would be able to survive the death of commercial logging. The Watershed Research and Training Center is a community-based nonprofit organization founded in 1993. The center is committed to finding new ways for Hayfork's residents to make a living from the forest and to reconstructing the social fabric of the town. Its initiatives include training for displaced forest workers, the creation of commercial ventures based on woods-related products, economic diversification, support for local community-building organizations, and the forging of linkages regionally, nationally, and internationally to bring the latest innovations in community-based forestry to this isolated corner of the Pacific Northwest.

The next two chapters focus on human assets. Particularly in the wake of welfare reform, it has become essential for low-income workers to acquire the skills and experience they need to earn a living wage. Job training, the subject of chapter 4, has long been a part of federal and state antipoverty programs. Often, though, these programs gave participants only the most rudimentary of skills and included little relevant work experience. Above all, they failed to connect people with jobs that paid enough money to support a family. Work force training organizations are developing new strategies to overcome these limitations. The Private Industry Partnership (PIP) of Wildcat Service Corporation has been successful in training many former New York City welfare recipients for entry-level white-collar jobs in the city's financial services, legal, advertising, and entertainment industries. It does so through a combination of skills-specific training, close collaboration with employers, and an internship program that enables workers and employers alike to make informed decisions about job fit. For one longtime welfare recipient, PIP indeed offered both new skills and a new set of opportunities, enabling her to find the first real job of her life.

An alternate route to independence through work lies in self-employment, the focus of chapter 5. Estimates suggest that more than 2 million poor Americans derive some or all of their income from operating a very small business, or microenterprise. As is true for wealthier individuals, owning a business can provide a family with income, serve as an asset to be borrowed against, and be passed on to one's children. Many low-income people have special skills, talents, and interests on which to build a business, but lack the resources needed to make a commercial venture a success. Among the most pressing of these are capital, credit, and business know-how. If potential entrepreneurs can be connected to these resources, self-employment may offer a promising avenue out of poverty. Iowa's Institute for Social and Economic Development (ISED), one of the earliest U.S.-based microenterprise training programs, has served nearly 7,000 people since it was founded in 1988. ISED provides its customers with training and technical assistance, while connecting them to private sources of capital and credit through a loan guarantee fund. In the process, it helps clients develop the skills and knowledge needed to run a successful enterprise. For a graduate of the program who operates her own cleaning company, this has made the difference between low-wage work and business ownership, between being dependent on government assistance and being able to provide for her son and herself.

Chapter 6 traces the idea of structured savings accounts for the poor from Michael Sherraden's first writings on the subject to its current place on the national agenda. The IDA story highlights one of the key strengths of the asset-building approach: its broad political appeal. Rarely has a policy aimed at reducing poverty enjoyed such vocal support by the leading lights of both political parties, including President George W. Bush, former vice president Al Gore, former president Bill Clinton, and House and Senate leaders on both sides of the aisle. Fighting poverty has generally been thought of in terms of building safety nets—spending the money needed to ensure that people do not fall below some agreed-upon standard of well-being. The standard and the resources needed to arrive at it have always been a source of political and budgetary contention, with liberals pushing for greater funding and conservatives challenging the very basis of a system that makes poor people dependent on government assistance. IDAs are an example of an asset-building strategy that bypasses this debate. By empowering low-income people to invest in themselves and their future, it is a strategy that both liberals and conservatives can and have embraced. To what extent IDAs make a real difference in the lives of the poor and whether current demonstration projects can be expanded to cover the millions of individuals who might qualify for such accounts remain open questions, but both are being energetically explored in the halls of Congress, in state and local governments, and by community organizations around the country.

The importance of social capital threads its way through each of these stories. Critical to the revitalization of Battle Creek's poorest neighborhoods are efforts to strengthen the social fabric and nurture local leaders who can serve as advocates for their community. The building of bridges between longtime opponents has been essential to the success of the Watershed Center in injecting some degree of dynamism back into Hayfork's economy. The network of connections that ISED and PIP provide their clients is as important to their achievements as their new jobs themselves. Even in IDA programs, where the emphasis is on accumulating economic assets, the resources to which clients are introduced often prove more instrumental in changing their prospects than their newly acquired savings.

Central to these efforts, too, are human assets. The website of the First Nations Development Institute, a community development organization that serves the Native American population, prominently displays the following message: "Access to and control of knowledge underlies the ability to control all other assets: business and financial capital, land, health, culture, and natural resources. Knowledge is the most crucial of all human assets, without which little can be done to control the physical assets and systems upon which we depend, and set a course for the future."[40] This is why training in economic and financial literacy is such an integral part of both home ownership and IDA programs for the poor. This is why successful job-training programs require high-quality information about employers' needs and why successful self-employment programs focus as much on building skills as they do on financing. And this is why the skills and knowledge of local residents have played such a critical role in efforts to resuscitate a dying town. It is not just the struggles and perseverance of program leaders and participants but their newfound knowledge that accounts for the achievements recorded here.

Despite their differences, the five organizations profiled in this book share some important characteristics:

—They are innovative and successful, representing the state of the art in antipoverty efforts. The unusual approaches they take are regarded highly by others within their field. Almost always, serious efforts have been made to evaluate the impact of their programs.

—The strategies they have developed can be used elsewhere and on a larger scale. There is no sense in reporting success stories if they cannot be expanded or reproduced outside their initial context. The work of these organizations has broader relevance, even if their achievements may not yet be widely known.

—They share a common emphasis on empowering people, while at the same time holding them accountable. Instead of doing for the poor, these programs work with them, enabling people to do more for themselves. In exchange, they require that beneficiaries assume responsibility for their own actions, whether that means repaying a business loan, showing up for a job-training program on time, or contributing to the health of the community.

—Their leaders have traded in the spirit of confrontation sometimes found in grassroots antipoverty efforts for an emphasis on partnership. They recognize that sterile debates will get them nowhere, that only through consensus and cooperation will the asset-building effort bring rewards. Most of these programs also enjoy support from across the political spectrum, making their wider adoption politically feasible.

The stories of these organizations are told through the eyes of individuals whose lives have been transformed by their work. These individuals are not the poorest of the poor. Most are employed, and some earn salaries that place them above the federal poverty line. All have graduated from high school or received an equivalency degree, and some have even attended college. But every one of the book's subjects has lived on the knife's edge, fighting to make ends meet and to cope with a set of problems that often extends far beyond the issue of economic well-being. Some have struggled with family members, experienced depression, or faced the battles of drug or alcohol dependency. Many have moved in and out of poverty as they have been subjected to forces beyond their control. Most have made bad economic decisions that carry with them long-term consequences.

Even so, this book is largely a record of success. Each of the individuals you will meet in these pages has materially improved the conditions of his or her life through the asset-building strategies discussed here. The psychological gains are, if anything, more impressive. Assets are not a magic bullet for America's poor families, and assets alone do not change a life. But they give people the confidence and self-esteem they need to cope with the challenges they face, economic and noneconomic alike.

"There are as many routes out of poverty as there are into poverty," says Robert Friedman, president of the Corporation for Enterprise Development, a think tank that was instrumental in putting IDAs on the national agenda.[41] One of the strengths of the asset-building approach is that it acknowledges that different strategies may be appropriate for different people, in contrast to the one-size-fits-all tendencies of income-based support. Job training may provide upward mobility for some workers, while others are best served by learning to run their own businesses. For some poor families eager to buy a home, it may be sufficient to give them the opportunity to save for a down payment through an IDA program. For others, a lack of economic literacy or poor credit history may require a greater investment in their money management skills. The answer to the economic plight of some rural communities may rest in better stewardship of the natural resources on which they depend, while other communities may need to diversify their economic base away from natural resource dependency. Asset-building strategies recognize these different needs and offer a range of approaches to meeting them.

An asset-building strategy also acknowledges that the journey out of poverty takes time. It was not until she was an elderly woman that my grandmother had the resources to live in her own modest home. My mother and her sisters spent their childhood in poverty, moving into the middle class after becoming adults. It is only their children, my generation, who have lived all of our lives without experiencing poverty. The ability to transfer assets from parent to child—the utility of assets in improving not just one's own life but the lives of one's descendants—suggests that ending poverty may very well be a multigenerational endeavor. The antipoverty efforts of the past have shown that there are no quick fixes to the plight of the poor. But there is much that can be done to set in motion the longer-term process of asset accumulation. Hundreds of innovative programs around the country are doing just that. Their success in helping the poor build assets shows that poverty *can* be fought, that the end of welfare as we know it does not mean the end of hope that a more just society can be achieved.

CHAPTER TWO

Coming
Home

Home ownership stands at the center of the American dream. Buying a home has long been a symbol of success, a sign of having made it into the middle class. Two-thirds of Americans own their homes and, among those who do not, a majority ranks home ownership as the highest priority.[1] For most families, their home is their single largest investment and an important source of security. Once a home is fully paid for, the owners can live in it rent-free or pass it on to their children. And, unlike rental costs that may increase each year, ownership makes housing expenses predictable. It also confers certain legal rights. Renters can be evicted from an apartment in ten days if they do not pay the rent. For homeowners, it takes between six and eighteen months for a foreclosure to work its way through the system. In this sense, homes act as a kind of insurance that gives those who are vulnerable a chance to get back on their feet.

Beyond these tangible benefits, home ownership confers tremendous psychological advantages. Most Americans say that owning a home helps them make a better life for their children and lends stability to a marriage.[2] Home ownership gives people freedom about such simple decisions as whether to plant a garden or own a pet. And homes represent an asset that can be borrowed against to finance an education, start a business, or cushion a family from economic crisis.

Like the other assets discussed in this book, home ownership is not distributed equally. Wealthier Americans are far more likely to own their homes than are low-income families. Home ownership rates for minorities, while rising, continue to lag behind those for whites. And families headed by single women are less likely than two-parent families to live in a house of their own.

The benefits of home ownership and the gaps in this area have led government agencies and private organizations to promote home ownership as a strategy for moving low-income families out of poverty. Unlike many policies designed to help the poor, this one has long enjoyed broad-based political support. Traditional antipoverty advocates welcome initiatives that enable poor families to leave behind overpriced rental housing and improve their living conditions. Those who emphasize self-reliance and personal responsibility as the keys to ending poverty also see home ownership as a desirable strategy. Initiatives designed to increase home ownership among the poor have proliferated in recent years among such diverse entities as Fannie Mae, Bank of America, the NAACP, and the nonprofit Center for Community Self-Help.[3]

While the emphasis on creating new assets embodied in these approaches is welcome, it is not enough just to help people buy homes. Many homes already owned by low-income families are in areas where property values are declining. In such neighborhoods, it makes little sense for owners to improve their homes because the money invested is unlikely ever to be recouped. A downward spiral sets in, with homes sinking into disrepair and property values falling further. As neighborhoods deteriorate, low-income families find themselves holding assets that are actually declining in value. This dynamic has led to a growing recognition that for home ownership to benefit the poor, it must be linked to strategies for keeping neighborhoods healthy. The difficulty lies in achieving this.

One place to look for answers is in Battle Creek, Michigan. Here, a nonprofit organization called Neighborhoods Incorporated has helped revitalize some of the city's most distressed areas by lending for home purchase and rehabilitation while strengthening the social capital of these same communities. Neighborhoods Incorporated's unique approach requires home buyers to invest in their homes and neighborhoods. By working street by street, not only to upgrade the physical quality of homes but also to build relationships among the people who live in them, Neighborhoods Incorporated has accomplished several goals. Property values have increased, providing many low-income homeowners with a new economic resource. Residents have organized to make their streets safer and cleaner, improving both the reality and perception of their neighborhoods. And the well-being of the larger community has increased as its stock of economic, human, and social assets has grown. These achievements are by no means comprehensive. With limited resources, Neighborhoods Incorporated has been able to focus on just a few target neighborhoods, and even in these areas much remains to be done. But the organization's efforts have resulted in positive change in the neighborhoods—and in the lives of their residents. The story of how this transformation came about offers lessons that can be included in other efforts to increase the assets of the poor through home ownership.

The Long Road Back

Greenwood Avenue was a frightening place for a young girl, yet Denise Washington had to walk down it each afternoon. The street, which runs through the heart of Washington Heights, a largely African American neighborhood on the northwest side of Battle Creek, had a long history of violence, drugs, and prostitution. On her way to and from elementary school and junior high, Denise managed to avoid Greenwood, but once she started high school it was the quickest route home. "When I got to that street," she remembers, "I would start running until I got through, and I wouldn't look back. Anything and everything was happening on that street."

A few years later, just out of high school, Denise and her baby daughter needed a place to live. An apartment on Greenwood was the only place she could afford. "I remember at night there was gunfire, there were drugs," she says. "There was always some kind of police action going on. Three people were murdered in the daylight on that street. This one guy was coming out of his house; he was just walking out of the house at eight in the morning and was shot. They just left him there." Elderly residents slept in their basements to avoid the gunfire. Even during Battle Creek's hot and humid summers, Denise kept her windows closed in fear.

Denise knew the neighborhood well. One of four children, she was raised by her grandparents just a few blocks away. She describes her father as a rolling stone; it seemed that after each of his visits home another baby was born. Overwhelmed, Denise's mother agreed to let her parents care for her eldest daughter. Denise is grateful to her grandparents for providing her with a safe and stable home, but nonetheless the family was marked by tragedy and upheaval. One of Denise's two sisters died in her late teens and her brother was killed in prison, where he was serving time for murder, at the age of twenty-seven. Denise graduated from Battle Creek Central High School and went to work at a local bank, but lacking a college degree could make little progress. A brief marriage that left her with a baby made it hard for her to return to school. Instead, Denise joined the military, serving for eight years in Germany. The stresses of military life took their toll on Denise's second marriage, which ended after seven years. She returned to Battle Creek in 1986, again divorced and now with two young children. The skills she had gained as a stock accountant in the army, however, helped her land a good job with the city, meaning that she could now afford an apartment in a nicer part of town. It seemed that her life was finally on track.

Within four years of her return from Germany, Denise was desperate. Things had somehow gone terribly wrong. Another short marriage had resulted in a third child; her husband walked out before their son was even born. Denise's grandfather became ill and moved in with Denise and her children. His medical expenses, coupled with the costs of caring for the family on her own, were more than she could handle. Just as damaging was Denise's propensity to help others even when she couldn't afford to. "I felt it was my personal duty to save the world," she says today. "My mentality was if you have a loaf of bread and somebody needs it, give them the whole loaf. You'll get some more." Credit card bills mounted and Denise found it hard to keep up. "I have this real personal spot in my heart for single parents," she explains. "I would see families who were less fortunate than myself and I would take my credit cards and buy them snowsuits and boots and whatever else they needed. I don't want to say I was stupid, but I wasn't very cautious. . . . I looked at it like, 'If I need [help], I know these people will come through for me.' I never intended on collecting, but you figure you have all these markers out there. . . . I trusted everyone. With that mentality, you don't expect anyone to take advantage of you." In 1990, Denise declared bankruptcy. Her fall from a sound credit rating had taken less than a year.

Denise's financial crisis was made worse by the relatively high cost of the family's housing. Ironically, it was her stable city job that had created the problem. Each cost-of-living raise Denise received had led to an increase in her rent. By now she was paying $500 a month for substandard housing that was going for $100 a month to families on welfare. She could not afford to go on like this. When she had first returned to Battle Creek, Denise had heard about a nonprofit housing organization based in Washington Heights. At the time, Neighborhoods Incorporated had not been able to help her, but five years later, with nowhere else to turn, she decided to give them another try.

Over six feet tall, her hair pulled back off her face, Denise Washington cuts an imposing figure. In her mid-forties, she dresses elegantly and wears a large cross. Although she is not a regular churchgoer, Denise considers herself a deeply spiritual person and credits her faith in God for much of the good that has happened in her life. The rest she attributes to Neighborhoods Incorporated. Denise's story emerges slowly—the big picture first, the painful details later on. Articulate yet soft-spoken, she is willing to share her story in the hope of helping others.

Kim Winfrey took Denise's call that day in 1991 and came out to see her the very same evening. Denise told Kim that she had recently filed for bankruptcy and did not see how she would ever be able to own a home. It was clear that Denise's financial woes had sapped her confidence as well as her credit rating. "I went through this thing of failure," she remembers. "I mean, it devastated me. When Kim came along, I had resigned myself to the fact I would never be a homeowner. I would always be mediocre. There was just nothing in store for me."

In Kim Denise found a powerful advocate. A woman of strong opinions and iron will, Kim had joined Neighborhoods Incorporated a few years earlier with a background in public relations. Initially she ran volunteer events and prepared the organization's newsletter but soon traded in her computer for a tool belt and began working on home repair. By the time Denise approached Neighborhoods, Kim had become the organization's housing counselor, responsible, among other things, for assessing whether new clients were ready for home ownership. Although many years have passed since their first meeting, Denise can recall Kim's words as though it were yesterday: "If you believe that I can help you, I can help you," Kim said. "It might not be overnight, but if you're willing to work with me on these issues I can get you into a house."

Denise's dream of becoming a homeowner was one most Americans share. But realizing this goal is harder for some than for others.[4] While the home ownership rate for whites stands at 74 percent, it is only 46 percent for Hispanics and 48 percent for African Americans. Only about half of those earning below the median income are homeowners, compared to more than 80 percent of those earning more than the median. And of single-parent women, only 31 percent own their homes, as opposed to 77 percent of married couples with children. Even apart from her bankruptcy, Denise faced formidable odds in buying a home. Kim Winfrey and the organization she worked for were there to help her beat these odds. To understand how and why, it is necessary to take a brief look back at the history of Battle Creek and the reasons Neighborhoods Incorporated came into being.

Battle Creek was once a boomtown. In the late 1800s, the city had become home to leaders of the Seventh Day Adventist Church who promoted a new kind of health regime that quickly grew in popularity. Wealthy individuals came from around the country to check into the Battle Creek Sanitarium. Run by the Adventist doctor John Harvey Kellogg, the sanitarium offered cures that included vegetarianism, massage, vigorous exercise, and the consumption of a newly invented grain-based food. It was John's brother, Will, who transformed the Adventist promotion of a healthy diet into a commercial venture and, along with C. W. Post and a bevy of other cereal entrepreneurs, turned Battle Creek into the mecca of the breakfast food industry.

By the standards of the day, W. K. Kellogg and C. W. Post were enlightened businessmen, committed to the flourishing of their hometown and their workers.[5] Post built a tract of two-story homes just south of his plant that were offered to employees of his Postum Company at cost. Payment schedules were tailored to income and down payments were as low as $5. Other Battle Creek residents could purchase the lots at slightly higher prices—although in a reflection of the racism of the day, black employees and residents were excluded from the development. Over the years, the company offered cash prizes for the best-maintained homes and gardens and, by 1915, more than 81 percent of Postum employees owned their homes. Battle Creek became known as a "city of homes"; even during the Great Depression, seven of ten residents lived in their own homes—a rate substantially higher than the national average.

In 1917, the U.S. government established a military base on a 10,000-acre tract of land just outside town. Fort Custer served for the next forty-five years as the site of induction and training for U.S. Marines heading off to fight in both World Wars and Korea. Able to accommodate up to 80,000 troops at a time, the installation played an important role in Battle Creek's economy. By mid-century, the city had become a hub of conventional and military manufacturing and home to a number of other important government facilities. Cutbacks in military spending and broader economic trends spelled an end to Battle Creek's boom. By 1964, Fort Custer had closed, costing the downtown business district the spending dollars of thousands of military personnel. Also in the 1960s, two of Battle Creek's largest manufacturers shut down, wiping out 5,000 jobs. Other firms relocated to the South or overseas in search of cheaper labor and more modern plants. Even the once-thriving cereal industry scaled back, as outdated production facilities, labor-management tension, and new competitors hindered profitability. A shopping mall was built outside of town and residents fled to the suburbs, taking their buying power with them. The city's population fell by one-fifth and downtown businesses faltered. By 1980, unemployment had risen to 20 percent. The city center was a shambles, with nine out of ten storefronts standing vacant on the downtown mall. One journalist described the scene as something out of the film *War of the Worlds*, "after the aliens disintegrated all the people."[6]

Beginning in the 1970s, Battle Creek fought back against decline through the combined leadership of the city, private businesses, and local philanthropies. These efforts met with limited success until a key turning point of 1982, when the Kellogg Company, which had been based in Battle Creek since 1906, announced that it needed a new headquarters but could not justify spending $70 million of shareholders' money in a dying town. Unless Battle Creek cleaned up its act, Kellogg would relocate. With the threat of Kellogg's departure hanging over their heads, city leaders set about doing everything possible to retain and attract business. A pivotal step was the merger of the City of Battle Creek with its wealthier suburban township, increasing the tax base and eliminating political rivalries. Local businesses, including Kellogg, plowed money back into an economic development fund and a downtown revitalization effort began. The old pedestrian mall was replaced by a landscaped street and new retailers moved in. The W. K. Kellogg Foundation, one of the nation's largest, built a gleaming new headquarters a few blocks away. An industrial park was established at Fort Custer and the city undertook a marketing campaign to attract foreign auto parts manufacturers and service firms to the area. Eight thousand people now work at Fort Custer, securing its reputation as one of the most successful military base conversion projects in the country.

David Rusk, a leading urban expert, says that Battle Creek has done as well with its physical environment as any American city he's seen.[7] But an even more important consideration in Rusk's view is the ability of community leaders to transcend particular interests on behalf of the greater good. Many of those involved in the renaissance of downtown Battle Creek claim it was the severity of the crisis—the sense of real desperation—that served as a catalyst for change and made possible a unified effort. Whatever the cause, these patterns of partnership would play an important role in efforts to extend that renaissance beyond the city's center.

As the downtown retail district began to revive, the contrast with the areas surrounding it grew stark. Denise's Washington Heights neighborhood, just a mile away from the center of town, had long been a trouble spot. In 1978, newspapers reported that drug use, prostitution, and alcohol abuse were the daily routine at parks in the area.[8] A decade later, residents of Greenwood Avenue were complaining to journalists that "13- and 14-year-olds have knife fights, parents stand like bodyguards while their children fight and youths smoke dope or drink while music blasts from car radios and boom boxes."[9] In 1989, Domino's Pizza announced it would no longer deliver to the area because of concern for the safety of its drivers.[10] By the early 1990s, the quality of life in Washington Heights was bleaker than ever. A community group estimated that there were at least fifty crack cocaine houses in the neighborhood.[11] And one summer night, Greenwood's worst elements closed off both ends of the street, stationed armed guards at the barriers, and charged people to enter a block party where drug sales and prostitution were among the chief entertainments.[12]

Residents clamored for greater attention from the city, and the city responded with stepped-up policing. But while a stronger police presence helped keep drug dealing and gang activity in check, it did nothing to alleviate the deteriorating physical condition of the northwest side, with its crumbling houses, vacant lots, and massive building code violations. As the overt violence subsided, city officials and residents turned their attention to these issues.

In 1991, Neighborhoods Incorporated was a small and underfunded operation. Formed a decade earlier, it had served mainly as an advocate for community groups seeking federal money for local projects. Its volunteers also worked in poor neighborhoods, painting, repairing, and weatherizing old homes. But nothing Neighborhoods did had any effect on the market and for every house that was fixed up, another deteriorated. As the city looked for answers to the continuing decline of its oldest neighborhoods, it consulted with several national housing organizations. The solutions proposed by the Neighborhood Reinvestment Corporation (NRC), a congressionally chartered nonprofit corporation, made the most sense to city leaders.[13] Instead of focusing on individual families and their homes, NRC advocates a neighborhood-based strategy that relies on resident leaders, community-building efforts, and the reclamation of abandoned and distressed properties. With substantial input from the community, a plan was created for a new Neighborhoods Incorporated that would be part of NRC's NeighborWorks network—a web of over 200 groups nationwide seeking to revitalize communities through partnerships of residents, government officials, and business leaders. The mission of the new organization would be tightly focused. It would not take on all the city's problems. The quality of the schools, the ability of the economy to generate jobs, downtown redevelopment—these tasks would be left to others. Neighborhoods Incorporated would do just two things: develop strategies to increase home ownership and stimulate the housing market in Battle Creek's inner city and work with residents of its target areas to improve their capacity to contribute to the health of the neighborhood. With a generous grant from the W. K. Kellogg Foundation and support from the city, the new Neighborhoods Incorporated set about its work.

Building Value

If you were to call Neighborhoods Incorporated today to inquire about buying a home, you would not find Kim Winfrey; after ten years with the organization, she moved on to start her own mortgage company. Neither should you expect a house call; Neighborhoods stopped making these years ago as lending volume expanded. You would, however, be asked essentially the same three questions that were asked of Denise in 1991. First, do you have a full-time job that pays at least $8.50 an hour, or $1,400 a month? For Denise, the answer was yes. She earned just over $20,000 a year at her city job, well above Neighborhoods' cutoff. Second, are you able to save between $1,000 and $2,000 for a down payment? This was a trickier proposition, since Denise not only had no savings but was in debt. And third, is your credit history reasonably stable? Having declared bankruptcy the year before, Denise's answer to this question was an emphatic no. But rather than turn Denise away, Neighborhoods offered to work with her to resolve her credit problems. The same would be true today.

In many respects, Neighborhoods Incorporated resembles a traditional lending institution. It buys and sells properties, charges interest on the money it lends, and sells its loans in the secondary market. But unlike a bank or mortgage company, Neighborhoods is willing to help potential clients address the barriers they face on the road to home ownership. And because Neighborhoods is not a profit-making organization, it can offer substantially more education and support to its clients than they would receive from a private lending institution. To ensure that customers have the skills and resources they need to succeed as homeowners, Neighborhoods staff counsels them before their home is purchased, during the transaction, and after the deal is closed. "They stick with you, they monitor you," says Denise. "If you have problems, they're there to catch you and help you get through it. They understand that life isn't peaches and cream all the time, you're going to have setbacks. Instead of just saying, 'Tough luck, we want our money,' they say, 'Let's work out a plan to get you out of this trouble.'" While Neighborhoods sometimes forecloses on a mortgage, it is far more common for a revised payment plan to be agreed upon.

Denise was a prime example of a client who had had little experience making major financial commitments and even less success managing those she had made. Repairing her credit was only the first step. If Denise was to assume responsibility for a mortgage, she would need to change her spending habits and learn how to handle her finances. Kim showed Denise a copy of her credit report and told her what she would need to do to qualify for a mortgage. "She said, 'This is what you need to work on in order for us to get ready. This is the money you'll need in order to get your down payment.' So I proceeded to start cleaning up," Denise remembers. "And as I got over another hurdle, then I would sit down [with Kim] and we would work on it some more."

Today, these lessons are incorporated into a series of training sessions that all prospective home buyers must attend. The classes are taught by members of Neighborhoods' staff of twenty-eight, dedicated individuals who endure long hours and low pay because they believe in the value of what they are doing. (Like many nonprofits, Neighborhoods Incorporated struggles with staff turnover and hiring difficulties because of a lack of resources for investing in its human and organizational infrastructure.)

First is an orientation session led by a member of Neighborhoods' home ownership team. Next comes Dollars and Sense, which introduces budgeting concepts, offers tips and tricks for saving, and asks participants to look at how their spending behavior can affect their ability to buy and care for a house. (Those clients with more severe credit problems receive one-on-one counseling, as Denise did.) As customers get ready to apply for their loans, they attend HomeRun, a session at which they hear about the different financial products available to them, assess what they realistically can afford, and learn what Neighborhoods expects from them as homeowners. In Kim Winfrey's words, "We take responsibility very seriously here. We expect families to be responsible for their own behavior, to be responsible for their house, to be responsible for their neighborhood."

Session leaders make it clear that they expect a reciprocal relationship with their clients. Neighborhoods will help you buy a house you can afford. In exchange, you must abide by the terms of your loan, improve your property, and contribute to the quality of life on your block.

A number of optional, one-time classes are also offered to Neighborhoods' clients. Often, it is the residents themselves who identify a need for training in a given area, such as landscaping, summer maintenance, or winterizing a home. Neighborhoods has also offered sessions on financial literacy wherein they warn residents about predatory lending—efforts by unscrupulous mortgage companies to encourage low-income homeowners to take out high–interest rate loans using their homes as collateral. These transactions can result in owners losing their homes if the loan payments cannot be met. And almost every year, one evening is dedicated to teaching residents how to decorate their homes for the holidays while staying on a tight budget.

With Kim's support, Denise began to come to terms with her credit problems. "She made it real," Denise says. "She was constantly reflecting personal experiences of her own so that you could relate and not feel so overwhelmed or feel so inadequate. . . . If I had a question or a situation, she was right there to keep me from getting off track." The first step was learning to say no to family, friends, and her own impulses. This task was made easier by the fact that when she declared bankruptcy she had lost all her credit cards ("the best thing that could have happened to me," according to Denise). With Neighborhoods' help, she learned to budget and buy needed goods on layaway. Highly motivated by the prospect of home ownership, she was able to save $700 toward a down payment.

The process was a long one. It was not until a year after Denise and Kim had first met that the call finally came from Kim saying she had found Denise the perfect house. Naturally, Denise wanted to know where precisely this perfect house was located. The reply came: "On Greenwood." "You must be out of your mind," Denise blurted out, as she remembered the nights spent with the windows closed and the doors locked, the trash, the gangs, the gunshots. "There's no way I'm going to live on Greenwood," she said.

Still, Kim persuaded Denise to keep an open mind. In an odd twist of fate, the house Kim had in mind was located across the street from Denise's old Greenwood address—a location that did not endear it to her any further. Since Denise and her daughter had lived there fifteen years earlier, Greenwood's most visible problems, especially drug dealing, had subsided.

But the street was still plagued by what Neighborhoods' staff and customers call "issues." Homes were in disrepair, garbage littered the street, and neighbors seldom spoke. One house on the corner saw a heavy traffic in half-dressed women and their male customers. Both apathy and fear were evident. As Denise says: "There were still issues that had never been challenged because, if a resident said they lived on Greenwood, nobody messed with them. It was still a really tough place."

Kim showed her the house and, much to her amazement, Denise fell in love immediately. "I can't explain it," she says, "but when I walked into the house, it felt like I had been there before. It felt like it was my house." Close to a hundred years old, the house had its problems, not the least of which was a driveway paved so badly that when it rained the runoff drained directly into the basement. But with four bedrooms, a large living room, a dining room, and an enclosed back porch, it was more spacious than anywhere Denise had ever imagined living. Best of all, these palatial quarters would cost less than the rent for her two-bedroom apartment. The possibility of owning a home, *this* home, outweighed Denise's fears and, to her own surprise, she found herself willing to return to her old neighborhood.

But before Denise could buy the house, she had to prove to Neighborhoods she was ready for home ownership. Under a lease-to-own program designed for higher-risk customers, Denise first moved into her Greenwood Avenue home as a renter, to live there for a year while Neighborhoods monitored her monthly payments. Only if she made them on time would she get a mortgage. Denise held up her end of the bargain and so did Neighborhoods. By the end of the year, her payment record was perfect and her savings had grown to $1,000—enough for the down payment and home insurance. Now the organization converted her rental agreement to a mortgage.

Neighborhoods makes loans in three ways. Most common is a tandem loan, in which the home buyer gets a first mortgage at the market interest rate from a commercial bank and a second mortgage, sometimes at a reduced rate, from Neighborhoods Incorporated. Banks are eager to make such loans because they count toward federally mandated low-income lending requirements and have proven to carry little risk because of Neighborhoods' involvement. But not every applicant will qualify for a bank loan. Banks do not look kindly on recent bankruptcies and often require customers with past credit problems to pay higher interest rates to make up for the greater risk. Neighborhoods has more flexibility than traditional lenders in determining whether to make a loan. It can take into account special circumstances, such as divorce or an illness, that might have contributed to the bankruptcy. It can also make judgments about whether a reasonable repayment plan is in place. If Neighborhoods decides to make a loan on its own, it has two options: the loan can come from a pool contributed by several local banks and operated by Neighborhoods, or it can come from Neighborhoods' own revolving loan fund and then be sold on the secondary market. In Denise's case, the organization felt she was ready to assume a mortgage. While Denise probably could have qualified for a bank loan by then, she opted to keep her mortgage with Neighborhoods.

Whatever the instrument, Neighborhoods operates as a sophisticated financial institution. It abides by conservative housing and debt ratios similar to those found in the private sector: a purchaser's monthly home loan payment must be within 28 percent of his or her income, and all debt combined (the mortgage plus any other debt, such as a car loan) may not exceed 36 percent of income. Neighborhoods has never lost money on a secured loan and, of the $17.6 million loan portfolio it manages, only $75,000 has been written off since the new organization was established in 1992.[14]

Lending plays a central role in Neighborhoods' activities, but it is only a means to an end. The organization's larger purpose is to build healthy neighborhoods, which it defines as places where people are willing to invest their time, effort, and money, and where neighbors manage the day-to-day issues that arise on their block. But converting parts of inner-city Battle Creek from neighborhoods of last resort to neighborhoods of choice after decades of neglect, white flight, and disinvestment is a tall order. To accomplish this task, Neighborhoods Incorporated differs in key respects from most community-based housing organizations. These focus on helping individuals improve their living situations; Neighborhoods Incorporated instead sees the neighborhood as the client. The goal is to restore its overall health in terms of image, market, physical condition, and the ability of residents to manage change. In other words, it was not enough to get Denise into a home. Neighborhoods also needed her to contribute to rebuilding the quality of life on Greenwood Avenue. Several strategies flow from this neighborhood-centered goal.

Unlike many housing programs that take a "scattered site" approach, renovating individual properties dispersed throughout a given area, Neighborhoods' efforts are concentrated geographically. When it began work in Washington Heights, Neighborhoods chose specific blocks on which to focus. Greenwood was one of these. Members of the organization's outreach staff learned about each and every property and developed a plan for the street. To date, around three-quarters of the homes on Greenwood have been affected by Neighborhoods Incorporated in one way or another. Neighborhoods deploys a variety of techniques in its quest for a healthier neighborhood. A dilapidated house might be purchased and torn down and a new one built in its place. Purchasers who can afford to take on major renovations might be attracted to the neighborhood by a low interest rate or down payment subsidy. Houses might be bought and rehabbed by Neighborhoods before being put on the market. Where underbrush needs to be cleared, a demolition contractor will be brought in. If neighbors express an interest in landscaping their yards, Neighborhoods will connect them with volunteer gardeners from the nearby arboretum. This geographically targeted approach allows for visible and often dramatic improvements in the look of a street. These changes, in turn, help convince residents of neighboring streets, along with realtors and others, that an area is improving.

Most community-based housing programs serve only low- and moderate-income households; Neighborhoods' programs are open to people at all income levels. Missing from the organization's publicity material is any mention of poverty, even though the organization works in some of the most troubled areas of Battle Creek, a city where the poverty rate exceeds the state average and where the percentage of children who qualify for free or reduced-price school lunches runs higher than the state average at virtually every elementary school.[15] Not surprisingly, Neighborhoods serves a largely poor population, with almost half its loans going to low-income customers.[16] But one of the organization's core tenets is that a neighborhood populated by residents of different income levels, age groups, and ethnic or racial backgrounds has the greatest prospects for success, and it strives for diversity in its lending. In 2000, for example, Neighborhoods Incorporated made loans to families whose incomes ranged from $18,400 to $97,000 a year, for properties with sale prices from $33,000 to $95,000.[17] Organizations that depend heavily on federal or state funds are restricted to making loans to households below a certain income level or to concentrating their efforts in low-income census tracts. Neighborhoods is bound by neither of these limitations, in part because its funds come from a diverse group of sources, giving it maximum flexibility in its lending decisions.[18]

Neighborhoods has a carefully considered strategy for choosing its target neighborhoods. When it began work in 1992, the organization selected areas where at least half the homes were still owner-occupied and no more than a quarter of lots stood vacant. There were worse neighborhoods in Battle Creek, but the idea—and it is one that remains crucial to Neighborhoods' work today—was to build from strength. Rather than beginning in the most distressed parts of town, where success would come far down the road if at all, the organization chose neighborhoods that still had some sources of vitality: long-term homeowners, interesting (if dilapidated) housing stock, residents who cared. By shoring up these pockets of relative strength, Neighborhoods could create a kind of firewall to keep the forces of decline from spreading. It could then move outward to focus on the weaker areas that surrounded its target neighborhoods.

This approach has drawn criticism from some residents of the city's poorest areas who believe that they should be first in line when it comes to revitalization efforts. Neighborhoods acknowledges the problem, but has resisted pressure to spread its resources too thinly. Pat Massey, the organization's CEO and a woman who has spent much of her adult life involved in community housing issues, reiterates, "The strategy can't be done in a shotgun approach. Therefore, if we are going to make it work, we have to have enough resources. That just defines some of the neighborhoods that we cannot yet tackle." In areas with more rundown or less appealing housing stock, the size of the subsidy provided by Neighborhoods would have to be that much higher. Like most nonprofits, Neighborhoods inhabits a world of limited resources and difficult tradeoffs. It must target its efforts for maximum impact and seek neighborhoods where its intervention will make enough of a difference to turn the housing market around.

Neighborhoods pays careful attention to the market in its quest to revitalize neighborhoods. Its work is based on a belief that market forces can be relied on to keep healthy neighborhoods strong. In places where the market is not working, Neighborhoods intervenes to bring values back into line with those that prevail in healthy neighborhoods. A generally accepted formula within the housing industry is that in a healthy neighborhood, houses should sell on average for about 150 percent of the residents' median income. In the early 1990s, values in Washington Heights and the other target neighborhoods were well below this level. The question Neighborhoods asked was, Why was the market not working? The answers were clear. The housing stock was old and in poor condition. Maintenance by existing homeowners was being deferred. Low housing values were attracting nonresident owners who bought properties to use as rental units, leading to greater density and lower standards. And the neighborhoods suffered from major image problems among realtors, prospective home buyers, and the general public.

Less obvious was how to tackle these issues. Scattered-site housing initiatives—building, rehabbing, or demolishing a house here and there—would do little to reverse such powerful trends. Instead, Neighborhoods needed to jump-start the market and create a dynamic that would lead to upward pressure on housing prices. If values could be induced to rise, residents would have a greater incentive to maintain their homes, prospective buyers would be attracted to the area, and the neighborhood's image would improve.

Its commitment to catalyzing the market led Neighborhoods Incorporated to break with one of the rules that prevailed among traditional lenders well into the 1990s. In making home loans, banks and mortgage companies are guided by a loan-to-value ratio, generally lending a borrower only up to 80 percent of the appraised value of the property. Unless special arrangements are made, the remaining 20 percent comes from the down payment. If the down payment is below this level, private mortgage insurance—an expensive transaction—is usually required. The reasoning is that if the borrower decides to sell the house tomorrow, or cannot make good on his or her mortgage payments, the bank will be sure to recoup the value of its loan. Neighborhoods Incorporated has from the beginning been willing to make loans that exceed the appraised value of a home, often going as high as 120 percent, provided the customer understands that he or she is making a long-term commitment to the property. This aspect of Neighborhoods Incorporated's lending appears less innovative now that traditional lenders have moved to more liberal lending standards, but most are still reluctant to go above a loan-to-value ratio of 100 percent. So the question remains: Why is Neighborhoods Incorporated not only willing but eager to lend its customers—including some like Denise, a woman with a troubled credit history—more money than their homes are worth? The answer lies in what Neighborhoods expects its customers to do in exchange for their loan.

Neighborhoods places a great deal of importance on the appearance and structural integrity of the homes its customers buy. Before any deal is signed, one of the organization's rehab counselors inspects the house. Working with the customer, Neighborhoods determines what work needs to be done and writes the improvements, along with their cost and a timetable, into a "spec." The amount of the loan is calculated to cover both the price of the house and the cost of planned repairs and improvements.

Renovations begin with the exterior—a paint job, new roof, or porch—and on structural repairs like Denise's flooding basement. When it comes to the outside of the houses it finances, Neighborhoods is very specific about what it will and will not allow. Driveways must be paved, storm windows and doors cannot remain unfinished, front porches are never enclosed. Only after the exterior and structural measures are complete may the customer begin any interior renovations he or she chooses (and can afford) to make.

The goal is to break a cycle often seen in declining neighborhoods, where homes fall into disrepair and the neighborhood deteriorates, taking housing values down with it. As housing values drop, those who can afford to do so move out. The poorest residents are left behind with homes that are quite literally falling apart. It is easy to fault the people who live in such homes for failing to take care of them, but in economic terms these homeowners are acting rationally. In a neighborhood where housing values are depressed, it makes no sense to invest money in maintenance or renovation, since the resident will not get that money back when the house is sold. So repairs go unmade, the housing stock deteriorates further, and the neighborhood slips into an even steeper decline.

Neighborhoods Incorporated has succeeded in reversing this downward spiral in Battle Creek through the strategy it refers to as "leading the market."[19] The premise is that once people begin investing money in their homes, values begin to rise. As the houses on the street get a fresh coat of paint or new windows, other residents start thinking about improving their own properties. By lending customers more than their home's appraised value and requiring that they spend that extra money on structural and cosmetic improvements, Neighborhoods is driving values up. This is a controversial approach and not suited to housing markets where prices are already high. But in many small and mid-sized cities of the Northeast, South, and Midwest, where the problem with housing prices is not how high they are but rather how low, this innovation can help ensure that the homes of low-income residents become appreciating assets rather than white elephants.

Leading the market is not a short-term strategy. Denise would not have broken even if she had gotten her loan, rehabbed her house, and put it on the market the following year. The staff of Neighborhoods stresses to prospective borrowers the need to make a multiyear commitment to their new home and neighborhood. The organization is looking for residents who will have a positive impact on their street, not those interested in a quick profit.

Some people in community development circles disparage Neighborhoods' approach as a "gentrification model" in which property values are pushed to the point where poor people are driven out of their homes. This argument falls flat when one visits Battle Creek's older neighborhoods. They are clean and well cared for, but they are worlds away from the kind of setting one associates with soaring housing prices and an influx of young professionals. These are neighborhoods where, on any given block, one can find houses that are affordable for people of a wide range of incomes. The difference is that a poor resident may now live next door to a middle-class family rather than an abandoned house or vacant lot. Jenna Tomalka, a consultant to Neighborhoods, puts it this way: "In most cities, it is an us-and-them thing. 'This is what *we* want. But *those* poor people, they want something else. And that is what we will give them.' Here, we decided that poor people want the same thing everyone else wants—safe, healthy, clean neighborhoods. And they will work for it."[20] Bill Jones, a housing activist from Chicago, agrees, saying, "I've never met a poor person who wants to live in a poor neighborhood."[21]

When people speak of gentrification, what usually lies at the heart of their concern is displacement due to rising housing prices. There is no sign that Neighborhoods' policies have led to such an outcome. Rance Leaders, the former city manager of Battle Creek who served as Neighborhoods' CEO in 2000–1, points to one target area, Park Hill, where the organization has built several new homes that have been appraised in the range of $80,000. "What that means," Leaders explains, "is, if you were one of the homeowners that stayed, the value of your property is going to go up as well. If you look at the number of homeowners who have lived there all their life, those folks are still there. There's a lady that lived in that neighborhood all her life. And because of what was going on there, she actually physically tore down her house on her lot and built a new house on that same site. And that is a lot different scenario than the gentrification model that I know of." As better-off residents—and those encouraged to do so by Neighborhoods Incorporated—invest in their homes, others on the block follow suit. Standards rise rather than sinking to the lowest common denominator.

This is what has taken place on Greenwood Avenue. Denise, an avid renovator, has helped raise the standards of her entire block. With money borrowed from Neighborhoods Incorporated, she has undertaken a series of improvements that have increased the value of her property. An alarm system was added when the house was purchased. When Denise moved in, her youngest child was a toddler. Her first rehab loan was for a fence so her daughter could play outside safely. With three children at home, she needed more than the one and one-half baths the house offered, so she had a shower installed in the upstairs bathroom. Over the years, she has added a new porch and a deck. In addition, the house has been painted, the chimney rebuilt, the yard landscaped, and the windows replaced. Denise has tried to balance high-quality, low-maintenance improvements with cost-effectiveness. When it came to replacing the pipes in the house, for example, she opted for the more expensive copper. Denise plans to live on Greenwood for the rest of her life, then pass the house down to her children. There's no point, she says, to putting in pipes that will wear out any time soon.

Denise's efforts seem to have made a difference. As she tells it, "In the summertime, I would literally have an audience. My neighbors would sit on their porches, they'd watch me clip my bushes, they'd watch me do all this landscaping. It would be 90 degrees outside and I'd be out there painting or whatever, and they'd be sitting on the porch sipping a beer looking at me and thinking, 'Is she an idiot, or what?'" Gradually, though, the other residents of Greenwood began stopping by to tell her what a nice job she'd done and to ask questions.

Soon Denise and a neighbor decided to work with Neighborhoods' outreach staff to install decorative iron post lights in the front yards of the homes on the block. Through a program called Building Blocks, Neighborhoods makes small sums of money available for community-building projects of this sort. With the assistance from Neighborhoods, the residents of Greenwood were asked to pay just $40 of the cost of the post lights. Even so, fewer than half of those who lived on the block signed up to participate. But once the others saw how the lights improved both the appearance and safety of the street, everyone wanted to join in. Landscaping projects followed, and the street grew greener and more welcoming. Recently a couple living in one of Greenwood's most ramshackle houses began installing new windows. Denise calls it "The Jones syndrome," as in keeping up with the Joneses. "I did it, then it started spreading, other neighbors started doing it. People say, 'I'm not going to let them outdo me.' I look at it as being healthy. People take pride now."

The house that Denise bought for $32,000 is probably worth around $75,000 today. This more than covers the amount of money she has borrowed for renovations. More striking, though, is the fact that houses in the area are now selling for $50,000–$60,000 *before* rehab, while a newly built house down the street from Denise recently sold for $112,000. Rising values, along with stronger building code enforcement by the city, have created an incentive for the owners of rental properties—usually the worst-maintained houses around—to take their money and run. Houses that had been chopped into several apartments have been returned to single-family status. Long-term residents are also improving their homes, sometimes with rehab loans provided by Neighborhoods Incorporated, sometimes with other resources. Greenwood Avenue is becoming a neighborhood of choice, not of last resort. It is also becoming more diverse. While middle-income people are among those moving in, the street's long-term low-income residents are staying put. And for the first time in years, their homes represent a valuable asset.

Neighborhoods' achievements extend beyond Greenwood Avenue and the streets around it. In Historic Northside, Neighborhoods' first target area, property values have risen substantially. An evaluation study of a small number of properties carried out by Michael Schubert, a former Chicago housing commissioner who consults for housing groups around the nation, gives some insight into the magnitude of the change. During the first three years of intervention (1992 to 1995), the average appreciation for the properties considered was almost $19,000.[22] This meant a substantial increase in equity for the residents of these homes, all of whom were low income. Housing prices in the area have continued to rise, and Historic Northside is currently one of Battle Creek's most desirable neighborhoods. Realtors, too, view the area favorably. One sign is that when properties come on the market, they generally sell quickly. In 1992, Historic Northside properties remained on the market an average of 124 days; by 1996, their stay on the market had dropped to half that, and today attractive properties in the area sell as soon as they are listed.[23]

In Post Addition, the second area where Neighborhoods became involved, the properties evaluated by Schubert had appreciated on average by $4,510 between 1992 and 1995. (The lower appreciation rate is due in part to the fact that Neighborhoods was less active in this area, but also to the nature of the homes, which are smaller and closer together than those in Historic Northside.) While the number of homes included in these evaluations is limited, another indicator of Neighborhoods' impact comes from a much larger sample. When Neighborhoods began work in 1992, the average selling price of homes in its target neighborhoods, before any rehab, was $25,783. By 1999, the average prerehab price had more than doubled to $54,685.[24] Finally, data from the 2000 Census show that in

Battle Creek the home ownership rate rose while the rental rate declined between 1999 and 2000—a change that city leaders attribute in part to the activities of Neighborhoods Incorporated.[25] These developments suggest that the organization's efforts benefit not just its customers but their neighbors as well.

There are other signs of revitalization. Citizen surveys commissioned by the city show that residents have a high degree of satisfaction with their communities, feel safe on their streets, and play an active role in beautifying their neighborhoods.[26] David Rusk says that Neighborhoods Incorporated is the only community housing program he has encountered whose beneficial impact can be seen in the public schools. Between 1993 and 1996, eight Battle Creek elementary schools showed a significant drop in the percentage of children receiving free or reduced-price lunches. Six of these schools were in Neighborhoods' target areas. (By way of comparison, in the nearby city of Kalamazoo, in every elementary school that showed a significant change in free or reduced-price lunches, it was an increase.) The number of low-income children attending Battle Creek's schools did not fall, but new students entering the schools came from higher-income families, a good indication that Neighborhoods' efforts were helping contribute to a better income mix in the central city.[27] An equally important trend is that the turnover rate has fallen at these schools, suggesting that Battle Creek's older neighborhoods are also becoming more stable.

For many years, Denise's mother and sister lived in San Diego. They often urged Denise to join them. But she has never had any intention of leaving. "They don't understand," she says. "Greenwood is my baby. I've seen so many changes on my street. I've got a vested interest. I know how it was when I moved on the street, I know how it is now. I have literally gone to bed at night with my screen door locked but the front door wide open. I'm not the only person responsible, but I feel like I've been a part of it. I've seen a beautiful change evolve right before my eyes. Why would I want to leave something like that?"

Learning to Lead

Until recently, Zoe Kimmel, an outgoing woman with short gray hair and lively eyes, lived down the street from Denise. Zoe and her husband got their home loan through Neighborhoods Incorporated, and Zoe later went to work for the organization. The Kimmels were also one of the first white families to buy a house on Greenwood. Zoe tells what happened when she went away for the weekend shortly after moving onto the block. She turned on the alarm, locked the doors, and left town. When she returned Sunday evening, her neighbors were waiting to speak to her. They told her in no uncertain terms never to go away again without telling them. On their block, they keep an eye out for each other. If she does not let them know she is out of town, how can they look after her property?

This sense of shared responsibility is part of what Denise loves about her neighborhood and part of what keeps her in Battle Creek. Today, Greenwood Avenue strikes the visitor as an unremarkable street in a quiet, older neighborhood—and that is saying a lot. Where teenagers once fought with knives, people are planting flowers and replacing windows. Where Denise once picked up trash when she returned from work each evening, the street is clean, and the neighbors that ignored her now let her know when they see someone unfamiliar loitering in front of her house. There are still rough spots, including a convenience store a few blocks away that attracts an unsavory crowd at night. But these days, as a local journalist writes, "It is almost as if the problems stick out because there are so few."[28]

The transformation of Greenwood Avenue suggests that for a neighborhood to remain healthy it is not enough for residents to have a stake in their dwellings. They must also have a stake in their relationships with the people next door and the larger community. Robert Putnam writes, "Homeowners who are also good neighbors take their social capital to the bank," citing a study showing that neighborhoods with high social capital were far less likely to decline in value than those with low social capital, regardless of other factors like racial composition, proximity to downtown, or residents' socioeconomic status.[29] The revitalization of Battle Creek's older neighborhoods has hinged not just on Neighborhoods' success in raising property values, but also on its ability to tap the talents and energy of local residents and increase their stock of social capital.

On a warm June evening, a graduation ceremony is under way in the airy, whitewashed sanctuary of Battle Creek's First Congregational Church. As in the many graduations taking place this month around the country, family members are in attendance, holding flowers and carrying babies. Inspirational speeches are given; then the graduates, dressed for the occasion, make their way across the stage, receiving certificates and gifts. But this is not your average graduating class. Its members range in age from twenty-three to sixty-nine. They work in factories, day care centers, and for the federal government. Some have two jobs and others are retired. One is a photographer and another is working on her doctorate. These 26 graduates are marking the completion of Community Builders, joining 140 alumni who have been through the program since it began in 1995.

When the new Neighborhoods Incorporated came into being, no one envisioned the need for a formal leadership training course. The organization's mission statement had called for residents to be able to manage the day-to-day issues that arise on their block, but all that was meant by this was that neighbors would be encouraged to communicate and share ideas about how to keep their street in good condition. Neighborhoods' staff members thought specific projects carried out by a block's residents might promote such communication, and they received a grant from the W. K. Kellogg Foundation to give the approach a try. In what became the Building Blocks program, Neighborhoods offered groups of residents grants of up to $5,000 if they met two simple criteria: do something positive for their block and then celebrate their success. Initially, projects focused on achieving immediate positive outcomes—in an afternoon, flowers might be planted, a fence painted, trash cleared. At the picnic or barbecue that ended the day, neighbors who had never spoken before would have the chance to socialize and take pride in their accomplishment.

In asking people to take matters into their own hands, Neighborhoods had to swim upstream against the prevailing idea that "others" were responsible for what was wrong in the community. Residents felt victimized and out of control and blamed the city for many of the problems on their streets. When Neighborhoods offered to provide them with the resources to carry out projects that they considered important, its efforts were met with distrust. People were suspicious of an organization that claimed it would respond to their priorities, not impose its own. Yet the desire to live in a cleaner, nicer neighborhood outweighed the skepticism, and the tangible changes wrought by block projects led to enthusiasm for larger-scale efforts.

Soon residents began to undertake more substantial projects, renovating parks, designing neighborhood banners, or installing post lights as Denise and her neighbors did on Greenwood Avenue. Residents also requested more training, new tools with which to improve their surroundings. In response, Neighborhoods offered occasional workshops on landscaping, public speaking, conflict resolution. But residents wanted more. They asked Neighborhoods to devise a longer-term training course and the Community Builders program was born. In evening and weekend sessions over two eight-week periods, Community Builders learn to set goals, make decisions, and develop other leadership skills. They also spend time thinking about how to market their neighborhoods, carry out block projects, and find community resources to help them in these endeavors. Perhaps most important, they have the opportunity to forge connections with their neighbors, connections that often endure beyond the end of the program. The course, which costs $40 per term ($25 scholarships are readily available), feels nothing like school. Concepts are presented through games, activities, self-reflection, and group discussion, and participants create relationships that carry over into later work in the community. As one recent graduate put it, "I don't know if we were supposed to have fun, but I did."

It took Denise four tries to complete Community Builders. Work, family, and other responsibilities intervened, but she stuck with it and eventually graduated in 1997. With her habitual tendency to look on the bright side, Denise says that every time she went through the program she learned something new. In fact, Denise became so familiar with the Community Builders curriculum that when funding for the program grew tight a year after she graduated, she volunteered to teach a session of the course. Neighborhoods had helped her buy a home, manage her finances, and develop leadership skills; this was her chance to give something back. In leading the class, Denise found that people related best to examples from her own life: "You need to be able to stand behind what you're saying. It's not that you read it out of some journal, but that you've been through it yourself."

In order to graduate from Community Builders, every participant must carry out a project. Denise's idea was to hold a workshop for homeowners in the community. She recruited speakers from city government and local insurance companies who could respond to common homeowner concerns and went door-to-door handing out leaflets. At the workshop, which was attended by about sixty people, homeowners heard suggestions about how to keep from falling behind in their property taxes and utility bills, how to find affordable insurance, and how to cope with other problems that might threaten the loss of their home. Through her growing community involvement, Denise has overcome her basic shyness, although she still describes herself as a quiet person: "If two years ago someone had told me that I'd be standing up in front of people and leading a class, I would have said, 'No way.'"

Like Denise, many of those who complete Community Builders go on to become more deeply involved in local affairs. One graduate, in his first foray into public office, won election to the Battle Creek School Board by one of the largest margins in recent history. His campaign manager had also been through the Community Builders program. Another has taken on responsibility for maintaining the renovated Quaker Park, a small park on the Historic Northside that had once been a magnet for dangerous and illegal activity. A third Community Builder, a longtime resident of the Park Hill neighborhood, remembered that a local park had once contained a rock garden built in the 1920s by a famous landscape designer and enlisted the city and the nearby arboretum to uncover and restore it. Community Builders volunteer at events throughout the city. They plant flowers, clear vacant lots, throw parties for the children on their block. As Marta Howell, a former director of Neighborhoods, summed up in her speech to the June graduates, "All the money in the world can't make a healthy neighborhood. It's people that make healthy neighborhoods."

Neighborhoods Incorporated is considered a model in the field of community building not just for its bricks-and-mortar achievements but for its work with resident leaders. The organization recently received a grant from the W. K. Kellogg Foundation to oversee a resident-driven planning process to increase educational attainment and create economic assets in Battle Creek's seven highest-risk elementary school districts. The project is a natural outgrowth of Neighborhoods' Building Blocks and Community Builders programs and marks a recognition of its track record in identifying and nurturing the resident leaders who can help increase the community's stock of social capital. The partnership with the W. K. Kellogg Foundation provides Neighborhoods not just with resources but also with a platform to disseminate its ideas nationally. A parallel initiative involves plans to market the Community Builders curriculum to other community organizations around the nation and offer training in its use. While some of the principles used to revitalize Battle Creek's older neighborhoods are not appropriate for every environment, the ideas that lie behind Neighborhoods' resident leadership training and social capital–building efforts are applicable everywhere. In big cities and small towns, in a climate of high or low housing prices, a healthy neighborhood requires the commitment of the people who live there. By bringing residents together and empowering them to manage change, local housing organizations can ensure that a neighborhood's vitality is more than skin deep.

With her financial situation stabilized and her housing crisis resolved, Denise's depression lifted. She went back to college to finish her associate's degree, applied for a series of better jobs with the city, and became an active volunteer and member of Neighborhoods Incorporated's board. In 2001, after eight years of night school, Denise finally completed her bachelor's degree, with a double major in accounting and business administration. Three weeks later, she started classes toward a master's degree in organizational leadership. She has had some setbacks at work, but continues to look for job openings with opportunities for advancement and recently received a promotion to the post of income tax collection agent.

Denise believes in people's ability to improve themselves, and she is well aware of how she has changed from the days when she was naive enough to run up her credit cards on behalf of others. "Now I know," she says, "if you've got a loaf of bread, you can give half of it away, but at least keep half for yourself." She has found another way to contribute. "Through educating myself, through becoming involved in the community, through all the things that I've learned being with Neighborhoods Incorporated, I've found that there's a different way I can help people. The way I help them now is by educating them, by helping them help themselves. The light was slow in coming on, but it came on." In January 2000, Denise's community work drew the attention of Spencer Abraham, then U.S. senator (R-Mich.), who nominated her for the prestigious President's Service Award, the top voluntary service award in the nation. While she did not expect to win, Denise took the nomination as a vote of confidence that, despite the setbacks and frustration she sometimes feels, her efforts are appreciated.

Denise is grateful to the people and principles of Neighborhoods Incorporated. "When they found a way for me to get the house . . . that was the turning point. Nobody ever took a chance on me before, except my grandparents. They [the people of Neighborhoods] didn't even know me, but they were willing to take that chance. They saw something inside of me that I didn't see but that was there. It was there all the time, I realize that now. But from them taking a chance on me, I started seeing it too, and it made me evolve. And I don't know when I'll stop. It's because of what they've done for me that I can be out there and do all the things that I'm doing. I always use myself as an example. I'm living proof that your life can change."

The lives of many individuals, Denise Washington among them, have been changed by the work of Neighborhoods Incorporated. Only a handful of Neighborhoods' clients have gone on to the same level of community involvement as Denise, but even those who are not activists have become responsible homeowners, good neighbors, and a source of stability in their community. Other housing organizations nationwide have developed similar approaches and still others look to Neighborhoods as a model. Even so, the lessons of Neighborhoods' experience deserve a wider audience and broader adoption. Not all of them will hold true in all cases—in particular, putting upward pressure on housing values in an already-overpriced housing market is a bad idea. But many of the core aspects of Neighborhoods' strategy point the way toward greater success in building assets for the poor.

First, Neighborhoods does not limit its services to low-income families. It takes seriously the adage that poor people should not have poor programs. Home buyers and potential resident leaders of all income levels are welcome at Neighborhoods, helping the organization achieve greater diversity in its target neighborhoods. A block that has a mix of homeowners of different incomes, ages, and ethnicities is one where homes are more likely to be maintained and a positive image projected to the larger community. These are key ingredients in ensuring that the housing market functions and that homes represent valuable assets to their owners.

Second, Neighborhoods takes a geographically targeted approach to strengthening neighborhoods. The scattered-site lending done by many other housing organizations may affect an equal number of homes while having little impact on a neighborhood overall. By working block by block to restore property values and achieve visible change, Neighborhoods has altered not just the reality but also the perception of its target neighborhoods among residents and the broader community.

Third, Neighborhoods is not concerned with just bricks and mortar. Its home buyer education sessions, block projects, and Community Builders program focus on people, not buildings. A new roof, paint job, or even a newly built house may increase property values, but such gains will not endure unless residents are able to recognize issues as they arise and work together to manage change. In the end, Neighborhoods' impact must be judged not simply in terms of economic assets, but according to the value of the human and social assets it has also helped build.

Fourth, Neighborhoods is willing to intervene aggressively to ensure that market forces work. The organization cooperates closely with market-based institutions, such as banks and realtors, and insists that its borrowers adhere to the same high standards imposed by traditional lenders. At the same time, however, it recognizes that the market does not function properly in many of the city's low-income areas. Neighborhoods works to reverse that trend by lending ahead of market value in an effort to jump-start housing price appreciation and by creating incentives for residents to raise standards on their block. Through block projects, rehab loans, and leadership training, Neighborhoods seeks to harness the power of peer pressure. As residents conform to the expectations of their neighbors, the image of the neighborhood improves, contributing to the successful functioning of the housing market.

Fifth, Neighborhoods pursues cooperative relationships. Early on, the organization's leaders decided, as they put it, "We're not going to be part of marching on anybody." This nonconfrontational approach has yielded results, and the same partners that succeeded in reviving Battle Creek's commercial center are now devoting themselves to rebuilding the city's older neighborhoods. As in all effective partnerships, each party plays an essential role. A nonprofit organization with roots in the communities it serves, Neighborhoods enjoys the trust of most local residents. The City of Battle Creek is a strong supporter of the organization and has responded readily to requests for more policing, street repairs, and other services in the target areas. Private philanthropies have contributed money to Neighborhoods and granted it unusual flexibility in how it may use those funds. Local banks, too, have supported the organization's efforts, providing mortgages to its customers and contributing to its loan fund. Bank representatives also sit on Neighborhoods' loan committee and serve on its board. Neighborhoods' emphasis on giving credit where credit is due has cemented these partnerships.

Finally, Neighborhoods continually strives to achieve a balance between helping people and holding them accountable for their actions. Kim Winfrey took a chance on Denise, providing her with the education she needed to become a homeowner and helping her buy a house she could afford. At the same time, Kim made sure Denise understood that, in exchange, she would need to manage her finances responsibly, improve her property, and give something back to the community. Like Denise, Greenwood's other residents have seen their street become safer and more desirable, but they know that these gains could evaporate if they neglect their homes or become unwilling to work together to solve problems. The people who live in the older neighborhoods of Battle Creek take pride in what they have achieved. And they know that if more is to be done, they will be the ones to do it. As Denise says about her street, "It can't get anything but better, because I'm going to do everything in my power to make it better." This dual message of empowerment and responsibility is Neighborhoods Incorporated's legacy to Denise and to anyone who seeks to make home ownership an effective tool in the fight against poverty.

CHAPTER THREE

On Common Ground

Two thousand miles away, the citizens of the tiny mountain town of Hayfork, California, are engaged in a struggle not all that different from the one being waged in Battle Creek. Here the forces of decline were not deindustrialization and a move to the suburbs, but a change in the fate of the forests on which Hayfork's residents depend for their livelihoods. Still, the goals are much the same: to stabilize the economic foundations of the town and bring residents together to develop a common vision for their future. And here, too, an organization with deep roots in the community is engaged in building the human and social assets necessary to realize these goals.

The story of Hayfork's decline illustrates one of the paradoxes of poverty in modern America: that some of the nation's poorest communities are found on or near some of its richest land. A rural society for much of its history, the United States underwent dramatic urbanization in the early twentieth century. As the locus of productivity and population shifted to the city, many rural communities were left behind, with earnings, employment, and educational achievement below that of urban areas. Today, from the coalfields of Appalachia to the fertile farmland of the Delta region, from the old-growth forests of New England and the Pacific Northwest to the mineral-rich lands of the Southwest, abundant natural resources form the backdrop for persistent poverty. One reason is that the people living in these communities are rarely empowered to manage the natural resources that surround them. Some of these resources are legally beyond their reach either because the land is owned by the government or by private interests or because it has been placed out of bounds by court rulings to protect the environment. Another reason is that resources have often been poorly managed—soil degraded, forests overlogged—with little regard for sustainable harvests. In areas where extractive industries such as logging or mining predominate, resources may have been stripped of their value long ago by industry or government agencies bent on maximizing short-term yields.

Like others who depend on natural resources for their well-being, people living in forest communities like Hayfork must reckon with forces well beyond their control. Property rights over natural resources are usually held by nonlocal owners, meaning that most of the benefits from the development of these resources go outside the community. Local residents gain only when benefits "trickle down" in the form of jobs or increased tax revenues for the provision of public services. Greater economic factors, such as timber prices and export levels, can create boom and bust cycles that wreak havoc on the local economy, while corporate decisions about production and investment can virtually determine the fate of a small town. Political factors enter into play as well. Much of the nation's remaining forested land is publicly owned, and policies regarding its use are set not in forest communities but in state capitals and Washington, D.C. The gains of the national environmental movement have come at a cost to many rural communities, as a series of court decisions seeking to address overlogging and threats to endangered species have restricted the use of public forests. Natural factors, too, can affect the health of these communities. No clearer example is needed than the forest fires that raged across much of the West in the summer of 2000, threatening homes and residents and overtaxing local and national firefighting budgets.

Can natural resources become a foundation for the wealth of rural communities, providing their residents with sustainable livelihoods? The answer hinges in part on the distinction between natural resources and natural assets. As economist James K. Boyce explains, "Natural resources are things: soil, water, air, minerals, and living organisms. Natural assets are relationships between these things and people."[1] Natural resources may or may not have any intrinsic value (a degraded resource, such as a contaminated stream, will have very little), whereas natural assets by definition represent some form of economic benefit. The critical challenge for rural communities is to ensure that the natural resources on which they depend can be converted into natural assets whose benefits flow to local residents.

There are several routes to enhancing or expanding the value of the natural assets held by the poor.[2] One is to invest in existing stocks of natural capital by, for example, making soil more productive or cleaning up a polluted urban waterfront. (A related strategy is to stop disinvestment in natural resources, such as their depletion through the dumping of hazardous waste or deforestation.) A second route is to broaden access to and control over natural resources by involving local communities in decisions over how resources are to be used and giving them a stake in the benefits that accrue . A third route is to ensure that local communities are rewarded for their efforts to maintain and manage the natural resources that surround them by, for example, compensating residents for watershed conservation or other environmental improvements. All these routes require the application of other kinds of assets—knowledge (a human asset), organizational capacity (a social asset), economic resources (if there is to be investment), and political power, a commodity in short supply in poor areas, rural and urban alike. In short, natural asset building must be recognized as a strategy that is linked to the development of other assets, especially human and social capital.

One approach to forest management that draws on all three of these asset-building routes is community-based forestry. The movement originated in developing countries among societies that depend almost completely on the natural environment for their livelihoods. In parts of India, Southeast Asia, and Africa, forest resources were being depleted at such a rapid rate that methods of renewing the health of the ecosystem needed to be devised simply as a matter of survival. The lessons of these efforts did not reach the United States until the late 1980s. Like microenterprise development (see chapter 5), community-based forestry is an example of how the United States can learn from antipoverty strategies devised in much poorer parts of the world. "They were simply way ahead of us," says Henry Carey, director of the Forest Trust in Santa Fe, New Mexico.[3]

Community-based forestry projects build assets in several ways. Ecologically, they involve local communities in restoring forest ecosystems and managing them for greater economic value, not just for the timber that can be extracted from them. Economically, they focus on the creation of sustainable natural resource–based livelihoods and value added at the local level (in this sense they represent the antithesis of commercial logging). Socially, they require that relationships of trust be built among local parties, thereby enhancing social capital. Community-based forestry is being practiced today around the country, but most projects are small scale and there is little communication across the field. "For all its promise, community-based forestry is still in its infancy, more a set of ideas than a reality," write Gerry Gray and Jonathan Kusel, two experts in the field.[4] Major questions remain: Can community-based forestry improve the sustainable management of forests? Can it reduce poverty by producing economically viable jobs and raising local incomes? If not, what are the options for communities that have few economic assets beyond what the forest provides?

The Watershed Research and Training Center is at the forefront of efforts to answer these questions. Since 1993, the Watershed Center has been helping Hayfork's residents make a living from the forest while rebuilding social capital depleted by the long-running battle between environmentalists and loggers. Small-diameter trees that commercial loggers would have treated as waste are being harvested, processed, and sold as paneling and flooring. A carpentry shop is turning some of this wood into furniture and fixtures for sale outside the region. Former loggers are working with the U.S. Forest Service to thin overgrown stands of trees, reducing the risk of catastrophic fire. A small-business incubator is being built to promote woods-related businesses and local entrepreneurs. Equally important is the Watershed Center's support for residents' efforts to improve the town's infrastructure, attract new industry, and enhance the quality of life. By working to build natural, human, and social assets in Hayfork, the Watershed Center has emerged as one of the town's hubs, a place where people who have long been divided are coming together and crafting solutions to the problems facing their community.

Casualties of the Timber Wars

They say that no one visits Hayfork by accident. Located in northern California's sparsely populated Trinity County, the town is not easy to reach. After flying into Redding on one of the two airlines that serve that city, you must drive for an hour and a half on winding mountain roads, up over the Buckhorn Summit (3,215 feet) and the Hayfork Summit (3,645 feet), then down into the valley. Once you arrive, there is not much to see: the abandoned mill site on the edge of town; a few stores, including Hayfork's single restaurant; the ranger station and volunteer fire department; two school complexes, the town park, and new library building; the Trinity County Fairgrounds. It takes just a few minutes to drive through town, then you are back in the forest, where every few minutes a ramshackle house or spectacular mountainside can be glimpsed through the trees. "It's not a cute town," says one longtime resident. "It's not a tourist town. People aren't gonna come here because it's a fun little place to shop. What you see is what you get."

What you see is a town whose economic foundations no longer exist. Eighty percent of the land in Trinity County is national forest, and the logging and milling of the timber found here formed the backbone of the economy for decades. Historically, most logging took place on privately owned land; indeed, as late as 1960, 97 percent of the public land in the county was virgin forest.[5] But driven by strong economic growth, a boom in home building, and the political clout of the timber industry, the U.S. Forest Service began allowing logging on Trinity County's public lands in the 1960s and managed them for maximum timber yield for the next thirty years. In 1988, 209 million board feet of public timber was produced, making Trinity the most timber-dependent county in California.[6]

Trinity County is huge and largely empty. The county encompasses 3,200 square miles of washboard ridges and isolated valleys that are home to only 13,000 residents, giving it an extremely low population density of 4 inhabitants per square mile.[7] There are no stoplights within its boundaries. Hayfork, with a population of 1,800, is Trinity County's second largest town. In terms of amenities, it is often compared unfavorably to Weaverville, the county seat forty-five minutes and one mountain pass away. Weaverville, which is located on the two-lane highway that connects Redding and Eureka, has become something of a tourist town, although the poverty rate in this, the wealthiest of Trinity County's communities, still exceeds the state average. No major transportation routes run through Hayfork, and it is in no position to compete for tourist dollars. Hayfork has always been a blue-collar kind of place, but while it was never prosperous, neither was it poor.

When the 1980s began, there were two sawmills in Hayfork and two more nearby. A half-dozen logging companies operated in the valley and logging trucks came and went daily. The town had four grocery stores, four restaurants, and three bars. Civic life was rich. Children could choose from any number of church youth groups, Little League, Girl Scouts, or Boy Scouts. The schools, which received a portion of the revenue from timber sales paid to the county each year by the federal government, were well funded and full.

Just a decade later, much had changed. Between the 1980 and 1990 censuses, the poverty rate in Trinity County rose by 62 percent, by far the largest increase in poverty of any county in California. By 1989, 30 percent of Hayfork's residents and nearly 50 percent of its children were classified as poor.[8] Unemployment rates still run close to twice the state average; in 2001, unemployment was 10.9 percent in Trinity County (and over 14 percent in Hayfork), compared to 5.3 percent statewide.[9] By the mid-1990s, virtually no logging was occurring on public lands. The county's annual timber harvest had plummeted from the 209 million board feet harvested in 1988 to 4.5 million board feet in 1994.[10] In the absence of ready access to timber, the local mills, which needed to modernize, opted instead to relocate to California's Central Valley. More than half the workers in town were unemployed; men were accepting jobs hundreds of miles away, returning to Hayfork only on the weekends. All but the one restaurant closed, along with two grocery stores and one of the bars. The Girl Scout troop folded, and enrollment at the elementary school dropped by almost half. The families who left town were those with jobs, meaning that a greater proportion of those left behind were poor. Four out of five children in attendance qualified for free or low-cost school lunches. Only a few church youth groups still meet.

One of the town's leading environmentalists has an explanation for what happened. Joseph Bower and his wife, Susan, live ten minutes from town, up a potholed logging road, down a long gravel drive, and behind a tall gate. Their solar-heated house and the garden in which they grow much of their food give them away as part of the "back to the land" movement of the 1970s. If that is not enough, Bower's full white beard and the psychedelic sun painted on one of the complex's outbuildings complete the picture. Bower came to Hayfork in 1973, in his mid-thirties and already retired. He had worked in Colorado, gone into business for himself, then consolidated his investments and moved to the mountains. The eighty acres on which the Bower home stands had what the couple was looking for—a creek, level ground, and an unobstructed view of the mountains. "We have Forest Service [land] on three sides now . . . and an unoccupied eighty acres on the other side. I've had lots of neighbors in my life and I thought I'd just as soon have a little more elbow room," says Bower, a congenial host, as he sits in the shadow of the water tower he built to guard his property against wildfire.

With the environmental movement that took hold across the nation in the 1970s came greater public scrutiny of the Forest Service's land management practices. The first battles in Trinity County were over the use of herbicides. The Bowers became aware there was a problem in 1976.

"A friend of ours was out picking wild berries in a clear-cut, where the black cap raspberries came up," Bower remembers. "Wonderful berries, but they grow in clear-cuts. She came and she had all these berries and she said, 'Strangest thing, look at the nice berries, but all the vines are dead.' And that seemed kind of strange to us. She ate the berries and got sick as can be. Then we started looking into it. The Forest Service was spraying Agent Orange all over the clear-cuts here. [They] spray it before their pine trees break dormancy, and it kills everything but the pine trees." (Forest Service veterans insist that Agent Orange has never been used, although they do acknowledge the use of other herbicides.)

It was not difficult to build a consensus in Trinity County against herbicide spraying. Many county residents live next to public land, and the government's chemicals drained off onto their property. In addition, virtually everyone's drinking water comes from creeks or wells whose source is in the forest. Even local loggers who depended on Forest Service work demonstrated publicly against the use of chemicals. In 1979, Bower helped form an advocacy group opposed to the spraying, and soon after the county adopted some of the most progressive herbicide ordinances anywhere in the country. The California state legislature later took away the right of local communities to regulate herbicide use; even so, the Forest Service no longer uses chemical sprays in Trinity County.

The next confrontation came when the Forest Service undertook a nationally mandated inventory of Trinity County's roadless areas to determine which sections of national forest should be set aside as wilderness. In a rare instance of cooperation, the county's environmentalists and industry supporters were able to agree on a set of recommendations to the local board of supervisors. But the incident led to environmentalists' growing distrust of the Forest Service when they discovered that the agency had neglected to count more than half the roadless areas in the county. "I don't hate the Forest Service," says Bower. "I think it's a wonderful concept to have these public lands and to have a public agency manage them. But they got captured around 1960 by the timber industry and they've totally served the timber industry will ever since."

New battles were in store as environmentalists on one side and supporters of the timber industry on the other—each now with their own advocacy organizations—sought to influence Forest Service policy. The conflict reached its peak in 1989 and 1990 over the federal government's anticipated listing of the northern spotted owl as an endangered species. Many biologists consider the owl an "indicator species" whose well-being reflects how other creatures and the ecosystem as a whole are doing. Logging and timber groups questioned the validity of data that showed an endangered owl population, going so far as to send their own biologists into the forest to "hoot" for owls—they reported that the species was doing just fine. One editorial writer noted, "The spotted owl, of course, is not the real issue at all; it is merely a 'surrogate' pushed to center stage by calculating environmental groups to prevent the cutting of ancient trees."[11] Others were even blunter: "We survived without the dinosaur. What's the big deal about the owl?" asked one industry supporter.[12]

The owl was not the only threat to the health of the timber-based economy. A timber recession earlier in the decade and record exports of logs overseas reduced the amount of work available to local mills. Technological advancements, too, led to cuts in the number of employees needed. But the spotted owl and the environmentalists who supported its listing as an endangered species were the easiest targets to blame. The debate was cast starkly, with environmentalists proclaiming themselves the saviors of the nation's dwindling old-growth forests and timber companies arguing that they would be unable to meet the growing demand for lumber unless they could log freely. Local residents were besieged with so much contradictory information that at times they did not know what to think. "To put it bluntly, we don't know what the hell is going on," said one sawmill worker. "We're being blackmailed and threatened from both sides. Industry is saying 'Support our side, or you'll lose your jobs.' Environmentalists are saying, 'Support our side, or you won't have clear air to breathe.' People are scared to death."[13]

In Hayfork, where most of the men either logged or worked in the sawmill, concern over jobs won out. It was a rough time for the Bowers. "People sort of characterized me as the spotted owl surrogate and they were darn mad with all these timber sales being injuncted and my name being in the paper," says Bower. "It got pretty heavy for awhile. I packed a pistol and some people called me up and threatened to kill me. When there were rallies in town the deputies would come out and say, 'Geez, it's really hot, you better stay out of Hayfork for a few days.' The sheriff's deputy got me a gun permit and told me in the meantime maybe I should carry my shotgun with me."

In 1990, the U.S. Fish and Wildlife Agency listed the spotted owl as an endangered species. A year later, U.S. District Judge William Dwyer ruled that the federal government had not done enough to protect the owl and issued an injunction that shut down most timber sales in the remaining old-growth habitat. By 1994, three separate court injunctions, including Judge Dwyer's, and over a dozen pending lawsuits had brought the timber program to a halt on federal lands in the Pacific Northwest. It was not until Judge Dwyer approved the Clinton administration's Northwest Forest Plan later in 1994 that some logging resumed, but at levels barely one-quarter of those of the 1980s. Court challenges, appeals, injunctions, and new petitions continue to this day. And bitterness from the worst of the timber wars lingers, more than a decade later. "There are still people around town, they flip me off, call me a 'green Nazi,'" says Bower. "They want to challenge me right there, run me over if they get the chance. You just have to accept that's the way it's gonna be if you're gonna live here. You've got a bunch of these lamebrains that are just so stuck where they're stuck, there's no explaining anything to them. None of them have ever talked to me about my forestry views. It's all this stuff they've picked up fourth-hand in the bar and coffee shop."

Those who do talk to Bower discover that his views place him as a moderate within the environmental movement. "An awful lot of the forest reform community has moved to zero cut," he explains, meaning that they advocate a complete end to commercial timber sales on public lands. Their position stems as much from distrust of the Forest Service and the timber industry as from their principles. "After the Northwest Forest Plan came in," Bower continues, "right behind it came the Gingrich Congress and they put through this thing called the salvage rider, which [said], 'To hell with the Clinton plan.' It prohibited appeals and exempted the Forest Service from all kinds of requirements, [saying] 'Just get on with cutting a lot of trees.' . . . I think a lot of us had a lot of hopes for the Northwest Forest Plan. . . . And then this salvage rider hit and, boy, I think the zero-cut ranks grew by probably 500 or 600 percent in short order. Organization after organization that had supported the plan and some reasonable approach to managing the forest went to zero cut. So now I find myself sort of at odds with a lot of the environmental community that in some form I'm supposed to represent."

At the other end of town, Keith McCollum can be found in his small office on the abandoned site of the Sierra Pacific Industries (SPI) mill— land he and a partner bought from SPI when the mill closed in 1996. With 160 workers, the SPI mill had been Hayfork's major employer and the largest business in the county. But it had been designed to process large-diameter logs, and by the mid-1990s the local supply had dried up. It made little economic sense to SPI's out-of-county owners to transport logs cut elsewhere to Hayfork's remote location for milling. Instead, the company dismantled the mill and moved parts of it to another facility several hundred miles away. Most of the mill's workers were invited to relocate along with its operations. Many took SPI up on its offer even though it meant leaving home and in some cases their families.

A large man with a handlebar mustache dressed in the logger's uniform of striped work shirt, jeans, and boots, McCollum looks like he would rather be in the woods than folded behind a desk. He and his father own J & K Logging, a company the senior McCollum founded in 1950. J & K built roads and logged for SPI in and around Trinity County for close to forty years. "For us [the business] was booming until, I would say, early '90s, '91, '92," says McCollum. "At that time is when we started with the spotted owl lawsuits, but nobody paid a lot of attention because it didn't make any sense. And it still doesn't make sense, but it's the law. People didn't think the mill would shut down, they didn't think that they would stop all the logging to protect a bird that doesn't even need protecting." Today, J & K Logging must scramble to find jobs for its three yarders (the large machine used for cable logging) and their crews: "It's made us move all over the country. We've sent a yarder to Utah to work. . . . It's real tough on the crew. They have to move all the time."

It's not just the environmentalists that are to blame for his predicament, says McCollum. "The Forest Service has most of the timber and it needs to be managed properly and they're not managing it properly. In my opinion, they're a totally dysfunctional agency and should be put to sleep. They spend a lot of money, for what I don't know. But they're a total waste. . . . It boils down to politics. The Forest Service, in my opinion, is what got the [timber] industry in trouble with the environmentalists to start with because of their clear-cuts and the mismanagement of them afterwards."[14]

McCollum has set up a holding company to diversify his business away from logging. "We want to raise fish in some of the ponds [on the mill site]," he says. "Hopefully, we'll get a rock plant in at the bottom of the site to sell crushed rock, gravel, sand. We've been kicking around a lot of different things." McCollum and his partner have also acquired a small hardwood mill to process wood imported from outside the county. And the company intends to rent parts of the old mill to other businesses (the log sort yard run by the Watershed Center is its first tenant). Anything seems worth a try, as long as it does not require access to the forest.

When asked if there is any middle ground on which environmentalists and loggers can meet, McCollum replies: "Some of those people you'll never satisfy. If they were concerned about the health of the forest, they would want salvage logging out there. They wouldn't leave it for bugs and fires. That's what they're after, zero cut, and that's what they're attaining."

There is not much on which Keith McCollum and Joseph Bower agree beyond this: the forests around Hayfork are dangerously overgrown. This is why Bower cannot support the zero-cut policies of some of the nation's major environmental groups. "The reality is I live in the forest," he explains. "I manage my own forest here, and I realize that we screwed up here for the last fifty years or more and now it's time that we have to fix the problems we created. Past logging and fire suppression have put the forest way out of balance and it's prone to catastrophic fire that's not natural here. . . . So as far as slamming the gate and saying 'Let nature take over,' I don't think we're at a point where that's the wisest decision." Instead, Bower supports limited logging of small-diameter trees to open up the forest floor and remove fire fuels. "I'm a very practical guy. I don't want to see wood go to waste. And, you know, we need to cut a lot of wood in the forest. Now, it isn't the kind of wood that the industry wants, and therein lies the rub, because the stuff that really needs to be cut out of the forest, some of it will pay its way out of the woods, but the vast majority of it won't."

The approach Bower describes is nothing new. In fact, it resembles elements of the Northwest Forest Plan developed in response to the Dwyer injunction. That plan called for replacing the Forest Service's emphasis on maximizing timber harvests with something called "ecosystem management."[15] An ecosystem management approach focuses on an area's environmental needs, such as reducing fire danger or restoring watersheds. Commodity outputs—in this case, timber—become a by-product of other management goals. It was clear that under such a system timber harvests would decline substantially and many forest-related jobs would be lost. The change would also hurt the finances of forest-dependent counties.

Under rules first established in 1908, counties with large concentrations of public land receive 25 percent of gross revenues from timber sales and other revenue-generating activities taking place on that land. The funds, which go into the schools and roads budgets of forested counties, are intended to make up for the land within county lines on which no property tax is paid. This arrangement has been crucial to the health of public services in timber-dependent counties, but critics fear it has also created an incentive for local communities to support as large a timber harvest as possible. Among its other goals, the Northwest Forest Plan sought to decouple county payments from timber receipts, while easing the transition of forest-dependent counties away from timber revenues.

As expected, timber receipts dropped precipitously in the aftermath of the Dwyer decision. To compensate for their loss, a special formula was devised under which funds allocated to forest-dependent counties would be calculated according to historically high timber levels, rather than the lower levels of the recent past. (A new financing mechanism must be agreed upon in Congress by 2003, when these special payments to counties in the spotted owl region come to an end.) The Northwest Forest Plan also provided funds for job retraining and economic development in communities adversely affected by the decline of timber harvests. The problem was that many of the most resource-dependent communities were not well enough organized to be able to apply for and utilize such funds. As Lynn Jungwirth, the executive director of the Watershed Center, puts it, "It was raining money and nobody around here had any buckets."

Plowing Common Ground

Lynn Jungwirth was not there for the worst of Hayfork's timber wars. She and her husband, Jim, who had grown up in the town, lived there from 1975 to 1984, then moved to Oregon. They returned to Hayfork in 1992 after Jim's father died. "We wanted to raise our kids in a small town," says Lynn, "because we think it makes strong people. You have to function as a member of a community. You can't pretend you're not." But the Hayfork they found on their return was different from the town they had left. The Dwyer decision had halted logging in the forests; jobs were scarce, and many of the Jungwirths' old friends had left town to find work. People were angry—angry with the environmental movement, angry with the Forest Service, angry with each other. The town even looked different. There were more empty storefronts, fewer people on the streets, and almost no logging trucks making their way up Highway 3. Lynn explains that the nature of poverty had changed as well: "It used to be that we had poor people, but they were the 'connected' poor: somebody's daughter, somebody's cousin, poor relations. People took care of them. . . . Not only do we have a larger percentage now in poverty, but they're also the unconnected, the disconnected poor, new people who've moved in." Substance abuse, particularly of the inexpensive and widely available drug methamphetamine, is a big problem among this newer population. "We also have a lot of the older people whose children used to live here and take care of them," Lynn continues, "and now their children have moved away. And a lot of the families that still live here, you have a lot of the husbands on the road—you know, being long-haul truck drivers or commuting on the weekends."

Yet Hayfork still had a nucleus of residents deeply loyal to their town and intent on ensuring its survival. The Jungwirths quickly rejoined this group. Soon after her return, Lynn was asked to speak to the high school's graduating class about the value of a college degree. (Lynn believes in the worth of the liberal arts education she received at the University of Oregon—"If you're going to live in a rural area, specialization will kill you," she says.) She asked the twenty-nine seniors, nineteen of them boys, what they planned to do after graduation. Many admitted they did not have a clue. The options they had long taken for granted— work in the woods, a job at the mill—had disappeared. One boy told Lynn that he wished he could stay in school for another year rather than face the future. Lynn came home and told Jim they had to do something. "This town is feeling like a victim," she remembers saying, "like they don't have anything to offer this world."

Tall, tan, and lean, with hazel eyes and graying hair, Lynn is plainspoken and resolutely informal (she has testified before the U.S. Congress dressed in jeans and a sweatshirt). Like many Hayfork residents, she prefers to be outdoors. A conversation is more likely to take place by the banks of a river or on the county's winding roads, which Lynn can navigate with just one hand on the steering wheel, than in her open office at the Watershed Center. Lynn is fiercely committed to Hayfork and, although a practical woman, can be moved to tears when speaking about what the town and its residents have endured.

Lynn likes to say that she came to natural resources through the social services door, not the conservation door. In the 1980s, a group of women from Hayfork, including Lynn and her friend Sally Aldinger, who runs the town's small natural foods store, had set up a rudimentary domestic violence program, complete with an emergency phone number and rotating safe house. Over the years the program expanded into a family health clinic that has since become a $3 million-a-year social service operation headquartered in Weaverville. A decade later, as Lynn pondered Hayfork's altered landscape, she turned to her friends once again. "The genesis of the Watershed Center started with this women's group," she explains. "They shut down the forests in '90. In '92 it was pretty clear. . . . It was like, 'Well, we have to figure out how to make this transition, and it's coming. So what should we do?' The first thing we did, falling back on our old skills, was to bring over the Health and Human Services people and try to reorganize the delivery of services through the school system to make that more efficient and more accessible to our people who up until that point had to get into their old beat-up cars and drive over to Weaverville to get services. So we did that and we organized food banks and talked to the churches about redistributing clothing, 'cause we just knew we were going to hit this wall."

The group's efforts were not applauded.

In the town it was unpopular to talk about [the coming crisis] because people just didn't want to face it. It was too painful, so you were kind of considered a traitor. . . . So we're sitting around one night about six months [later]. . . . We had done the organizing, people had pitched in, and it was cool, we had systems set up. And Sally said, "You know what we've just done? We have figured out a way to subsidize poverty. We're trying to make poverty acceptable." And we all kind of went, "Ah, shoot. That's not what we wanted to do." So I said, "OK, Sally, so what do we do?" And she said, "Well, what do you know about economic development, because we have to do that." And I said, "I don't know, let's get a book." And then that led me to natural resources, because when you look at economic development you have to look at your assets, what you have to build with. So I said, "Well, there's the Forest Service. You know, they're the major landowner, so if we learn how to work with them, if we change that relationship and be useful to them, then maybe we have some future."

With this goal in mind, a small group of residents led by Lynn formulated plans for a center where people could learn how to do world-class forestry. With a start-up grant of $5,000 from the Trinity County Resource Conservation District, the group rented a large storefront that had once housed the town's variety store. "It was terribly empty," Lynn remembers, "and I brought over a desk. And people said, 'Why are you in this great big building when you have that little tiny desk?' And I said, 'Because we are going to fill it up.' And then I went down to Costco [in Redding] and spent $32 apiece on six eight-foot long tables. And I went down to the elementary school and I borrowed thirty chairs. Because it was people sitting down at tables and working together that we needed.

And I don't care whether you're rich or poor, you can't do anything unless you do that."

In assembling a board of directors for the new organization, Lynn looked for people who had made a commitment to the community. "I wanted people who cared about schools, I wanted people who cared about senior citizens, I wanted people who cared about conservation on private lands, I wanted people who cared about Indian tribes." While the board brought together a diverse set of stakeholders, Lynn tried to avoid re-creating the environmentalist-industry split that had so scarred the town. The lack of prominent environmental leaders on the board did not endear Lynn to the Bowers or to Hayfork's other activists, already suspicious of her motives since both she and Jim came from logging families. But Lynn and her associates stuck to their plans for an organization that would transcend the town's deep divisions. "The Watershed Center has been very careful to work in areas where people can plow common ground," she explains. "We try not to do controversial stuff because we want to show people that there's enough here that is not controversial."

In short order, the group had sketched a vision of what the Watershed Center would do, arriving at the mission of integrating healthy communities and healthy forests through research, training, education, and economic development. The center's activities have emerged from this mission. "It wasn't just my board or me sitting down with a vision and trying to impose it on the community. It was sensing what the community wanted and then trying to staff it," says Lynn. In all its activities, the Watershed Center has strived to meet the two challenges facing many natural resource–dependent communities: how to convert natural resources into natural assets from which people can derive a sustainable livelihood and how to diversify the economy to reduce dependence on natural resources.

Finding Value in the Woods

Lynn understood that the shift from timber harvesting to ecosystem management was going to happen quickly. "We don't have much time to make this transition and we're not making it very well," she says. One way to speed things up was to build on the knowledge and experience of others. Connections to academics from the University of California at Berkeley, five hours away, proved especially useful. Yvonne Everett, a landscape ecologist, was interested in helping Trinity County residents learn about local forest plants that have commercial value as herbal remedies. Cecilia

Danks, a sociologist, wanted to focus on the social and economic health of the area. Both women became valued members of the Watershed Center's staff. "They just showed up, like a gift from God," Lynn explains. "They said, 'We think we have the skills to raise our own funds. Here are the skills we have. What can we do to help?'" Cecilia and Yvonne introduced Lynn to the community-based forestry movement nationwide. A series of Forest Service grants provided funding for the Watershed Center to build a new kind of relationship with the agency and link to other groups engaged in sustainable forestry. "We knew we needed to do two things," Lynn says. "We had to link people internally, but then we also had to make our linkages—because we're so damned isolated—to the resources and the new ideas on the outside."

Lynn has been successful in connecting the Watershed Center to regional, national, and even international initiatives. The center participates in the Lead Partnership Group, designed to provide a regional voice for community-based resource management, and the Collaborative Learning Circle, a group of twelve organizations in northern California and southern Oregon devoted to the ecological and economic health of the region. The National Network of Forest Practitioners, of which the Watershed Center is a member, facilitates the transfer of technical information among forest-dependent communities. Lynn also chairs the Communities Committee of the Seventh American Forest Congress. (The congress, which met in 1996, brought together over 1,400 citizens interested in promoting collaborative approaches to forest management.) As a participant in the international Forest Stewardship Council, the center has hosted visitors from abroad and presented its work at international conferences. These linkages have accelerated the learning process for Lynn and her colleagues, while providing them with collaborators, insight into the policy process, and a broader context for their work.

But the focus remains local. Geographic Information System (GIS) mapping is being used to better understand the forests of Trinity County. Among other GIS projects, the Watershed Center staff has mapped data on fire hazard conditions and fuel breaks for use by the Forest Service and local fire prevention agencies. Ongoing social and economic monitoring has enabled the center to assess the impact of the Dwyer decision and mill closures on the community. One discouraging finding is that the proportion of children attending Hayfork Elementary School who qualified for free or reduced-price school lunches—an indicator of poverty levels—rose from 54 percent in 1990 to 84 percent in 1997.[16] Monitoring also allowed the Watershed Center to identify the beneficiaries of Forest Service activities in Trinity County. The news was not good. Data showed that between 1991 and 1996, only 7 percent of the value of timber sales and 6 percent of the value of reforestation/restoration contracts had gone to local contractors.[17] In other words, almost all the activities taking place in the forest were benefiting companies and individuals based outside the county.

But the historical analysis concerning the relationship between timber harvests and poverty drew the greatest attention from the community. Residents had long believed that their community's economic health was tied tightly to the fortunes of the timber industry; it surprised many to learn that, since the mid-1980s, poverty in the county had grown even in years when the timber harvest was high.[18] In fact, most of the value of timber-related activities had been leaving the county even before the 1991 Dwyer decision. If the Forest Service ever did allow higher timber harvest levels, as many in town clamor for, this alone would not be sufficient to rejuvenate Hayfork's depressed economy.

Although poverty may have risen independent of the timber harvest, there was little doubt that the shutdown of work in the forest and loss of the Hayfork mill had cost many local men their jobs. Some of the 160 workers laid off when the mill closed took Sierra Pacific Industries up on its offer to transfer them to another site. Charlie Bramlet was among them. Charlie had been logging for more than twenty years, the last seven in SPI's log yard, "decking" (stacking) logs for winter storage. With the closure of the mill, he felt he had little choice but to follow SPI to its new location in Lincoln, 300 miles away. It was not an easy move. Charlie's family has been in Trinity County for generations—one set of grandparents homesteaded on the Trinity River in the early twentieth century, while the presence of his Native American ancestors dates back even further. When Charlie left town, his wife stayed behind to care for their elderly parents. After a year in Lincoln, Charlie returned home. "There were a lot of reasons," Charlie says now. "I didn't care for living down there, and we had two old people at home." Charlie is one of the fortunate few who has found part-time work through the Watershed Center. "We can pay his health insurance and we pay him $15 an hour," says Lynn. "He was probably making $14 and had health insurance and a retirement plan at the [Lincoln] mill, and it was year-round work and this isn't. So he's made a lot of sacrifices to come back in terms of money. But he didn't have to give up his home and his heart."

Enabling displaced workers like Charlie to find jobs in Trinity County was one of the main reasons the Watershed Center was founded. "If they want Eden," Lynn has said, referring to the environmental restrictions on logging, "they're going to have to have gardeners."[19] Roger Jaegel is one of those chiefly responsible for developing the center's training program. Roger is over six feet tall and his cowboy boots add another inch to his height, while his jeans, baseball cap, and boyish face make him seem younger than fifty-five. Roger grew up in Hayfork, where his dad ran the pharmacy. He and Jim Jungwirth have known each other since childhood. Roger left town to attend college at the state university in nearby Chico, where he studied biology. But when he got out of school he decided he would not be happy working in a lab and instead enlisted in the U.S. Air Force. After his military service, Roger joined the Forest Service where, over a twenty-eight-year career, he rose from an entry-level job in fire management to the senior position of district engineer. By the mid-1990s, Roger had grown tired of the infighting and struggle for resources and left the agency: "When the spotted owl situation came up and the Northwest Forest Plan, I really did not see an end to the fight, so when they had the early out, I said I'd take the retirement."

With his Forest Service connections and long-standing ties to the town, Roger was in a good position to understand what it would take to retrain displaced forest workers. With funding from the Forest Service and in collaboration with the nearest community college a county away, he and Yvonne Everett designed a seven-month curriculum for an ecosystem technician certification program. "We took ecosystem management at face value," explains Roger. "We said, 'If we're going to do ecosystem management, this is how it should be done.'" In the four years of the training program, fifty to sixty workers learned how to replant natural slide areas, reduce the underbrush that serves as fuel for wildfires, improve wildlife habitat, and process the small-diameter trees taken out of the forest in the thinning process. "When we designed our classes, we promised people that we would not put them in a room without windows and make them listen to a talking head," says Lynn. Most of the training took place on the job. Even the one day of formal instruction each week was often held in the forest.

The Forest Service estimates that 40 million acres of national forest are at risk of catastrophic fire due to dense underbrush, thickets of small trees, and low branches that make it possible for a ground fire to move to the tops of trees and spread rapidly.[20] The main culprits for the forest's dangerous state are the government's long-standing policy of across-the-board fire suppression and commercial logging that has removed the largest and most fire-resistant trees while leaving behind the smaller and more flammable trees, which are considered commercially worthless.

Environmentalists and industry supporters alike acknowledge that fire historically played a crucial role in sustaining the health of the forest environment. Most estimates suggest that natural fires swept through the Hayfork district every ten to fifteen years. Native Americans, the region's first residents, used fire to keep trails open, enhance hunting, and promote the growth of plants that produced edible seeds and basketry material. The ranchers who took their place also relied on fire to keep grazing areas and livestock trails clear. Not until the early twentieth century did fire suppression become the norm. As people built their homes closer and closer to forestlands, pressure grew to extinguish fires as soon as they were detected, resulting in a buildup of flammable material on the forest floor responsible for the large scale of many recent wildfires. In the mid-1990s the Forest Service abandoned its policy of wholesale fire suppression and began to use "controlled burns," or fires set intentionally, to manage the landscape. The fire that burned out of control in Los Alamos, New Mexico, in May 2000, taking with it 2,000 homes, drew public attention to the change, although the Forest Service is quick to point out that only one-half of one percent of its prescribed burns ever get out of hand.[21]

Agreement on the reasons for overstocking does not imply that there is any agreement on the solutions to the problem of catastrophic fire. Timber industry supporters advocate a return to logging as part of any effort to remove fuels from the forest, rejecting evidence that suggests large-scale logging is partly to blame for the problem. Environmentalists, on the other hand, fear that policies intended to reduce fuels will be hijacked by industry interests and that thinning the forest will simply serve as an excuse for renewed logging. The lack of trust among the parties and the politicization of the debate over forest health have made the logging of small-diameter trees a complex and controversial endeavor.

It is this endeavor that has claimed much of the Watershed Center's attention. In an effort to restore the health of both the forest and the community, Roger and his colleagues set about investigating whether small-diameter trees (generally anything under ten inches in diameter) could be processed in a way that would make them commercially valuable. Because such an experiment would take place on Forest Service land, the Watershed Center first had to enlist the support of agency personnel—not an easy task in a climate of tight resources and political infighting. Still, with the help of supportive local rangers, the Watershed Center was able to set up several pilot projects to test the economic viability of removing small-diameter material and to find markets for products made from it.

Lynn calls the men she works with "geniuses at applied physics." Their ingenuity can be seen in the equipment they have developed to carry out the forest thinning and the products they have created from the harvested wood. Felled timber can be removed from the forest either by tractor or cable. Tractors work best on fairly level ground; to log steep slopes you need a yarder. But most commercial yarders are huge and their impact on the forest profound. Most often, the crew sets up in a single location and cuts all the large trees within a radius of 1,000–1,500 feet. Using the yarder's system of pulleys and cables, the felled trees are dragged to a landing area and hauled out of the woods by truck. Large yarders also represent a substantial investment for their owners, costing on the order of $300,000 to $500,000 and requiring a crew of as many as six to run. The Watershed Center needed something cheaper and more portable to remove small trees selectively and economically without harming the rest of the forest.

With financial support from the James Irvine Foundation, Roger and a group of men set about designing and building their own small-diameter yarder. One of these men was John Porritt, a wiry Englishman who came to the region some twenty years ago. John is a rigger; he climbs trees to set pulleys and hang cables for yarding crews. The work is difficult and dangerous and, despite the drop-off in logging, John's services remain in demand (although he admits to being attracted to the "easier" jobs now that he is in his fifties). John had some early experience with small-diameter yarding in his native Yorkshire and was able to advise the group on the best configuration for the yarder. Tom Blackburn, a local machinist, constructed the machine from spare and used parts, even designing his own system of hydraulic drums. The yarder that emerged from their work has a 35-foot tower and 1,500-foot cables mounted on a trailer. It is quick to set up and can be moved easily.

The first site to be logged with the new equipment was twenty-seven acres of densely overgrown forest in the China Gulch area—nicknamed "Chopsticks" by the Forest Service. The Watershed Center crew thinned Chopsticks from a density of around 300 trees an acre to 120 trees an acre. Roger is immensely proud of the condition of the site. "We took off an amazing amount of material that's generally considered 'slash,' or worthless wood," says Roger, yet Chopsticks shows virtually no signs of recent logging—just a clearer view through the forest understory and considerably less brush on the ground. While some of the larger logs were sold to mills, the cut trees averaged 7.3 inches in diameter, well below the size needed for conventional saw logs. In the past, these trees would have been converted into low-value pulp, chips, or fuel wood. The Watershed Center hoped to do better. "For me, the most exciting [part] is trying to utilize this material that has . . . had a negative value," says Roger.

The logs from the Chopsticks operation were hauled to the Watershed Center's sort yard on the site of the old mill, where Charlie Bramlet oversaw their placement. Most of the small-diameter trees harvested were Douglas fir that had grown slowly in dense, shaded stands. This "waste" wood produced over 90,000 board feet of lumber—nearly five times what the project plan had estimated. Even more surprising, the wood had a strength, density, and grain reminiscent of old-growth trees. It turned out that the small Douglas fir could be milled into attractive paneling and flooring, as well as posts and poles used in construction. The Watershed Center teamed up with Jefferson State Forest Products, a woodworking company owned by Lynn's husband, Jim, and his partner, Greg Wilson, to explore whether even higher value-added products could be manufactured from the small-diameter wood. The answer was yes. The craftsmen at Jefferson State were able to use the small Douglas fir, as well as hardwoods removed in the thinning process, to build furniture, display cases, and other finished products.

The next challenge lay in marketing these goods. Here Lynn's regional connections proved invaluable, as the Watershed Center joined forces with several other community-based forestry groups in the Pacific Northwest to create a collaborative business network. The Healthy Forests Healthy Communities partnership is managed by Sustainable Northwest, a Portland-based nonprofit organization. The partnership works with rural communities to promote ecosystem management and help market its members' small-diameter wood products. Through the partnership's efforts, the material produced by the Watershed Center's small-diameter utilization program is finding its way to home products companies like Environmental Building Supplies in Portland and the Environmental Home Center in Seattle.

Since 1997, Watershed Center crews have thinned a total of 110 acres on five separate sites in and around Hayfork. The center has tracked the cost of each operation, the number and size of trees harvested, the products manufactured from the wood, and their market price. It has discovered that small-diameter logging is economically viable only if there is a steady supply of wood. "We've pretty much established that there's a market out there for almost any of this material," says Roger. "With a program of 2.5–3 million board feet a year [of supply], I could thin and make a positive cash flow." Such a program would help the local unemployment picture by requiring the efforts of about fifteen people for eight months of the year among the sort yard, the milling equipment, and the woods. Secondary and tertiary manufacturing—the processing of lumber into flooring, paneling, and furniture—would add more value and more jobs.

But it is unlikely that the Watershed Center will ever see anything approaching a steady supply of wood from public lands. The timber wars have subsided but they are not over. Even salvage sales (the removal of trees that have been burned, blown down, or are on the verge of rotting) have been challenged repeatedly in the courts by local environmental groups. The situation is frustrating for the Forest Service and local residents. Joyce Andersen, the district ranger for the Trinity River Management Unit, explains, "Pretty much everything we do is scrutinized and appealed. We have so much process to go through that often it takes us one to two years to plan a project. Then when we get to planning the project, it's usually cut off and held up due to . . . court orders, appeals, litigations, holds because we're going to have reviews with panels to see if we can negotiate differences. The purpose of the Northwest Forest Plan was to basically stop the gridlock and I would say we're as much in gridlock as we were before." Roger Jaegel agrees: "We have zealots on the environmental side, we have zealots on the industry side, and they have the power, so they're driving the situation politically. And the people who live in these communities and want to see the forest managed in a sustainable way agree with ecosystem management, but the dynamics of it [are that] it's just not gonna happen. So it's frustrating for the people around here."

Jim Jungwirth, who needs a regular supply of wood to fill the orders for flooring and paneling coming in to his company, cannot afford to wait for the gridlock to end. He has concluded that he cannot depend on the Trinity National Forest for small-diameter materials and has enlisted a mill in eastern Oregon to serve as a secondary source of supply. Like Keith McCollum, Jim is in the odd position of importing wood for processing from outside the region while living in the midst of the forest.

The Watershed Center, too, has felt the impact of the gridlock described by Jaegel and Andersen. After five years of work on national forestland, the center's training program ground to a halt in the summer of 2000. The Forest Service had failed to make any new parcels available for thinning or fuels-reduction projects. One reason is that the agency is tied up with the survey and manage activities required under the Northwest Forest Plan, assessing the habitats of snails, fungi, and other species. In an atmosphere of shrinking resources, the time and energy needed to maintain a special relationship with the Watershed Center was simply not a priority. Another reason is that Forest Service personnel who had served as advocates for the center within the agency hierarchy moved on, leaving Watershed Center programs in the hands of others who were less familiar with its work. As one of the center's reports puts it, "When a program is supported by agency personalities and not agency policy, it is very vulnerable."[22]

Roger and his crew were back in the woods in the summer of 2001, but the ups and downs of the small-diameter business have underscored the need to find other ways of working with the Forest Service. One possibility is "stewardship contracting." Under a program authorized and funded by the Clinton administration in 1998 and subsequently supported by the Bush administration, stewardship contracting aims to provide incentives for local contractors to improve the condition of Forest Service land. In keeping with the principles of ecosystem management, what is taken out of the forest is a by-product of stewardship services, not their end goal. "When we do these projects," Roger explains, "we emphasize that it's much more important what you leave than what you take out." But even though stewardship contracting is being promoted at a policy level, more could be happening on the ground. Joyce Andersen elaborates: "Even if people [within the Forest Service] talk the language of stewardship contracts, there isn't a lot of patience with the amount of time it takes or the targets that you can supply. It's costly. I think the government in general talks about risk-taking and doing things differently, but there's very little reward or support within the system to do that. So the people who struggle with this are usually out on their own." She notes that the Forest Service still needs technical assistance in determining how best to offer stewardship contracts, while local contractors remain reluctant to bid on them because of the mix of skills required, the variety of equipment or subcontracting needed, and their unfamiliarity with the bidding process.

Durand Mortensen, another Forest Service veteran who helps Roger run the Watershed Center's work crews, agrees: "Loggers are used to bidding on logging. They know what it's going to cost to maintain a road, they know what it'll cost to skid the logs . . . , they know what they'll get over at Weaverville for Doug fir, they know what the haul cost to Weaverville is, they know what it's gonna cost if they ship this stuff to Anderson [in the Central Valley]. But most of them have never thinned a plantation or done roadside brushing, and now they have to take all those costs and come up with an estimate. Not for just this year, because you're buying into a five-year plan." Local contractors do not necessarily have on hand the right people with the right skills to undertake the range of tasks involved in stewardship, such as data collection, mapping, watershed restoration, wildlife survey protocols, habitat enhancement, and, as Cecilia Danks puts it, "a light touch with heavy equipment."[23] The Watershed Center has begun training local contractors to bid on stewardship contracts—efforts that have met with some success. Early on, Roger and Durand set up their own partnership to bid on contracts and keep local people employed if contractors were unable to gain a share of Forest Service work. The partnership has not been needed thus far. As the Forest Service intensified its efforts to recruit local contractors, three groups of Watershed Center trainees formed their own businesses and became successful bidders on stewardship contracts.

In the meantime, the loggers who work for the Watershed Center find themselves in an awkward position. They are grateful for work that keeps them in the woods and allows them to continue to live in Hayfork. But their logging buddies look askance at them for teaming up with the center and, by extension, the Forest Service. "The older loggers think we're just playing around," says Charlie Bramlet. John Porritt agrees: "A lot of the loggers don't like the Watershed because they think they're hand in hand with the Forest Service. [They say] the Forest Service is giving some jobs straight to them instead of putting them up for bid to the private sector. That's the common complaint . . . [but] there isn't another small yarder. Nobody with a big yarder can afford to do [this work], so in actual fact there really isn't any competition."

Lynn is aware that the Watershed Center takes flak from many quarters. "Some places we get written up as cutting-edge conservation," she says; "Locally, because I'm from a logging family, I know that there are a lot of people who think that's what I want to do in life, cut big trees." But Lynn is less interested in how the center's work is labeled than in its impact on Hayfork and its residents. The small-diameter utilization program and stewardship contracting are both part of an effort to capture added value from forest work for the local community. When logs are shipped out of the area for processing, the higher prices paid for finished products go to firms and individuals based outside Trinity County. By investing in equipment and training so that production can be done locally, the center is trying to keep the value associated with secondary and tertiary manufacturing within the community. Similarly, when Forest Service contracts go to large companies outside the region, scarce resources and job opportunities are diverted from the local economy. Efforts to build the capacity of local businesses to bid on contracts are designed to reverse this trend.

Unfortunately, success in achieving the goal of adding value locally depends on decisions over which the Watershed Center and Trinity County have little control. Forest Service funding and strategies, often determined in Washington or at the regional level; the presence or absence of advocates within the agency; environmental challenges to Forest Service plans; and court decisions that can allow a forest project to go forward or postpone it indefinitely are among those variables that shape the ability of the Watershed Center to pursue its value-added strategy. Even though the center's leaders are well aware of this problem, they can still be taken by surprise: "I was feeling really good these last few years," says Lynn. "We built this capacity, we had the sort yard going, we had the small-diameter utilization, we brought in all these resources, then, bang, the Forest Service just stopped. All of our projects stopped. . . . And we had no control over that, we couldn't do anything."

Broadening the Base

The limited room for maneuver when it comes to forest projects has increased the urgency of finding economic development strategies that do not depend on the county's natural resources. "You don't want to be leading people to a future that doesn't exist," says Lynn. In this light, the Watershed Center's efforts to broaden the community's economic base have taken on greater importance.

The main component in the center's plan for economic diversification is a small-business incubator that focuses on value-added wood products. Two sources of funding were critical to the project: a five-year grant of $150,000 a year from the Ford Foundation's Community-Based Forestry National Demonstration Program (the Watershed Center was one of twelve organizations nationally to receive such funding) and a $300,000 Community Development Block Grant (CDBG) to Trinity County. The CDBG money, which was contingent on receipt of the Ford Foundation grant, was dedicated to constructing a building to house the incubator. The building, located on county land near the fairgrounds in Hayfork, is owned by Trinity County and leased to the Watershed Center for a nominal fee. The first few years of the Ford Foundation grant will go toward purchasing equipment, including kilns to speed the drying of wood, a log loader, a log sorter, and various saws. The equipment will serve three purposes: job training, custom leases for business start-ups or expansion, and custom jobs for existing businesses. "We'll have real machinery that people can have access to and lease time on, and that [they can use] to be trained on," says Lynn. "And if it is industry-standard machinery, then they can learn the skills and go other places. If there are businesses that come in who need customized training, or who could expand but they can't capitalize their own equipment, then we could make that available to them." Once the equipment is in place, the remainder of the grant will be used to support the development of local businesses and a for-profit subsidiary of the Watershed Center itself. Along with the grant comes technical assistance from the Pinchot Institute, a leading national conservation organization, and information sharing among grant recipients. The funding and support is designed to enable the Watershed Center to help local companies reach self-sufficiency through research and development of high value-added products, market development, and the recycling of wood wastes.

One of the challenges in putting together plans for the incubator is that collaboration does not come easily in places like Hayfork. "People who live here are fiercely independent," says Jim Jungwirth. In the early 1990s, Jim had explored the idea of forming a marketing cooperative among the twenty-six small sawmills then operating in Trinity County. He had discovered that independent sawmillers could get twice as much money for their wood if small lots were combined and sold outside the region than if the lots were sold individually and closer to home. "The further away from the stump," he explains, "the more valuable it is." But most independent operators could not afford to spend time marketing their wood to faraway buyers. Jim reasoned that by joining together in a cooperative the owners could double their production, reduce costs, improve quality control, and sell their wood by grade to the highest-value market available. Jim visited the sawmill owners, presented his plan, and quickly realized it had no future. "They just didn't like the idea of having to sit together as a group and having to make decisions," he says. One owner told him that this was the kind of arrangement he had fought against in Vietnam. The incubator takes a different approach. By acquiring equipment in its own name and leasing it to small businesses, the Watershed Center is creating the same kind of economies of scale as Jim's proposed marketing collaborative—but it is doing so through traditional market mechanisms, not cooperative ownership.

The incubator's first tenant, Jefferson State Forest Products, moved in at the end of 2001. Until then, the company had worked out of rented space at the fairgrounds. The problem with this arrangement was that the firm's entire operation, including its storage of raw material and finished product, had to be moved each year to temporary quarters for the short period in August during which the county fair takes place. Jim and his partner, Greg, are excited about the prospect of facilities they can use year-round. They also expect to benefit by leasing time on the incubator's equipment, particularly the kilns, which will cut the drying time for their wood by three-quarters. Jefferson State currently employs twelve workers and expects to add more once the incubator is finished. While considerable training is required when new workers are hired, there are advantages to operating in an environment where unemployment is high. "I'll tell you," says Greg Wilson, "one of the nice things about being here in this location is people stick like glue to you." The company's largest client is Whole Foods Markets, which relies on Jefferson State to provide booths, chairs, tables, and counters for its in-store cafés. As Whole Foods has expanded nationally, Jefferson State has grown, too, and turned its first profit in 2001.

The goal of the incubator is to support the entrepreneurial impulses of Trinity County residents and help firms expand to employ more local workers. Before finalizing plans for the incubator, the Watershed Center surveyed all the businesses in the county involved in wood products and asked what equipment they would like to see in a shop where they could buy time. The results of the survey were used in selecting equipment and designing the shop. And the fit with the needs of the community was further enhanced by the appointment of an incubator board that includes representatives of the local economic development agency and job-training programs, along with the owner of the town's lumber store and the wood shop teacher at Hayfork's high school.

In addition to Jefferson State, tenants include a company that makes straw wattles for erosion control and landscaping and a sole operator engaged in saw filing and knife sharpening for the wood products industry. The Watershed Center has also installed a line of equipment for making flooring products, which can be rented by whoever wants to use it.

Lynn points out that there are individuals throughout the county, some in Hayfork itself, who operate home-based businesses and could benefit from the low-cost office space and services to be provided by the incubator. Woodworkers, craftspeople, even a pair of residents intent on promoting ecotourism in the area—all could take advantage of the accounting, secretarial, and business analysis capabilities the incubator will eventually have in place. They will also have the opportunity to participate in the collaborative marketing arrangements under the umbrella of the Healthy Forests Healthy Communities partnership.

The Watershed Center staff hopes that the potential for entrepreneurship will be limited only by the imagination of Hayfork's residents. Some point to the example of one thriving enterprise in their midst—Boom Boom Productions, a fireworks producer with a national, even international, reputation. Fred May, the company's owner, started Boom Boom as a cottage industry, assembling fireworks on his dining room table and presenting small displays during the summer months. The company has grown over the years to become one of Hayfork's largest employers. Along the way, May bought one of the town's old sawmills and converted it into a fireworks depot. In the summer of 2000, May was hired by the Hungarian government to produce a fireworks display celebrating a thousand years of Hungarian sovereignty and traveled to Budapest with a crew of twenty. As Joseph Bower says, "He's a good example how people can come here and through their own ingenuity can figure out not only a way to make a living but employ other people and create an industry no one ever thought of." The Watershed Center's success in procuring funding for the incubator should make it possible for other local entrepreneurs to expand their businesses, hire local workers, and create an economic base in Hayfork that does not depend on access to the forest.

Building Buckets

Even now, one of the Watershed Center's most important asset-building activities has nothing to do with the forest. Since it opened its doors, the center has supported Hayfork's community organizations by offering them meeting space, staff time, grant-writing advice, and other services. Cecilia Danks says of Lynn, "She has brought so much money into the community that wouldn't have been here otherwise." When the Northwest Forest Plan was introduced, along with it came economic assistance funds for communities that would be adversely affected by the loss of timber receipts. "Nobody had any savvy about collecting money," Cecilia explains. "We have quite a few groups around here that haven't bothered to go through nonprofit status. They raise money when, say, somebody's house burns down, and they do that by having yard sales or bake sales or something like that. The idea of going to a foundation to get money is very foreign. So [Lynn] developed that capacity here, which is one reason people come to us. It's like, 'Oh God, we have no way to feed the seniors lunch. What do we do?' And we help them."

The mill closure in 1996 marked a low point for the economy, and those who moved away took with them much of the town's social capital. "They were the ones who coached Little League, were involved in civic affairs, gave to charities," says Jim Jungwirth. But, happily for Hayfork, there are many who stayed and, for some of them, the crisis led to an upsurge in civic involvement. "When the mill shut down and we saw what the impacts were . . . , the community formed a whole series of Hayfork Action Teams," explains Bob Mountjoy, a retired architect and avid volunteer who serves on the Watershed Center's board. The teams, made up of various community representatives, were charged with developing ideas to help the town. "[The Watershed Center] has been the nucleus of the real power movement of getting things going economically here and bringing together in a network a lot of different groups," according to Bob. He and his wife, Jan, are leaders of the tourism and recreation team, which has been meeting at the Watershed Center for over five years. Among its achievements are the promotion of local trail systems and construction of a visitors' lounge at the tiny Hayfork airport. But the group's most lasting contribution may well be its crafting of the Hayfork Downtown Revitalization Master Plan.

Few residents believe that Hayfork will attract either new businesses or tourists without a change in the look and infrastructure of the town, but until the action teams were formed there was little effort to grapple with this problem. Hayfork's main street is Highway 3 and, like much else in town, it is strictly utilitarian. One reason is that even though the highway is only two lanes wide, the state's transportation department, Caltrans, owns a 100-foot right-of-way through town. This means that storefronts are set far back from the road, behind a no-man's land of empty pavement generally used for parking. The town grew up with no sidewalks or landscaping and little sense of cohesion among the buildings of the central business district. The tourism and recreation team hoped that a downtown plan could address these issues through attention to the architectural character and historic value of buildings, landscaping, lighting, signs, and a pedestrian/bikeway system. The team applied for and received a $25,000 grant from the Forest Service's rural community assistance program to begin the planning process. A landscape architect was hired to work on a design and group members began discussions with Caltrans and other state and local agencies. Caltrans agreed that if space for a center turn lane were set aside, the rest of the right-of-way could be used for bicycle paths, parking, sidewalks, and landscaping.

But resistance to change on the part of some business owners meant a scaling back of the initial plan. In consulting with the community, the action team discovered that there was strong resistance to the new parallel parking arrangements called for in the plan. The debate over parking became surprisingly emotional, with some business owners unwilling to relinquish any of the empty pavement in front of their stores. The result was a two-phase plan, with the first phase covering only two-thirds of the downtown area. The team hopes that once improvements are made to the west side of town, the rest of the community will come around. By the fall of 2001, the first set of improvements was in place, with sidewalks built and landscaping completed. Jan Mountjoy, who works as a librarian in the newly built public library, expresses wonder at the sight of an entire class of elementary school children with their teachers walking down the sidewalk from the school to the park—a seemingly unremarkable sight, but something new in Hayfork. As part of the downtown revitalization project, Caltrans will fund and build a new storm drainage system to address Hayfork's chronic flooding problems. This investment comes on the heels of a new sewer site and treatment plant completed in 2000. (Until then, all of Hayfork's homes and businesses relied on their own septic systems, another obstacle to attracting new industry.) Overall, the downtown revitalization plan and accompanying public infrastructure improvements will bring into Hayfork investments on the order of $1.6 million to $2 million—a staggering amount of money to have been leveraged from a $25,000 grant and the vision of a few local residents.

Affordable housing is also a priority for the town and another area where the Watershed Center believes it can play a role. While some of Hayfork's neighborhoods are tidy and comfortable, a drive through the town and its environs reveals families living in shacks with tin roofs, their yards littered with old cars, trailers, and broken-down machinery. The community has worked hard to make social services available to Hayfork's poor, but little has been done on the housing front. "We've created all kinds of programs for teen moms to teach them about child development and how to treat children, create opportunities for them to mix with other teen moms and older women, and [then] they go home to a hovel. The further you get back in the woods, the worse it is," says Lynn. "If they just had a clean place that they could keep warm for their children, that would improve their quality of life. That alone can make a difference." Lynn hopes the Watershed Center will eventually expand into the home-building business: "We'll have the material because we're going to mill it, we'll have a training institution that can train people to build and can link with the high school, we'll have the economic development capacity so that we can tie to the affordable housing industry."

The idea of building new housing in Hayfork has special resonance for the Jungwirths. "My dad came from Oregon in 1956," says Jim. "He had fairly extensive logging operations there and was part-owner in a sawmill. He came down [to Hayfork] with his brother logging salvage. . . . My dad believed that one of the most important ways you can stabilize a worker was to ensure he had a home." The elder Jungwirth bought a large tract of land in town and subdivided it into lots. On one he built the house where Jim and his six siblings grew up. (Lynn, Jim, their children, and Jim's mother live there today.) He sold the other eight lots to his workers, lending them money for the down payments, sometimes even co-signing their notes. "Every person who worked for him ended up with their own home," says Jim. The houses themselves were built from kits that arrived on the back of a flatbed truck. Reminiscent of the barn raisings of old, the Jungwirths and their neighbors helped each other with the construction. All the families are still there, in what has come to be known as the Jungwirth subdivision. Speaking of the Watershed Center's affordable housing plan, Lynn says, "If we design it right and cluster it, then there'll be communal space and you've got to have that because you've got to have a neighborhood and neighborliness. They've got to be watching out for each other."

Downtown revitalization, the business incubator, and plans for affordable housing are signs of hope for Hayfork's economy. Two other initiatives have contributed to the sense of progress. The U.S. Department of Housing and Urban Development has announced it will fund an independent living facility adjacent to the library. The overall plan calls for a cultural center on the same site, perhaps including an arts and crafts center, museum, and performing arts facility. One possible future tenant is a recently established nonprofit organization called the Rural Arts Guild and Gallery (RAGG), which is seeking a home. The second development is the establishment and growth of a distance learning center operated by Shasta Community College, the nearest institution of higher learning, located a county away. The center is attracting more students each semester and has worked out collaborative arrangements with Hayfork's library involving the sharing of a full-time assistant librarian and online services provided by the college but accessible to all of Hayfork's residents. These developments are a tribute to what Roger Jaegel calls the "hard core" of people still committed to their town. "People in these small rural communities are pretty hard to beat down," he observes. "They're pretty resilient."

The Watershed Center is one of the focal points for those invested in Hayfork's future. The public schools are another. Jan Raffety runs the parents' center at Hayfork Elementary, a position that affords her an up-close view of the problems plaguing many of the town's families, problems that include poverty, substance abuse, and domestic violence. "People on meth[amphetamine] can't remember if they've given their kids dinner, if they've given them a bath," she says. "It kills any hunger, so they forget to eat." Jan sees a lot of abused children and works closely with the state's Child Protective Services Agency. She has also helped turn the schools into a resource center for Hayfork's troubled families. A funny, fast-talking woman, Jan came to town for a visit eighteen years ago and stayed. She rattles off some of the volunteer activities she has helped put in place over the years. Schoolwide head checks for lice carried out by parent volunteers, which have cut the infection rate from 64 percent to less than 10 percent. The Etiquette Dinner held each year to socialize Hayfork's teenagers to the rituals of dating and going to restaurants. A drop-in center that stocks shoes and winter coats for needy families. A play group for teen mothers and their babies. A fund started by a local child's well-off grandmother to aid the town's poorest residents with food, medicine, and clothing. A reading program. A database of volunteers. Jan's friend Sally Aldinger says of her, "She's really skilled at inviting people to participate in their community. It helps people realize that they can contribute."

Hayfork's economic assets were severely depleted in the 1990s by the shutdown of the forests and the mill closure that followed, while the ability to draw value from the natural resources that surround the town is limited by forces largely beyond the community's control. In part to make up for this loss of tangible wealth, the Watershed Center has sought to increase the human and social capital of residents.

It is clear that Hayfork's future depends on its residents. "If you want stewardship, you have to have people who are committed to the place, who care about the place," says Lynn Jungwirth. "We talk about community-based forestry, community planning, community this and that, but you know what? Communities don't do anything. It's people. It's individual people who take their skills and their talents and make something out of nothing." "The people are what really make Hayfork what it is," says Jan Raffety. From time to time, forest fires have burned out of control and threatened residents' homes. "All of a sudden you'll see this line of trucks heading out," she continues. "They load everything in the pickup and they take it someplace safe. And, I mean, you just don't find that in a lot of communities." "There's something about the community of Hayfork," adds Sally. "Unless it's put its arms around you at a time when you really need it, you would never fully understand it, but it's just something that you want to bequeath to others."

Hayfork has another asset that provides wealth to its inhabitants: the beauty of its environment. Lynn has no illusions that the natural wonders of the mountains, streams, and forests translate automatically into economic benefits. "But when you talk about natural assets," she says, "you can't just talk about, 'Will it produce cash?' The reason people can live here, and live on the median income of $18,000 a year, is because they do have a beautiful place to live. Half the kids in town think venison is the only meat there is, they have access to the forest in terms of recreation, and so they're willing to say, 'You know what? I would rather live here on $18,000 a year than go to the city where I could earn twice that and have to live in an apartment building in the middle of the city. I don't want to do that.' So it is their value of the natural assets in terms of clean water and clean air, and no gangs for their children, and when they wake up in the morning the world is a beautiful place. It's a conscious trade-off for most of the people who are here."

The Watershed Center's mission is to be "a catalyst for positive change." It is difficult to be a catalyst in an environment that does not have a lot of resources to catalyze, just as it is difficult to build assets in a community where residents have been compelled to leave town for jobs elsewhere and where conflict over the use of resources has led to bitter infighting and a fraying of the social fabric. The Watershed Center has sought to overcome these limitations by providing the people of Hayfork with a place where they can work together to create new sources of dynamism for their community.

Several attributes of the organization underpin its effectiveness. The Watershed Center has staked out the middle ground in a highly polarized community. Rather than replicate the divisions between environmental groups and the timber industry that had been a source of acrimony, the center has sought to highlight practical concerns about Hayfork's future around which residents of differing opinions can unite. Those involved with the center also understand that, because of the battles of the past, trust must be rebuilt slowly. By proving its mettle in small-scale pilot projects, the Watershed Center has gradually gained the support of much of the community and shown that it can be entrusted with larger and more ambitious endeavors.

In Lynn Jungwirth, the Watershed Center has a leader with strong local roots. "That's one of the things that scares me about a lot of these programs I see that want to do place-based conservation and they advertise for an executive director," she says. "You know that if they're gonna bring in somebody, they're gonna do that for a few years, then they're gonna go someplace else." Hayfork has always been Lynn's central concern: "That was the goal, that was the object to start with. And the center was just a tool for doing it. I live here and I'm committed to being here."

At the same time, Lynn is a policy entrepreneur who has succeeded in linking to broader networks at the regional, national, and international level. The Watershed Center also willingly serves as a resource center for others. It has hosted visits by community-based forestry groups from the United States and abroad, congressional delegations, journalists, and others. Its staff members and supporters are unfailingly generous with their time, a generosity all the more remarkable in a climate of tight funding and careful accounting for time and effort. The linkages built by the organization have given it access to state-of-the art knowledge about community-based forestry as well as relationships and resources that have enabled it to increase its own capacity.

Perhaps most important, the Watershed Center has been able to draw into its circle some of Hayfork's most committed and talented individuals. Whether they are designing and building equipment suited to a new kind of forest work, marshaling public resources for downtown revitalization, creating employment opportunities for local residents, devising ways to collaborate with the Forest Service, or attracting funds for community projects, the people of Hayfork and their ability to work together are the assets on which the town's future rests.

Will Hayfork's residents succeed in converting the natural resources that surround them into natural assets that benefit the community? Will they meet on common ground and repair their tattered social capital? Will they be able to craft a new foundation for the local economy? These are ambitious tasks and success is not a foregone conclusion. But the progress already made and the continued engagement of Hayfork's most valuable asset—its people—offer reason for hope.

CHAPTER FOUR

Work with
a Future

If there is any consensus among the American public about the route out of poverty, it is that work must play a central part. Welfare reform, enacted in 1996, had as its centerpiece strict rules that require all able-bodied recipients of public assistance eventually to leave welfare for work. The success of these policies in cutting the welfare rolls has only reinforced the notion that virtually all Americans can and should be gainfully employed. The new rules, however, have been far less successful in reducing poverty. Former welfare recipients earn on average just over $7 an hour. Three-fourths of them receive no medical benefits. One-third have had to cut back on meals because they do not have enough money for food. And many have returned to public assistance, with almost one out of three welfare recipients who left the rolls from 1995 to 1997 returning by the end of that period.[1]

The evidence shows that simply getting a job is not enough to lift welfare recipients out of poverty. If work is to open the door to upward mobility, the focus must be on increasing the skills and earning potential of the poor.[2] Job training itself is nothing new. For four decades, it has been a central part of federal and state antipoverty efforts through legislative initiatives such as the Manpower Development and Training Act of 1962, the Comprehensive Employment and Training Act of 1973, and the Job Training Partnership Act of 1982. Much of the training carried out under this legislation, however, gave participants only the most rudimentary of skills and provided little relevant work experience. The greatest weakness of traditional training programs was that they failed to connect people to good jobs. As a result, graduates of such programs frequently found themselves cycling through low-wage jobs, in menial or "make work" situations, or even unemployed.[3]

In recent years, job-training organizations have developed new approaches that respond to the needs of the labor market while offering low-income workers marketable, real-world skills.[4] One such program is the Private Industry Partnership (PIP) of Wildcat Service Corporation. Based in New York, PIP trains welfare recipients for jobs in some of the city's leading industries: financial services, law, advertising, health care, and entertainment. The program's success rests on several elements: PIP works closely with employers to identify available positions and the skills they require, then tailors its training course to give students precisely these skills. PIP relies on professional development classes, workshops at private sector outplacement firms, and work experience in city agencies to socialize trainees to the workplace and reinforce the personal habits they need to succeed. Upon completion of the program, trainees are placed in internships with prospective employers; the decision whether to offer the trainee a permanent position rests with the employer and is based on performance. The result has been a win-win situation for job seekers and employers. More than 400 former welfare recipients have completed the program and landed jobs that pay a decent wage, offer good benefits, and hold out the opportunity for advancement. In turn, participating employers have gained access to candidates who are well prepared for their new positions and exhibit a substantially lower rate of turnover than other entry-level workers.

Programs such as PIP are not for everyone. People who lack basic reading and math skills may find it difficult to gain admission to the training course, while problems such as substance abuse or illness may make completion impossible. Child care and transportation are other potential barriers; unless adequate arrangements are in place, performance in both the training program and the workplace will suffer. Despite these limitations, the innovations in job training described in this chapter hold out hope to those just entering the work force as well as to workers in low-paying, insecure jobs. Skills-based training and a direct connection to employers can help make job training not just a way to reduce the welfare rolls but a doorway into a new life.

A New Beginning

Sandra Bradford approached the basement store of Dress for Success that Saturday afternoon with trepidation. The staff at Wildcat Service Corporation, where she had just completed four months of job training, had said she should dress for her interview in conservative clothing—something black, brown, or gray, they advised. There was the brown blazer that had hung in her closet for five years, a black skirt, and gray slacks, but none of it matched. Besides, fixing hems and sewing on buttons was one source of stress she did not need as the big day approached. To find a new outfit, she had been sent to Dress for Success, a nonprofit venture that provides low-income women with appropriate business attire. With the help of the volunteers who staff the store, Sandra chose a deep red designer suit and white silk blouse in a plus size to fit her 289-pound frame. The outfit looked so good she decided just this once to go against the training center's advice. The color might not be conservative, but she looked like a professional. Before leaving, she found shoes and jewelry to match—all donated by working women to help others on their way into the white-collar world. The entire outfit had cost her nothing. Relieved, she whispered another word of thanks to those who had helped her reach this point and turned her attention to the challenge ahead.

In a few days, Sandra would take the subway from her Brooklyn housing project to the Manhattan offices of Salomon Smith Barney to interview for an internship. *If* she got the position, and *if* she performed well, she would have a shot at landing a real job with a good salary at one of the world's leading financial firms. The whole process was fraught with uncertainty. Sandra had never held a full-time job. Not only did she know nothing about the ins and outs of Wall Street, she had never had anything to do with a financial institution before. She had no checking account, no credit card, no savings. Her only financial transactions involved taking her monthly card from the city's welfare agency to the local check-cashing store. Here she received the cash and food stamps with which she had supported her family for most of the past fifteen years.

On second thought, the stakes were too high to take a chance on a red suit. Sandra's sister had a brown skirt and jacket she was willing to part with, so Sandra put her new outfit back in the closet. Maybe she would have the chance to wear it later.

Sandra, a vivacious African American woman in her forties, was born in Brooklyn and has lived there almost all her life. Her mother died when Sandra was two and her grandmother stepped in to raise her and five older siblings. When Sandra graduated from high school, she enrolled at La Guardia Community College. But at the end of her first semester, she found out she was pregnant and quickly got married. By the middle of the next term she had dropped out. (She later received an associate's degree from the college.) The first of her four children was born a few months later and another daughter the following year.

The family lived in Red Hook, one of Brooklyn's poorest and most violent neighborhoods. Sandra's husband worked as an emergency medical technician, and Sandra took care of her two little girls. All was well for a few years. Then Sandra's husband started using drugs, straining both the marriage and the family's finances. In 1979, a few days before Christmas, he walked out. Pregnant again, Sandra went to her grandmother's for the holidays. "It gave me that time to say, 'What are you gonna do? You have kids, you're not working.'" It was not easy to decide whether to end her marriage. "I'm a religious girl," she explains. "You're married for the sanctity, the safeness of the home. And if you feel that you cannot protect all your kids if something happened, then it's time to go." Her grandmother said to come home, and she did. Sandra's first step after moving in was to apply for public assistance. A responsive social worker got her emergency food stamps that very day and started the paperwork necessary for her to receive Aid to Families with Dependent Children (AFDC).

When Sandra's third daughter arrived six months later, she and her husband reconciled. They lived together for the next five years, but his drug use continued and Sandra found it hard to tolerate his circle of friends. Then, in 1985, Sandra got pregnant for a fourth time and the reality of her situation finally took hold. "When I seen that my kids was in danger, I was like, 'Stay with the husband and fight it off, or protect the kids?' It was kind of a pull. Then things started disappearing [from the house] and I thought, 'No, we can't have that.' . . . I guess that mother instinct kicked in and I said, 'Hello! You've got to protect the kids!'" When her son was born the following fall, Sandra left once and for all and moved back into her grandmother's apartment, where one of her brothers was also living.

With food stamps, AFDC, and her brother's wages helping to pay the rent, Sandra made ends meet. She devoted her energies to her four young children, volunteering at their schools and at church. Unable to afford to enroll her daughters in the local after-school program, she offered her time in exchange for their attendance. One thing led to another, and soon Sandra was an active member of several community- and school-based organizations. "I was PTA everything," she says. Her volunteer work also led to one of the only paying jobs Sandra ever held—assistant director of the Crispus Attucks Educational Community, the after-school program where she had first volunteered. Her $5,000-a-year salary reduced her welfare payments but fell far short of what she would have needed to leave the system altogether.

In 1990, the day before Easter, Sandra's grandmother died. The woman who had raised Sandra, then taken in her children a generation later, was eighty-four years old. Even so, Sandra was not prepared for the loss. And worse was in store. Although Sandra had lived in her grandmother's apartment for years—had, in fact, grown up there—her name had never been on the lease. After several years of fighting to stay, a final eviction notice arrived in the fall of 1995. The family would need to be out by February.

Sandra blames the welfare system for what happened next. When she learned that eviction was pending, she began the search for an apartment, but with a housing allowance of only a few hundred dollars a month, she could not find one large enough for her family. Finally, she came across the ideal place—four bedrooms on Ocean Avenue for $540 a month, a bargain by New York standards. But because the amount exceeded her housing allowance, she could not get her social worker's permission to move in, nor could she get access to the assistance with rent and moving expenses to which she believed she was entitled. At the same time, she was interviewing for a part-time job at a local after-school program. The position of homework specialist would pay $362 a week, enough for Sandra to leave public assistance and be able to afford the new apartment. With the expectation of higher earnings, she moved to Ocean Avenue in October 1995, deciding to give it a shot without any help from the housing authority. But by January, she had fallen behind in the rent and had to return to her grandmother's apartment, where her brother was still living. When the eviction date arrived the next month, Sandra put her belongings in storage and, with nowhere else to go, entered a city shelter. Sandra and her children were homeless.

Sandra has mixed feelings about the welfare system. She relied on public assistance for many years and appreciates the system's benefits. But she also feels betrayed. An ongoing conflict with the social worker assigned to her case in the period following her grandmother's death seems to have worsened a series of bureaucratic mistakes. Sandra's recounting of this time is filled with stories about the denial of benefits to which she was entitled along with gratitude toward those caseworkers who went out of their way to help the family. Sandra's outspoken nature and community involvement have made her a vocal critic of the system, but at the same time she understands that without it she and her family would have been much worse off. Oddly enough, her time in the city's shelter system is one of the bright spots. Not only did it keep Sandra and her children off the streets, the accommodations were ample and the premises carefully patrolled. In fact, with a ground-floor apartment from which she could keep an eye on the playground, the shelter was the first place Sandra had ever lived where she could allow her ten-year-old son to play alone outdoors.

Sandra was scheduled to start her new job just days after moving into the shelter. But here her housing arrangements fell short. The commute— a multiborough trek from the last stop on the F train in Jamaica, Queens, to the after-school program in Williamsburg, Brooklyn—was a killer. She managed from March to June, while her son learned to ride the subway to school and back on his own. But the commute, along with the pressing need to track down an affordable apartment, was too much to take. She left the job before the summer session began.

Finally, a three-bedroom apartment opened up through the housing authority. It cost $212 a month, which would be covered by Sandra's housing allowance. She and her children moved out of the shelter in mid-September. With her son old enough to be on his own after school, Sandra began to think about what to do next. She had been on public assistance since before her youngest child was born. Sandra thought it might be time to let him see a different side of her.

From Welfare to Wall Street

Sandra's association with Wildcat Service Corporation began when her former sister-in-law told her about a flier she had seen posted at the local housing office. It mentioned a program run by Wildcat in which trainees could learn computer skills and get work experience at a city agency. In December 1996, Sandra visited Wildcat's headquarters in lower Manhattan, took a basic skills test, and met with Margie Torres, one of Wildcat's intake counselors, to discuss her situation.

Margie, a compact Hispanic woman, is a Wildcat veteran who has been doing intake for many years. A bundle of energy, she flies through the forms that are filled out for each client, asking delicate questions about drug or alcohol dependency in the same matter-of-fact tone she uses to inquire about one's date of birth. The other counselors on the bustling, open floor call out to her with questions, relying on her experience to solve thorny questions about placement needs. Wildcat's intake counselors are charged with directing clients toward the program that is most appropriate for their background—a complex undertaking since, in addition to welfare recipients, Wildcat serves ex-offenders, prisoners in work release programs, former substance abusers, noncustodial parents, crime victims, youth dropouts and delinquents, and Latinos with limited English.

The program Margie first mentioned to Sandra was one in which she would work four days a week at the city's housing office and receive training in computer skills on the fifth. Sandra was not impressed. "That's it?" she asked. "It's OK, but you're being trained in clerical at [the] housing [authority]. So you're going to be trained just for that. For me, I went to a vocational high school where you're supposed to be trained for everything. I know how to do nails, I know how to do hair because I took cosmetology. Yes, I know how to repair my own VCR, and, yes, I do know how to fix my iron and wire a toaster. I wanted something that would let me say 'see you later,' and I didn't just have to stick with housing, where everyone knows you have to take a [civil service] test to work there. That way I could move on. I could say I got training." Sandra was well aware that she needed to upgrade her skills to find a good job, in part to make up for her lack of work experience. "On a résumé it looks funny," she says. "You graduated in 1976 from high school, you went to college and had your kids. What did you do since then besides your community involvement?" Sandra had used the computer at the after-school program where she worked, but she knew she had much to learn. She asked Margie whether there was any way to get more intensive computer training. Margie directed her to a relatively new program that offered sixteen weeks of classroom instruction followed by the possibility of an internship at a private sector firm. Classes began the next month.

The first thing that comes to Sandra's mind when asked about her training program is the cold. Wildcat was located in a drafty, old building with an unreliable heating system, and it was January in New York. "There was many days we walked around wearing extra clothing inside," Sandra remembers. Some of the women became discouraged by the dilapidated look of the place. She told them, "It's not what you see on the outside, it's what you're gonna get in your brain. Listen, wear extra clothes, put on extra stockings, don't give up, just keep on coming." (Wildcat has since moved to a well-equipped—and warmer—headquarters just steps away from many of the financial service firms with which it works.)

The rules of the program are clear to attendees from the beginning. The most important is attendance: three unexcused absences during the four-month training period and a trainee will be asked to leave. (While classroom instruction and the chance at an internship are lost, clients may still use Wildcat's résumé and job placement resources.) The second rule concerns dress. Sandra learned quickly that students were expected to look like professionals. "Whatever boots or sneakers I would have on my feet to get there, I would have a bag and change," she recalls. When it came to dressing up, she was in better shape than some of the other trainees. "I grew up in church, so I always had to have a skirt, stockings, and a jacket and a blouse. Some mothers there didn't have [these] since they never went to church. All they had was stretch pants, dungarees, and sneakers." The emphasis on attendance and dress are intended to build some of the habits needed for success in the workplace. Such rules also help weed out those who are not fully committed to the program or who have demands in their outside lives that might interfere with their keeping a job.

Most attrition occurs within the first month of class and is the result of poor attendance. The most common reason people miss class is because their child care arrangements have broken down. "It's one thing to have your child in a day care center," says Gloria Williams Perez, director of Wildcat's training center; "but when your child is sick the center won't take the child. Now what do you do? You need to have a back-up system in place." Trainees' own health may also restrict attendance. Many welfare recipients have health problems and do not always get the medical care they need. Absences due to illness can make it impossible to stick with the training program. There is also the matter of attitude. Albert Farina, head of the training center when Sandra attended Wildcat, puts it this way: "There are expectations and it's about them stepping up to the expectations. I'm not your social worker, I'm not your baby-sitter. Guess what? It's time to help yourself." These lessons are not lost on the trainees: "You had to be to school every day, you couldn't be late," Sandra says. "If you come in late you must have a valid excuse. It's just like any job, you know. It's a school, but everyone dresses nice. Everyone seems to have respect." Building this respect—respect for self as well as respect for the norms of the workplace—is one of the most important steps in crossing the cultural divide that separates new trainees from the white-collar world.

It is hard to imagine an odder juxtaposition than welfare mothers working on Wall Street. Public assistance is generally thought of as the realm of bureaucracy, entitlement, and payments barely adequate for survival. The businesses in which these women hope to find jobs are, in contrast, among the most fast-paced, cutting-edge firms in the private sector—places where raises and promotion are based on merit, where a job can be lost in the blink of an eye, and where the possibility of great riches is not far out of reach. The seemingly audacious idea that these two worlds could be bridged came about because of two broader developments, one economic, the other political.

The U.S. economy began an unprecedented expansion in 1991. As the unemployment rate fell to a thirty-year low by the end of the decade, it became increasingly difficult for employers to find and retain qualified workers. It is expensive to recruit, hire, and train new employees, and the costs multiply when they do not stay for long. The problem is most acute at the entry level, where workers tend to move on frequently in order to move up. In a climate of strong economic growth, it was harder than ever to keep entry-level positions filled. The second development was congressional passage of the Personal Responsibility and Work Opportunity Reconciliation Act of 1996. The new law ended the federal guarantee of cash to poor families and required welfare recipients to work in exchange for benefits. States were given block grants and greater authority to run their own welfare programs, but were required to cut their caseloads in half by the year 2002. In response, most adopted a "work first" philosophy that emphasized finding a job over additional education or training.[5] Clearly, most welfare recipients would be going to work, and if they were to be able to support their families, they would need decent jobs. With welfare recipients looking for jobs and employers clamoring for trained workers, it was not a huge leap for existing job-training programs to begin to think more carefully about how to match the needs of these two groups.

When the economic expansion began, Wildcat Service Corporation had already been in the business of job training for close to twenty years. Wildcat is the nation's oldest and largest supported work program, meaning that it combines work experience with classroom training and other forms of support. Wildcat has long considered itself New York City's "program of last resort" for individuals with limited work histories and few job skills. It has an impressive track record, with over 80,000 city residents having enrolled in its training programs since 1972, about 70 percent of whom have found unsubsidized, mainstream employment.[6] Even with this wealth of experience, the challenge of placing long-term welfare recipients at elite private sector firms required a retooling of the way Wildcat did business.

For most of its history, Wildcat had operated like most other jobs programs. Once students completed their classroom training and work experience assignment, they were directed to a job developer who would help them find a position. Placement was usually ad hoc. A job developer might have a network of contacts in place, but there was no ongoing effort to build long-term relationships between the training program and specific firms. One of the weaknesses of this approach is that little prior attention was given to the fundamentals of the local labor market—in other words, who is hiring and for what jobs. The lack of input from employers, in turn, led training organizations to develop programs based on what they could most readily offer rather than on what the labor market needed. The result, all too often, was training that was outdated, generic, and out of sync with the marketplace. At Wildcat, for example, until 1996, trainees were still spending two hours a day, five days a week practicing their typing skills—this at a time when virtually all companies were using computers.

Among the questions Wildcat confronted was how to make its programs more demand-driven—in other words, how to construct a training program that would respond to the market and serve employer needs.[7] The organization identified a crucial component lacking in most job-training programs: a failure to market services to the private sector as an employment resource. "Most programs still carried the mantle of being good because they helped welfare recipients," says Jeffrey Jablow, one of those involved in designing the program under the direction of Amalia Betanzos, president of Wildcat.[8] "What [we] confirmed with the employers is that, to be successful, employers had to go about their business with a certain set of criteria." Those criteria are simple: cost, quality, reliability, and service. "And the truth was," Jablow continues, "if they hired somebody who had previously been a welfare recipient, that was fine. And if they weren't a previous welfare recipient, that was fine too. It really didn't enter into the equation. So there was no point in using that as part of the marketing strategy since it was irrelevant to the customer. That was one of the core departures."[9]

Wildcat would need to become, first and foremost, an employment resource. Its competitors would not be other welfare-to-work organizations, but public and private employment agencies. And Wildcat would offer services that were at least as good as what employers were getting from the competition and that matched market conditions. "It was our choice," Jablow explains, "to have welfare recipients, or ex-offenders, or whoever the population was we were serving . . . as the recipient of this process."

With this in mind, Wildcat arrived at three goals for the Private Industry Partnership. First, welfare recipients would be connected to the job market at points of entry that were most likely to promote economic self-sufficiency and that were generally unavailable or unknown to them. Second, Wildcat would become an integral part of the recruitment and hiring process for an industry. Jablow explains: "Just like employers think, 'If I'm going to buy my printers, I'm going to Hewlett-Packard. If I'm going to buy my soft drinks, I'm going to Coca-Cola,' we want them to think, 'If I'm recruiting for entry-level employment, Wildcat is right up there.'" Third, Wildcat would offer private employers a set of operational and financial benefits such as training tailored to the needs of the individual employer, access to qualified interns at a low cost, and information about the federal tax credits available to companies for each former welfare recipient hired.

To meet these goals, Wildcat had to determine the best point of access to the workplace for its trainees. After surveying the range of entry-level job opportunities and with input from senior officials at Citigroup and Smith Barney (now Salomon Smith Barney), Wildcat decided to focus its training efforts on job categories it classified as requiring moderate skills and offering moderate pay. Low–paying jobs were rejected as being at odds with the goals of creating an avenue to self-sufficiency, while high-skill, high-paying jobs were rejected because of the substantial barriers to entry. Working with Drake Beam Morin, a national career management organization, Wildcat identified industries and companies whose entry-level jobs matched the target for skills and wages and for which growth was forecasted. Eventually, the financial services industry was selected as a place to begin, and Smith Barney agreed to collaborate on the project. James Dimon, Smith Barney's CEO at the time, helped publicize the program to leaders of other financial firms and, as a result, Wildcat's list of partners has expanded to include companies such as Morgan Stanley Dean Witter, Citibank, PaineWebber, McCann-Erickson, and Chase Manhattan Bank.

The next step was to retool the existing training program to better prepare students for jobs with these employers. One issue was achieving the right balance between hard and soft skills. Hard skills are subjects generally taught in school; at Wildcat, they include English, math, accounting, business communications, and computers (both keyboarding and applications such as word processing, spreadsheet, and presentation programs, and Internet training). Soft skills refer to the personal attributes needed to be a successful worker such as attendance, punctuality, proper business attire, and good interpersonal communication. Many job-training programs, particularly those designed for people who already have some work experience, emphasize hard skills—what a worker actually needs to know in order to be able to do a job. However, people tend to lose their jobs not because of what they can or cannot do, but because of how they conduct themselves. (In fact, the most common reason people are fired is simply because they are habitually late to work or have too many absences.) Training organizations that serve welfare recipients have come to realize that having the necessary skills to perform a job is only half the battle. Those with little work experience may never have learned the importance of punctuality and attendance, how to dress for an office job, or effective ways of resolving conflicts with co-workers or managers. These skills need to be taught, just like accounting or word processing.

At the same time, it is possible to go too far in the direction of emphasizing soft skills. Employer surveys regularly identify the most important attributes in a worker as reliability, punctuality, and honesty, with hard skills coming toward the bottom of the list.[10] But such rankings can be misleading. Employers often assume that workers have a core set of basic skills and are surprised when they do not. Once a person is on the job, the employer may call Wildcat and say, "This is a great person, but she can't do anything." With input from employers, Wildcat has been able to sharpen its hard skills training, giving students the precise skills employers require. Wildcat provides its own instruction in soft skills and sends trainees to workshops at career outplacement firms. But the staff is convinced that soft skills are best acquired through actual work experience, not classroom training or even private coaching. Because of this, all of Wildcat's programs have evolved to include a substantial amount of time spent in the workplace.

When Sandra came to Wildcat early in 1997, the organization offered several different training formats. Sandra's program entailed four months of full-time classroom training followed by the possibility of a four-month internship. (Hers was Wildcat's final class that did not include a paid work assignment as part of the training.) All the other formats involved some kind of work experience, with trainees placed in paid or unpaid jobs at city agencies. Work experience was emphasized not only because it helps build soft skills but also because federal welfare-to-work legislation required that trainees spend time in a work setting. The approach Wildcat eventually settled on is a four-month period during which trainees alternate between one week of paid work experience (whether at Wildcat, another not-for-profit organization, or a public agency) and one week of classroom training. This has become known as the "one-and-one" model, and all training for welfare recipients is now carried out under this format, whether or not participants are internship candidates. For those who are selected to participate in the Private Industry Partnership, the training period is followed by the opportunity to interview for a four-month internship.

When it began, the PIP program was restricted to those receiving public assistance. Although funding restrictions have since eased, PIP still serves welfare recipients exclusively, in part because New York City has so many people still on public assistance. And because public assistance is awarded only to those who are custodians of children—overwhelmingly mothers and grandmothers—almost all PIP participants are women. (A recent class, which included 4 men among the 240 people admitted, was representative.) The makeup of the welfare population in New York City also means that almost all the participants are African American or Hispanic. These demographics represent an added challenge for Wildcat. Trainees destined for jobs in Wildcat's target industries will often find themselves working within cultures that are largely white and male. The one-and-one program is thus designed not just to help trainees land a job in these industries but to ensure that, once hired, they have what it takes to succeed.

Skills for Success

In George Black's classroom, fourteen students are working their way through an accounting problem. All are African American or Hispanic, thirteen are female, and one is male. Accounting meets every day during the weeks the trainees spend in class. Black, a courtly African American with a quiet demeanor, has taught adults in a variety of settings for many years and is well prepared for the task at hand. During eight weeks of instruction, he takes his students—most of whom have no accounting experience—through the accounting cycle from journal entry to the preparation of financial statements. Computer-based accounting is taught toward the end of the course. "He's so thorough with his work," says one former student; "It's so hard to find a teacher who can get the teaching done and still have a good relationship with the students and induce them to work." Students are tested after each chapter and take a final exam. Those having problems are tutored by Black or by their more advanced colleagues. Although standards are rigorous, extra help is available and, as Black says, he gets everyone through.

Like the other teachers at Wildcat, Black started out with more limited expectations. Initially, the accounting course was designed simply to qualify students to be accounting clerks. But his students kept asking for more information so he added new topics, such as payroll, to the curriculum. Even though most graduates do not wind up in the accounting field, the skills they learn in class help them in their jobs. Another important function of the class is to provide some background on the financial services industry—a sector in which many of the trainees will find internships and then, hopefully, jobs. Mr. Black's classroom is where most students first learn about the stock market and are introduced to terms used in the financial industry.

According to Black, PIP's main strengths are teachers who genuinely want their students to succeed and will do whatever is necessary to help them, and students who recognize the internship opportunity as the gateway to a real job. Students are motivated not just by the internship but also by each other. "A lot of the ladies are very competitive," Black explains, "especially when someone is sitting next to them saying, 'Why can't you do this?'" But even those who perform well in class may lack the confidence needed to land an internship. "Many of [the students] are scared to death [to go from Wildcat to the workplace], especially at a company the size of Salomon Smith Barney. It's a heck of a transition." Still, some of his students surprise him: "I had a girl with tattoos and body piercing who applied for an internship at Salomon Smith Barney. She was one of the first ones they took."

Hard skills like accounting make up most, but not all, of the PIP curriculum. The soft skills that are so important to job success are taught in a class called Professional Development. As part of this morning's class, nine students—eight women and one man—have been asked to interview each other for a hypothetical clerical position. Their energetic and sharply dressed instructor, Will Robles, gives them a list of questions to ask each other and offers some tips: Think about your body language. Sit forward, smile, keep your hands still, make eye contact. Try to say "excuse me" instead of "um." Offer some personal information, but nothing too private. Don't talk about your kids. And convey that you are looking for more than a job; give some picture of your career goals or at the very least, use the word "career."

It is a lot to remember. The students pair off to begin their interviews, and Robles's helpful tips quickly fall by the wayside. By the end of class, everyone is a bit more relaxed, but they have a long way to go. Three more sessions and an outside workshop will be devoted to interview skills, and students will have at least one opportunity to practice interviewing one-on-one with Wildcat's professional development instructor. As the session wraps up, one of the students has a good suggestion for the class. Try to do some research about the company where you are interviewing, she tells the others, so you can ask the interviewer some questions about it. Go to the library, use the Internet (available at Wildcat), and make sure you understand the basics before you walk through the door. That way the employer will know you are truly interested.

The business communication class is another venue where soft skills are taught. One of the goals of this class is for students to learn how to make their point without becoming overbearing or hostile. "A lot of people, they're so used to dealing with ignorant people or caseworkers that have attitude, sometimes they get angry and they don't know how to [express] themselves. They taught us how to speak without having to be rude," says one participant. In a session on business etiquette, students learn how to answer phones in an office setting and the importance and techniques of networking. They are also required to carry out group projects to prepare for the emphasis on teamwork found in many business settings. For people who have had little occasion to work constructively with others, the group process can be difficult. "I found out that you have to learn to listen sometimes to get your point of view across," a student recalls.

Some of the training at Wildcat is designed to help students assess their own capabilities. Sandra clearly remembers the first meeting of what was then called the Life Skills class. Each student was given paper and markers and asked to draw a shield with four squares representing what her life is about. Sandra quickly filled the first three squares with representations of God, her children, and her community work. She was stumped when it came to the last square. Some of the other women had put "my man" front and center, a decision for which Sandra had little regard. "If your man is so great, how come you're on public assistance?" she wanted to ask. Finally, Sandra found the right choice for the last square and filled in the words: "Me getting a job."

The PIP program was fairly new when Sandra participated and, in the spring of 1997, Smith Barney's demand for interns was outstripping Wildcat's supply. Sandra was doing well in class and, after only one month of training, she was asked whether she would like to interview for an internship. She did not feel ready. Despite repeated offers of an interview, Sandra held out for the full length of the training program.

Wildcat's method for assessing student progress and deciding who will be considered for an internship has become more systematic since Sandra's day. Students are evaluated after two months, at the midpoint of the training session. They get a grade in each class, and every teacher provides a comment about the students' work. Case managers add information about attendance and punctuality. The director of the training center, Gloria Williams Perez, then reviews all the evaluations. Perez is a soft-spoken woman with a background in childhood education. It is hard to picture her teaching high school equivalency degree preparation courses behind bars at the Bronx House of Detention, something she did in the 1970s. She joined Wildcat in 1999, after many years as head of an adult vocational education program and a stint with the board of education. She knows what to look for in evaluating Wildcat's students for internships. Grades are used as an initial cutoff, but attendance is equally important. Perez explains, "You can have a 95 average, but if you've been out ten times . . . we can't send you on an internship because apparently whatever is happening in your life that's keeping you from being here is going to keep you from being there."

Wildcat's PIP coordinators interview each potential internship candidate to start making matches between trainees and firms. This is a crucial stage, since Wildcat has found that job retention depends largely on good job matching. Where someone ends up will depend on her knowledge, aptitude, and attitude. An extroverted person with computer graphics skills might be a good fit for an advertising agency, while someone with strong math skills and a grasp of brokerage house jargon would be directed toward one of Wildcat's financial service partners. Now internship candidates begin more specialized training to prepare them for specific work sites.

Before trainees interview for an internship, they attend a day-and-a-half-long workshop at the offices of a leading career management firm: Drake Beam Morin (DBM) or Mullin & Associates (Mullin)—both experts at selling a service to the white-collar employment world. As Wildcat intended, the journey from the familiar surroundings of Wildcat's headquarters to a Park Avenue office is itself an experience designed to socialize trainees to the professional world. The first day of the workshop focuses on presentation skills: how to dress, how to conduct oneself in an interview setting, and so on. The second day consists of a series of mock interviews with DBM or Mullin trainers. The PIP coordinators attend the sessions and can see firsthand how candidates perform. At the conclusion of the program, a luncheon is held for the trainees, who receive certificates of completion. Students say that the workshop boosts their confidence. "You're selling yourself when you do an interview," one trainee explained. "The hurdles we had to go over, they made them seem easy." The workshop is timed to come just before the internship interview so it will be fresh in the students' minds.

As the training program nears its end, Wildcat's PIP coordinators schedule interviews for the internship candidates. Many trainees, Sandra included, find themselves gazing out the window of a modern glass building in the office of Salomon Smith Barney's director of employee relations high above the Hudson River.

What Employers Want

As director of employee relations until 2001, Barbara Silvan was responsible for Salomon Smith Barney's 38,000 employees, and her corner office reflected her stature within the organization. She is one of the chief reasons for Wildcat's success in getting its trainees through the doors of Wall Street's top firms. After joining Shearson Lehman Brothers in 1987, Silvan worked her way up through the ranks of a succession of companies, as Shearson merged with Smith Barney and then with Salomon Brothers. Surviving—indeed, thriving—amid this series of corporate mergers requires a professional savvy that the calm, elegantly dressed Silvan has in abundance. At the same time, her warmth and commitment to employees are rare commodities in the cutthroat world of finance, making her an ideal person for her job. Silvan's department (now headed by Robin Leopold) is the locus of many of the benefits Salomon Smith Barney offers its employees. The firm runs child care centers; offers tuition reimbursement, scholarship programs, and an on-site master's program; and provides counseling to assist employees with problems ranging from marital issues to substance abuse to work-related conflicts. It is no surprise, then, to find that Salomon Smith Barney's welfare-to-work initiative is also located here.

Silvan first learned of the Private Industry Partnership when her contacts at Drake Beam Morin, which did outplacement work for Smith Barney, mentioned that they were also doing some work for Wildcat Service Corporation. They told her that Wildcat was looking for a private sector firm as a partner in a new kind of training program and asked if Smith Barney would be willing to participate by taking on a single trainee as an intern. She agreed to take four. The first interns arrived in mid-1995. Two were placed in

Silvan's own human resources department and two others with a friend in the controller's office. "It was shaky," says Silvan. Two of the four left before their sixteen-week internship was over; the others stayed and were hired as permanent employees. The 50 percent success rate was nothing to write home about, but Silvan and her colleagues were willing to stay involved provided Wildcat made some changes to its program. Wildcat had been teaching its trainees to use Lotus spreadsheets, but Smith Barney used Excel; the interns knew their way around WordPerfect, but the firm's word processing program was Word. "So that's how that conversation started," Silvan remembers. "And [Wildcat] said, 'No problem, we will train them on what you need.' And that was unique. They weren't the first company that ever came to us, but they were the first ones that were willing to, at the snap of a finger, change the way they were doing things."

Between 1995 and the end of 1999, Salomon Smith Barney provided internships to 135 Wildcat trainees, 91 of whom it hired into permanent jobs. Eighty-five of these employees were still with the firm at the end of 1999, a retention rate of 93 percent. (This compared favorably to Salomon Smith Barney's overall retention rate of 87 percent for all categories of employees, as well as the industry's historical rate for entry-level job retention of about 75 percent.)[11] "The failures we've had," Silvan reflects, "the turnover we've had, when I look at it, it's no different than what happens with our regular population. The number one reason we end up terminating people around here is attendance, and that's the number one reason we terminate at Wildcat."

During the sixteen-week internship, Salomon Smith Barney pays Wildcat $8.50 an hour for the time worked by the interns. The interns receive $6.50 an hour, and Wildcat uses the difference to pay taxes, modest benefits, and administrative costs. Interns are placed in a variety of departments, including human resources, finance, operations, technology, and research. In encouraging the firm's managers to accommodate Wildcat interns, Silvan assured them that they faced absolutely no risk. "If you like the person, they work out, and you want to hire them, fabulous," she told her colleagues. "We'll help you work out what you're going to pay them. If you don't like them and wouldn't recommend them, you tell me that, they go back to Wildcat, Wildcat places them elsewhere. If you really like them but don't have an opening, then I shop them around and get them interviewed in different places around the firm." For several years, Salomon Smith Barney hired about thirty people annually from Wildcat, although the economic slowdown and layoffs in the financial services industry have since led to a sharp decline in these numbers. "It's not like, 'Let's see how many welfare-to-work people we can place here,'" Silvan explains. "It's servicing a business need."

Nonetheless, Silvan recognizes the tremendous impact of the internship program on the lives of the women hired. "I feel very close to these 91 women and they feel close to me," she says. "I love to see them in the hall and exchange a wink and a smile and say, 'How's your kid?' You get close to them and when they share their stories and say how their lives have changed, you can't help but think [that] these 91 women average three kids each, so when you start doing the numbers there's probably 400 or more people who now have very different lives than they did four years ago. It is doubtful that the children of these women will ever end up on welfare, because now they have role models that their mothers never had." Silvan is not alone in her positive feelings about the program. She explains, "Although I like to sell it from the business perspective because there's an incredibly good business case to make for it, people here feel very good about doing something to help another human being and to give them an opportunity. They feel like they're mentoring someone, nurturing someone. . . . I hear that all the time when managers talk about it. But the fact is, that has nothing to do with why we're doing it."

Salomon Smith Barney and the other employers that participate in the Private Industry Partnership are doing it because it makes good business sense. While employers play no formal role within Wildcat, the lines of communication are wide open. "I literally talk to them every day," says Silvan. The feedback can sometimes be very specific. On one occasion, for example, Silvan told the PIP coordinator that the last two interns placed had some problems with the spelling of people's names and asked whether they could do some skills practice along those lines. Wildcat complied. Salomon Smith Barney has learned to make the most of Wildcat as an employment resource. Silvan elaborates: "I would say to them, 'Gee, we're about to have a lot of call center jobs'—let's say because we're introducing a new stock option plan—'so we need to train them on phone skills. But we have a great phone skills program, so we want you to train them on *our* phone skills program.' So we would take our trainers, bring the program to Wildcat, train their trainers, and then their trainers could train the group. We wanted them to get exactly what they would get if they were employed here."

The core skills needed for an internship at Salomon Smith Barney are computer proficiency and the ability to speak articulately on the telephone.

But there are even more basic things every employee needs to know that cannot be taken for granted. Silvan explains: "If you're a manager running to a meeting and say [to your intern], 'Get me ten copies of this collated and stapled' [and you hear], 'What's collated mean?'—there is no patience for that. So I have to make sure that everybody coming in has that minimal level." But the most important ingredient is attitude. "You can teach them skills," she says; "you can teach anyone skills. But you can't teach them how to speak nicely to somebody, how to not get angry, how to work as a team member." Part of Wildcat's role is to identify people who have these traits and then help polish them. "The visual is very important, and they spend a great deal of time on that. If you look at someone the day they walk into Wildcat for the first time and the day they come to my interview, it's like night and day. They have nice suits, they're having their hair done differently, they're having dental work done," Silvan says, referring to the occasions when Wildcat has arranged for a trainee to have her teeth fixed before going on an interview. "If you're missing your front teeth, it's hard for people to be comfortable with you."

In June 1997, Sandra met with Silvan. She had abandoned the idea of wearing her red suit and was dressed in brown instead. "When I walked into 388 Greenwich for the first time I just looked around and said, 'Man, how many elevators do they got in this building?' [I] had to take the escalator to the elevator just to get to Barbara's office. Then, when I got there, I seen nothing but water outside her window." Sandra is afraid of heights and tried to avoid looking out at the river. Even so, she was less intimidated than some of the other trainees. Through her community work, Sandra had visited City Hall and other imposing buildings. Many women in the program had not, and occasionally Sandra would hear word of people who got lost on their way to an interview or even after starting work. Sandra mentions one intern who wound up on the roof when she took the wrong staircase.

The interview went smoothly. Silvan told Sandra that she handled herself well and would be a good candidate for the internship if a position could be found. Sandra remembers the moment vividly. "She had a beige folder, I'll never forget it, and a stack of paper, maybe twenty-five or thirty pieces. She got all the way down to the bottom of the pile. She kept saying, 'Not for you, no, not for you.' I think it was the next to the last [piece of paper] when she said, 'I found something for you.' And that was the reorg department." Sandra had her internship.

Salomon Smith Barney's reorganization department was Sandra's home for the next four months. She learned to handle stock and bond transactions, send letters to banks and brokers, and speak with the firm's other branches by phone. "I was lucky, I was able to get into a good department. The manager was perfect; he made me feel really relaxed. His senior assistant made me feel even more relaxed. And the woman who was training me said, 'I want you to get hired, so this is what we're going to do. Talk to me, let me know what you need.'" She also told Sandra that no one apart from her managers needed to know she had come from Wildcat. Sandra decided nonetheless to be open about her status. Recognizing that a lot of people within the firm had misconceptions about welfare mothers, Sandra felt it was her job to help prove them wrong.

Halfway through the four-month period, the interns met for a luncheon at Wildcat where speakers addressed issues like handling stress on the job and dealing with difficult colleagues—and Wildcat's case managers passed along to the interns their employers' evaluations. It was a stressful day for some, but the message to Sandra was positive. Her supervisors liked her; she was doing well. With newfound confidence, Sandra returned to work. Then she made a mistake. Sandra mentioned in passing to a co-worker that she had been told she would be earning at least $24,000 if she were hired. As it turned out, some of Sandra's colleagues—including a few who had been at the firm for years—were earning less. An awkward period followed, as Sandra discovered one of the most important rules of the workplace: never discuss your salary with your co-workers.

Two weeks before the end of her internship, Sandra got a call from a human resources specialist, who sent her around the firm for interviews. The chemistry was off with one pair of managers. The second interview went better, but she shied away from the idea of handling customer phone calls, feeling that the pressure would be too much for her first position. One of the jobs she interviewed for seemed as if it might be too repetitive. The fourth interview was with Michael Ward. By now, Sandra was feeling fairly confident that she would indeed land a job. Maybe it was time to break out the red suit that had been hanging in her closet since June. It turned out to be a lucky move. She and her future boss hit it off immediately. Looking at Sandra's record of community involvement, he said, "You're interested in education? You know, my wife's a teacher," and they were off and running. Ward told Sandra he was hiring for a new department. Sandra found this appealing, even though the work was a bit less challenging than some of her other opportunities. "I think I would rather start a little lower just to get my feet wet," she told one of her supervisors. If all the other employees were new, too, her mistakes would be less obvious.

Sandra joined the limited partnerships department of Salomon Smith Barney in October 1997, at a salary of just over $24,000. As a service representative, her job was to reregister clients, handle files, and update computer records. Merit raises increased her pay to more than $30,000 by 1999. Along with the salary came health insurance, vacation, sick time, and stock options offered through the Citigroup WealthBuilder program.

Each June, every employee with at least one year of service at Salomon Smith Barney is awarded Citigroup stock options equal to 10 percent of his or her salary for the year (Salomon Smith Barney is owned by Citigroup).[12] Over the course of her employment, Sandra's account accumulated close to $6,000 worth of shares. "I don't think anybody here really understands the significance of what that's gonna mean to them twenty years from now," says Michael Ward. Sandra was among them. "You know, I never really gave it any mind about the WealthBuilder," she says, until she had spent several years on the job. Sandra's shares would have been fully vested in June 2003, meaning that she would have been able to exercise her options at market value. If she left her job before then, she would take only those shares that were vested, forfeiting the rest.

All went smoothly for the first few years and, as of the end of 1999, both Sandra and her boss expected her to be around when her options matured. "It's worked out very well," said Ward at the time. "You should know that the department was eleven people, and today there's only four people left and she's one of them." Sandra had gained confidence on the job. "I'm not gonna tell you she was a shy woman when she walked in here," says Ward, "but her tone has changed." One of Sandra's colleagues was a big help in acclimating her to the department. Billy Summers, a longtime employee, showed Sandra the ropes, put her in touch with people in other parts of the firm, and taught her about the kind of behavior expected in the workplace. "Her communication skills have greatly improved," according to Ward. "She handles the phone desk; that's part of her job. That group takes 400 calls a day and . . . on an average day you can say she takes 100 calls. And like I said, I usually get nothing but a nice comment. Every now and then someone will call me up and say, 'Well, so-and-so really isn't that nice, but, you know, I like talking to Sandra.' And that goes a long way. We are in a service business. And maybe she doesn't have that piece of paper hanging on the wall like a lot of other folks have, but you would never know it by talking to her."

Ward had changed, too. When he was first asked to interview Sandra, he agreed only because he trusted the manager who recommended her.

Today, if asked whether he'd like to interview another Wildcat trainee, he would say, "Yes, by all means, I want to see her." Sandra also changed his ideas about the kind of background needed to succeed in his department. Ward points out that Salomon Smith Barney virtually never hires an applicant without a bachelor's degree for its white-collar positions. In fact, in the financial services industry overall, about 85 percent of those hired into moderate-skill entry-level jobs are university graduates. "I'll tell you what has changed," says Ward; "If I had a job open in mutual funds three years ago I probably wouldn't have opened up myself to interview her for the job without a degree. But now, since seeing her and being around her and having her work for me for this period of time, I wouldn't even think twice about bringing someone into mutual funds without the B.A."

Getting It Together

Success on the job can have a profound effect on women who have never worked before. "They feel like they've died and gone to heaven," says Barbara Silvan. "You don't know how bad you have it when you don't know what's out there. When they first come into this building, they've never seen anything like this. They look at the marble. They sit right where you're sitting and look out the window and say, 'Ahh. . . .'" It is not just the buildings that make an impression, it is the people. "With this population [welfare mothers], fitness has not been a big part of their lives," Silvan explains. "When they get into the working world and they see the beautiful people all around them, they want to get in shape and get their act together." Some of Salomon Smith Barney's buildings have on-site fitness centers. After she was hired, Sandra began exercising and eventually lost more than a hundred pounds. Sometimes when she shops for clothes she finds herself at the plus-size rack, having forgotten that she now wears a size 12.

To ensure that the transition to regular employment goes smoothly, Wildcat stays in close touch with its former trainees.[13] For the first year after placement, PIP staff telephones each new employee weekly to ask how things are going. The calls are made in the evening or over the weekend to ensure that the trainee can speak freely about what is happening at work. If issues arise—conflict with a manager, a poor evaluation, an attendance problem—Wildcat can intervene to try to prevent the situation from worsening. The PIP coordinators also receive regular feedback from employers throughout the first year and often beyond. If a manager raises a problem that an employee has not mentioned, PIP staff can bring it up in conversations with the employee. After a year, regular contact with former trainees ends. Wildcat's managers resist the idea that postplacement services must be provided forever—the goal, after all, is self-sufficiency. Nonetheless, Wildcat wants trainees to understand that if there is a problem they can contact the organization for help. As for employers, they too have learned the value of maintaining a relationship with Wildcat. If problems can be identified and addressed before they get out of hand, new employees will be more likely to succeed.

But success on the job does not guarantee that everything else will fall into place. An illness, a financial crisis, or a child's health problems can get in the way. Even in the absence of crisis, a new job is not a panacea for someone unused to steady work or a regular income. Sandra has struggled financially, even with her new salary. "I still live from paycheck to paycheck," she reported two years into the job. "I just got paid yesterday and I'm broke. I got about $60." Sometimes she feels like she is still on welfare. "You know what I miss?" Sandra asks. "Medicaid!" When she was covered by Medicaid, Sandra could go to any doctor or emergency room. Now she needs to make a $10 co-payment to see a doctor and alert her health maintenance organization about any visit to the emergency room. She also lost her prescription drug coverage. When her son got sick, Sandra was in a bind: "I don't have no $30-some-odd dollars to pay for his medicine."

It seems to be a law of nature that as earnings rise, so do expenses. Housing costs took the biggest bite out of Sandra's budget. When she was hired into a full-time position, not only did her welfare payments cut off immediately, her rent went up to $619 a month for a three-bedroom apartment, an outlay she found hard to handle. The several-week gap between Sandra's final welfare payment and the arrival of her first paycheck is responsible for some of the rent arrears she still owes. Sandra's position at Salomon Smith Barney, along with her weight loss, also required her to invest in a new wardrobe. Her transportation costs rose, too, since she now needed to pay for daily subway fare to and from work. The cheapest way to do this is with an unlimited fare Metrocard bought at the beginning of the month, but the up-front cost was sometimes too much for Sandra's budget. Instead, she would opt for a weekly unlimited fare card at a slightly higher price.

Of course, a full-time salary has its benefits as well. When she did her taxes for the first time after starting her job, Sandra was thrilled to learn that she would receive a refund of almost $5,000. She used the money to buy a living room set. She also bought a new bed frame, but had to wait to get the mattress. She did not have enough cash for a complete bed, and she did not have a credit card. Being on public assistance for so many years, Sandra had never established credit in her own name. When she started work at Salomon Smith Barney, she tried to get a credit card, but was denied by every bank she called. "They want you to have a prior credit history, and I don't," she explains. In 1999, Sandra finally got a credit card, her first, from Stern's Department Store—with a $100 limit, she could not buy much. Responding to an offer to employees of Citibank financial services, Sandra filled out an application for a credit card, but learned that Citibank would provide her with a no-fee card only if she kept $500 in a Citibank account—resources she did not have. She also applied for a loan that would consolidate her debts, but Citibank turned her down because she did not have enough money in the bank to qualify for its loan program. Sandra has come up with a few cost-saving measures on her own. For example, when she noticed that her phone bills had risen sky-high (thanks in part to her daughters' phone habits), she cut off her phone service and got a cellular phone to carry with her. And she finally found a company that would issue her a credit card for an annual fee instead of a minimum balance.

Sandra also learned more about her 401(k) account. During her first few years of employment, she had contributed only a tiny fraction of her salary each month and the account still held less than $1,000. Sandra discovered that she could borrow against her 401(k) only if it amounted to more than $1,000, and she wanted to have this option in case of an emergency. With the raises she received, she decided she could afford to contribute more and increased her pretax deduction to 10 percent of her salary.

Particularly interesting in light of Sandra's story is the experience of her oldest daughter, Athena, who spent several months in a housing shelter with her four-year-old son. As her mother was for much of Athena's childhood, she also was on public assistance. But unlike Sandra, Athena stayed in school, resisting pressure from her caseworker to drop out and find a job. Instead, at the urging of her mother, she entered Wildcat's training program while taking college classes at night. "I told her," Sandra says, "that even though you're in college and you'll be getting your associate's degree, it's still good for you to have the training." Sandra was pleased when Athena conceded, "A lot of stuff [the teachers] be telling me, I know you said that." In June 2000, Athena received an associate's degree in public administration from Medgar Evers Community College, and she has already amassed many of the credits needed for a bachelor's degree. Athena loved Wildcat but had to leave before she completed the program in order to finish her last semester of school. Because of this, she was not eligible for an internship, but she could use Wildcat's job placement resources to look for a job. She benefited from Wildcat in other ways as well. Her work assignment at a city agency was a high-quality experience that went on her résumé. The bookkeeping skills she learned in Mr. Black's class, along with the intensive computer training she received, also increased her marketability. The workshop at Mullin & Associates helped her conquer most of her nervousness about interviewing. With these assets in hand, Athena found a job as an assistant supervisor at a child development agency.

The Next Move

The longest economic expansion in U.S. history came to an end in 2001, and the financial services industry was among the first to suffer. Brokerage houses and investment banks responded to a slowing stock market and projected slump in corporate earnings with a wave of layoffs. Charles Schwab, Bear Stearns, Morgan Stanley, Merrill Lynch, and others together shed thousands of workers. Salomon Smith Barney and its parent company, Citigroup, were not immune. In April, Sandra was told she was being laid off. As is the practice in the industry, no two-week notice was given; employees were handed their belongings in a cardboard box and escorted to a cab. After three and one-half years, Sandra suddenly found herself unemployed. Michael Ward explains that as part of the firmwide reduction in force, he was required to cut his staff by 10 percent. At her year-end review, he had told Sandra she had gotten a bit too comfortable in the job and was not nearly as motivated as she had been a year before. She ranked toward the bottom of his staff and was among those let go. Still, without the reduction in force, Ward says she would still be employed today. Sandra was one of about 150 people in her building to lose their jobs that day. According to both Ward and Sandra, she took the news well, saying she felt much worse for the people who had worked at the firm for many years.

Sandra received two months' severance pay plus two weeks of pay for each year on the job. Her WeathBuilder shares were only partially vested, and the value of the shares she needed to sell upon leaving the firm was lower than in the past because of the falling stock market. Her 401(k) account was large enough that she could borrow against it, but she now needs to repay the loan at a cost of $22 a month—an expense that is hard to meet without an income. Because the financial services industry as a whole is in a slump, Sandra has been unable to find a similar job at another firm. Companies that expected to resume hiring later in the year were further hit by the September 11, 2001, terrorist attacks on the World Trade Center, and the New York economy as a whole has since slipped into a true recession. Sandra participated in a three-day job search workshop paid for by Salomon Smith Barney, has attended job fairs, and has had some interviews, but thus far she has not found a new position. After trying for several months on her own, she has returned to Wildcat to use its "job readiness" room and the services of its job developers.

While New York City extended unemployment benefits for those who lost their jobs after September 11, it opted not to do so for those laid off before the attacks. Without unemployment benefits and unable to afford the high cost of her medical coverage, Sandra has had to return to public assistance. She finds a system different from the one she had left—a system where she must report regularly to a city agency and carry out a full-time job search in order to receive her benefits. The differences between the welfare system's approach to finding a job and Wildcat's depress her. She comments that no training is offered; you are just pushed to go ahead and find something, anything, in the way of employment. Still, Sandra remains fairly upbeat about her prospects and hopes that once the stock market and the economy pick up, her experience and skills will enable her to find a good job.

Employed or not, Sandra's life has undoubtedly changed since she saw Wildcat's flier on the wall of the housing office. The Private Industry Partnership's training program gave Sandra marketable skills and an internship opportunity at a top-flight employer. With these advantages, she was able to land an entry-level position that came with a good salary, benefits, and the potential for savings. Hopefully, three and one-half years at Salomon Smith Barney will enable her to find another job before long. Her training, internship, and work experience also brought Sandra a new level of self-confidence that carried over into other areas of her life. By losing weight and exercising, she improved her health and appearance. By setting an example for her children, she reduced the odds that they will repeat her mistakes. "Since she's been working, she's much happier than I ever saw her," said Athena while Sandra was still employed. "She holds her own, takes care of the bills on her own. . . . She has much more freedom and doesn't have to answer to anybody."

It was the skills and connections offered by Wildcat's Private Industry Partnership that gave Sandra and hundreds of other former welfare recipients their first shot at full-time employment. The program's impact can be traced to several of its most innovative elements. First, PIP set out specifically to serve the needs of employers. The program's leaders recognized that most jobs for welfare recipients would be in the private sector and that firms would base their hiring decisions on cost, quality, reliability, and service. Wildcat has positioned itself as an organization that can meet these criteria, not as a social service provider. Wildcat also carefully assesses an employer's needs by looking at the mix of entry-level jobs, comparing formal job descriptions with real jobs, becoming familiar with the company's culture, learning about the main reasons for turnover, and carrying out site visits. Working with the employer, Wildcat then develops a specialized training curriculum that gives trainees the skills they need to succeed in a particular position. "Employers often take on risks and additional expenses when hiring less-skilled workers, which can result in increased turnover," says Richard Bonamarte, Wildcat's executive vice president for planning and development. "Wildcat reduces these costs and risks by tailoring our job training and support services to specific employer requirements."

Central to the process of signing up partners is a recognition that doing so is neither a quick nor an easy task. Discussions may go on for several months before a firm agrees to participate in the program. Wildcat has found that relationships with employers require just as much maintenance as relationships with trainees.[14] Wildcat remains in contact with firms after they begin accepting interns, offering ample opportunity for feedback and retooling its training in response to changing job needs or specific requests—a flexibility that makes the program of continuing value to its private sector partners.

Second, the Private Industry Partnership holds its trainees to high standards of accountability while offering them the opportunity for long-term gains. The program enters into a kind of social contract with participants: If you take the training seriously and conduct yourself appropriately, we will connect you to a job that holds out the promise of upward mobility. Along the way, we will give you the resources you need to succeed, such as training in hard and soft skills, intensive work on interviewing and personal presentation, high school equivalency degree study for those who need it, and ongoing support during the internship phase and beyond. The Private Industry Partnership does not just train people and send them into the marketplace to sink or swim. It stays in touch, tracks their progress, and makes its job placement services available for those who need help down the road.

Third, the Private Industry Partnership lowers the stakes for both employers and trainees through its internship program. It is a big step for former welfare recipients to enter the world of white-collar work. Likewise, it is a big step for leading employers in highly competitive industries to feel comfortable hiring former welfare recipients. The four-month internship serves as a kind of trial run for both parties. For employers, the internship makes hiring a no-risk process; they have the opportunity to bring in Wildcat trainees at minimal cost and offer jobs only to those who perform well. For trainees, the internship gives them the chance to get on-the-job experience with some room for error; managers understand that for many of these women this is their first full-time job, and most are willing to offer a little extra support. The internship also plays a networking function for trainees, introducing them to employment opportunities that, without Wildcat's intervention, would be outside the realm of their experience. Academic research has shown that only a small fraction of jobs are obtained through formal mechanisms. Most people find jobs—especially good jobs—through personal contacts or informal networks. "Some individuals have the right contacts, while others do not," writes Mark Granovetter, an expert on job networks. "If one lacks the appropriate contact, there is little he can do about it."[15] As a group, welfare recipients are among the most bereft of contacts. Often, they come from families or live in neighborhoods where few people work, and they are unlikely to find a job through their personal acquaintances.[16] Wildcat's Private Industry Partnership creates a network for them, connecting them to available jobs and introducing them to contacts who may be able to help them find employment later on.

Since the mid-1990s, Wildcat has expanded its own network of employers to firms in a variety of fields. PIP staff members continue to sign up new partners, including some that will be able to accommodate interns with lower skill levels. The program has been successfully replicated elsewhere. PIP is held up as a model by the Welfare to Work Partnership, a national initiative that encourages private companies to hire welfare recipients. (Since it was founded in 1997, the partnership's 20,000 member firms have hired an estimated 1.1 million welfare recipients.)[17] In 1999, the British government enlisted Wildcat to provide technical assistance to the United Kingdom's welfare reform task force. The PIP staff is working with task force members to develop the same kind of demand-driven training approach used at Wildcat in partnership with London-based financial services and information technology firms.

The Private Industry Partnership is likely to remain a model for other job-training programs, despite the challenges of such an approach. It took two years to shift Wildcat's internal culture and behavior in a more demand-driven direction and, even now, maintaining existing relationships with employers and cultivating new ones is an ambitious task. But the approach is worth the effort because of the results it yields. The Private Industry Partnership has managed to achieve for a deeply disadvantaged population what economists call "labor market attachment"—a systemic connection with employers that allows for the ongoing placement of trainees in positions that offer the opportunity for advancement. A whole range of assets has been created in the process. For most of those hired out of the program, their new jobs have translated to an increase in economic assets, including higher salaries and the potential for savings. Many of these assets have value across generations. Economic resources allow workers to provide their families with a more secure life-style. More education and better job skills enable them to set a good example for their children, an example that often leads these children to higher levels of educational and professional attainment of their own. Even connections can be passed along, just as Sandra encouraged Athena to enroll at Wildcat.

While Sandra faces the daunting task of finding a new job in a depressed economy, her experience with the Private Industry Partnership made it possible, at least for a while, for her to break the pattern of welfare dependency and lack of economic opportunity that seemed destined to repeat itself in her children. A virtuous cycle was set in motion for Sandra and her family, one that holds out the promise of a brighter future for them all. As Athena says when asked about the impact Wildcat has had on Sandra's life, "We're doing the right thing with our lives, she's doing the right thing with hers." While Sandra is not employed at the moment, a permanent return to public assistance is no longer an option both because of changes in the welfare rules and changes in Sandra herself. She knows that work is her future and it is a future she welcomes.

CHAPTER FIVE

Making It
Her Business

Low-income people have few options as they seek to find a place in the work force of the twenty-first century. As recently as the 1970s, a high school diploma opened the door to a stable job at a decent wage. Even those who had not completed high school could earn good pay and excellent benefits through union membership and employment at one of the nation's manufacturing firms. But by the 1980s, the avenues that had provided economic security to people with limited skills were blocked. A shift away from manufacturing and toward services eliminated many unionized jobs. The globalization of the U.S. economy led to downsizing and widespread layoffs. Rapid technological change drove up the premium on education and training, benefiting higher-skilled workers. High school dropouts, and even graduates, faced a dwindling supply of jobs offering the earnings potential available to them only a decade earlier. Today, the pay gap between those with a college degree and those without is at an all-time high.[1] Even with unemployment at historically low levels, people who lack both skills and education remain at the margins of the economy, working in dead-end jobs for the minimum wage and minimal benefits.

Job-training programs offer one route into the mainstream economy. Self-employment offers another. In 2000, 9.9 million Americans, or 7 percent of the civilian work force, were self-employed.[2] Some of their stories are legendary. Philip Knight founded Nike in 1972 with $1,000 in cash; today the company earns $9 billion. Michael Dell started Dell Computer in 1984, also with $1,000; annual revenue is now $32 billion. Ross Perot's Electronic Data Systems, Apple Computer, Ben & Jerry's Ice Cream—all are successful companies created from almost nothing apart from the vision and energy of their founders. Beyond these high-profile successes lie the realities: self-employment does not make many people millionaires, but it does provide millions of Americans with gainful work and a degree of flexibility hard to find elsewhere.

But can it work for the poor? The Aspen Institute, a leader in research on microenterprise programs, estimates that more than 2 million low-income Americans currently run their own small businesses.[3] (A microenterprise is defined as a business with fewer than five employees that can utilize a loan of less than $25,000 and has difficulty accessing the commercial banking sector.)[4] Many more low-income individuals supplement their wages with income from self-employment. Some of these microentrepreneurs opt to work for themselves because they have a particular skill or interest on which to base a business, but most become self-employed out of necessity, starting their businesses after having been laid off or as an alternative to low-wage work.

Antipoverty policies should be flexible and varied enough to serve diverse populations. While job training may be appropriate for many, participants have a limited say over which skills they will learn and in what kind of job they will be placed. Self-employment provides greater freedom in choosing a line of work, gives people more control over their hours of employment, and makes available the option of working from home—an important consideration for parents trying to balance work and family responsibilities. For someone who is highly motivated and enjoys operating independently, self-employment may offer a more promising route to economic security than even the most innovative job-training program.

Numerous organizations have emerged in recent years to support low-income entrepreneurs with training, technical advice, and capital. Like job training, microenterprise programs help the poor build not only economic but also human assets. Those who start successful businesses usually increase their income and may eventually build equity in their company. But clients also gain the skills, connections, and confidence that can lead to a better life, whether they end up working for themselves or for others. In this sense, microenterprise training is an asset-building strategy even for those who choose not to become self-employed.

This chapter focuses on the work of Iowa's Institute for Social and Economic Development (ISED), one of the nation's leading microenterprise development organizations. Several features set ISED apart from other organizations in the same field. ISED works in many rural areas, its client base is largely nonminority, and it operates statewide rather than in a single city or region. Nonetheless, ISED's experience holds valuable lessons for promoting self-employment as a strategy for fighting poverty. First, ISED is among the largest U.S.-based organizations involved in training low-income entrepreneurs. How it achieved this degree of scale is instructive for other groups intent on expanding their reach. A second distinctive feature of ISED is its emphasis on training over lending. Recognizing that low-income microentrepreneurs need training and technical assistance above all, ISED's programs discourage clients from taking on debt right away—a departure from the lending-based orientation of many other programs. ISED provides an example of a successful program that engages in almost no direct lending and is a valuable model at a time when the microenterprise development field as a whole is moving in a more training-led direction. Third, ISED's performance has been enhanced by its commitment to program evaluation. With data collection and assessment capabilities that are among the most advanced in the field, the organization has been able to learn a great deal about which approaches to microenterprise development yield the best results. As its program matures, ISED is grappling with many of the same issues as other organizations. The evolution of its program and plans for expansion represent a serious attempt to achieve more fully the twin missions of poverty alleviation and community development that lie at the heart of microenterprise development.

On Her Own

Marguerite Sisson was twenty-seven years old when she boarded an airplane for the first time. Growing up poor in the Mississippi River town of Clinton, Iowa, most of her energy had until very recently gone toward bare survival. On her own at the age of thirteen, a single parent by the time she was twenty, a low-wage worker, a welfare mother—this had been the trajectory of Marguerite's life. But everything had changed in the past two years, and this trip was proof of it. She was on her way to Washington, D.C., to testify before a congressional committee about the importance of federal funding to help low-income individuals go into business for themselves.

An outgoing woman with fair, flyaway hair and pale blue eyes, Marguerite understands the significance of her journey. "I had never even been to Chicago, nothing ever, nowhere," she explains, sitting on the couch in her dingy living room dressed in a T-shirt and shorts. "I went from being on welfare, to going to Chicago, jumping on a plane, and going to Washington, D.C., of all places. Then the next day I testified in front of Congress. I was very nervous. I thought they could hear my heart pounding over the microphone." In Washington, Marguerite toured the White House, visited the reflecting pool, which she had seen in the movie *Forrest Gump*, and ate at the Hard Rock Café. She also met her half-brother, Charles, who lives in nearby Delaware. "He drove down and I met him for the first time ever in my whole life," she says. "It was weird. He sounded just like my father, and he looks just like my father. I had longed to see a piece of that."

Marguerite had lost her father, also named Charles, not once but twice. "My father left when I was five. He said he was going to the bank and he never came back." Marguerite's mother worked as a nurse's aide, but her job did not bring in enough money to support the family so they went on welfare. Her parents' separation and her mother's subsequent relationships uprooted Marguerite. "I was drug [*sic*] through schools like you wouldn't believe. I don't think I had too much schooling after third grade because my mom moved all over, and I guess they just kept passing me. When I got up to sixth grade, I was a good student; I had honors and everything. But then when I went to seventh grade I started being kind of rebellious." Marguerite dropped out in the eighth grade.

She missed her father terribly. "I'd never had a man in my life," Marguerite says. Her mother has been married many times and, out of all her husbands, "nobody ever treated me like a daughter." Marguerite met her father again when she was a teenager, but they did not have long to get reacquainted. "My father died when I was fifteen, right after I met him. He had six months to live. He was a really bad alcoholic and he died from cirrhosis of the liver. I was devastated when he died. I was devastated."

"I was basically on my own when I was thirteen. I taught myself a lot of things. . . . My mom didn't even drive," Marguerite recalls. "I ended up getting $9,000 from Social Security back pay after [my father] died and I gave my mom some money. I gave her half of it, and she got a house. She always wanted a house so I gave her money for the down payment on a house at the age of sixteen. And I bought myself a car and taught myself how to drive."

Marguerite also went back to school, entering the ninth grade when she was eighteen years old. She stuck it out for two years despite being so much older than the other students. Then she got pregnant with her son, Will, and dropped out again (she later received a high school equivalency degree). "My relationship with my son's father . . . just went downhill and he left me just after he was born. Then my mom ended up moving away. And I remember I went to work down at the railroad crying because my mom was gone, my dad was dead, I didn't have anybody else to turn to."

For two years, Marguerite drove a van for a transportation company that served the town's railroad station. She worked the third shift—10 p.m. to 6 a.m.—earning $5.35 an hour. "I missed two years of my son's life. He would get out of school at three. I would have to go pick him up, so I would wake up about two in the afternoon, get ready and go get him, come home, and fall back asleep. . . . The weekends would roll around and I would be exhausted, I'd never want to go anywhere or do anything. I had my own housecleaning, my own laundry, everything to do, and I was struggling really bad. A lot of times I can remember just crying because I had Skippy peanut butter but no bread to eat it on. It was really, really hard."

Marguerite had gone on welfare when her son was born. Her job driving the van paid so little that she continued to receive partial public assistance even though she worked full-time. "I was getting all these letters and notices from the welfare office that said, 'You've got to get a job because you're not making enough money on what you're doing now,'" she remembers. "Then they would send me down to this Promise Jobs program [Iowa's welfare-to-work agency] and I'd say, 'What do you want from me? I'm working forty hours a week.'"

Marguerite took a new job in a factory that paid a slightly higher wage of $7 an hour. But she still had to work nights. "I said to myself, 'Darn it, I have to spend time with my kid, so I need to get something else.' And I said, 'The first job I get in Clinton I'm taking it, I don't care what it is.' And it was cleaning." Marguerite enjoyed the work and she was good at it. Doctors at a medical facility she cleaned complimented her on her thoroughness. Some of the people she worked for even asked why she did not start her own business. "That was really the furthest thing from my mind," she explains. "I thought, 'Yeah, give me a break, how could I ever do that?'"

One day, half in jest, Marguerite said to a co-worker, "I think I'm gonna start a cleaning company." The co-worker promptly told

Marguerite's boss and he confronted her, accusing her of competing against him. She protested, "'Well, I talked about it, but I'm not cleaning for anyone. It's not like I have an ad in the paper.'" She was fired anyway. "I walked out of there and cried, thinking, 'Now what am I going to do?'" With her last paycheck, Marguerite paid for some insurance coverage. The night yardmaster at the railroad, an older man whose family had befriended Marguerite, helped her buy some cleaning supplies. She put an ad in the paper and in a matter of days got a call from a woman who needed her house cleaned. Her second call was from the Foley Construction Company. "I couldn't believe it," Marguerite remembers. "I was actually getting a phone call from a company. They said, 'When can you come out and give us a bid?' I went out there, did not know what I was doing at all. I said, 'I can clean it for $50 a week.' And I'm still there." Marguerite was in business.

After a few months of cleaning for a small number of clients, Marguerite decided to get serious. In March 1998, she applied for a tax identification number, purchased more insurance for her company, bought stationery and a briefcase. "That's when I said, 'I'm a businesslady.'" Marguerite's Promise Jobs caseworker helped her apply for a waiver from Iowa's welfare program that would allow her to continue to receive cash assistance and medical benefits during her first year of self-employment. The caseworker also told her about ISED and asked her to meet with one of its trainers, Jane I. Duax, who was based in Davenport, about forty-five minutes away. "I thought, 'I don't want to go down there.' I gave her some excuse, 'Oh, my car. . . .' I didn't want to do it. I thought, 'This is just another dumb program and I don't want any part of it.' I was really reluctant and I was really angry the day I met Jane. And she's like, 'Fill out these papers,' and I'm like, 'Yeah, yeah, whatever.'" Jane, too, recalls that Marguerite was anything but enthusiastic: "Our first meeting was on the run. She said, 'OK, I'll come down and look at the stuff you want me to look at.' She really couldn't be bothered." At the time Marguerite had only a few clients, most of them house-cleaning accounts. Jane had some thoughts on how she might expand her business and reach out for commercial cleaning contracts. Marguerite was impressed. "I started talking to Jane and she started telling me all this stuff and I was like 'Wow, *Wow!*' . . . She was helping me. . . . And then things started happening."

Self-Employment for the Poor

Marguerite's newfound enthusiasm was no surprise to Jane I. Duax or the organization for which she worked. Since 1988, the Institute for Social and Economic Development has been helping people like Marguerite learn how to make a living working for themselves. Founded by Dr. John Else, then a professor of social work at the University of Iowa, ISED was one of only a handful of microenterprise development organizations active in the United States in the late 1980s. The microenterprise movement was still new, the product of several different kinds of efforts to help disenfranchised groups expand their economic options. Women's organizations, community action agencies, and community development corporations had all played a role in bringing the field into being. Despite their different origins, these groups shared a commitment to helping people who were not being adequately served by existing business assistance organizations and financial institutions.[5]

Inspiration for the microenterprise movement had also come from overseas, both from European governments experimenting with self-employment for unemployed workers and from nonprofit organizations in the developing world that had hit upon a strikingly successful antipoverty strategy. One of the best-known foreign models was Bangladesh's Grameen Bank, founded by economics professor Mohammed Yunus in 1979. Yunus had been looking for a way to help Bangladesh's landless poor finance their own businesses without having to rely on moneylenders, who charged exorbitant rates. The solution he devised was "peer lending," a system under which several owners of tiny businesses, almost all of them women, would form a group, receive training and a small amount of capital, then decide together who should receive the first loan. The trust of the group's members served as collateral; if all members kept their payments current, the other members would be eligible for loans. The program spread like wildfire; by 1994, Grameen operated over 1,000 branch offices serving 35,000 villages and 2 million customers. By 1997, more than $2 billion had been disbursed, with a payback rate on loans of over 93 percent.[6]

While the peer lending model worked well in densely populated nations like India and Bangladesh, where self-employment is common, different approaches were needed for other parts of the developing world. Acción International, the leading microenterprise organization in Latin America, chose to promote self-employment by making loans to individual entrepreneurs. Since 1992, Acción has lent more than $3.2 billion in loans averaging $600 to more than 2 million borrowers in fifteen Latin American and Caribbean countries and, more recently, the United States. Its repayment rate is 98 percent.[7] The impressive results achieved by a range of organizations working in different environments elicited support for microenterprises from both left- and right-wing governments of developing countries, foundations, and grassroots organizations. The U.S. Agency for International Development, the World Bank, and other foreign aid donors have since jumped on the microenterprise bandwagon.

John Else learned about microenterprise development in Zimbabwe, where he spent two years developing training materials for Africans who would be assuming leadership positions from whites in Africa's newly independent states. Aid donors were interested in promoting self-employment there, but the context was very different from Asia or Latin America: the economies of sub-Saharan nations were characterized by subsistence agriculture and lacked an entrepreneurial tradition. Else realized that the lending-driven strategy that had characterized microenterprise organizations elsewhere would not work in Africa unless a strong training component was added. During his stay in Zimbabwe, Else helped write the curriculum for a microenterprise training program. At the same time, it struck him as strange that Western governments, including the United States, were giving grants for self-employment as a poverty alleviation strategy in Africa but not in the United States. When he returned to Iowa, Else decided to apply the lessons he had learned abroad to the problem of poverty at home, and ISED was born.

In translating the microenterprise development idea to the United States, practitioners like Else saw a fundamental similarity between the needs of the poor in developing countries and those at home: in both settings, there is a segment of the population that has long been inadequately served by mainstream financial institutions. It is almost impossible for a poor person anywhere to get credit at market rates, and banks are not set up to lend the very small amounts of capital needed by most microentrepreneurs. But the differences between the U.S. and developing country settings outweighed the similarities. The informal economy is much smaller in the United States, a fact with several implications. Many of the participants in Grameen's peer lending circles already worked for themselves and could use a small amount of capital to expand or stabilize their businesses. In the United States, most participants in microenterprise programs are building their businesses from the ground up. This means that they require more training, which costs more money. The regulatory environment surrounding business ownership in the United States is also more complex than in countries with a large informal sector, further increasing the need for training. In short, successful microenterprise development in the United States is a more expensive and training-intensive proposition than in the developing world.

It took some time for U.S. organizations to adapt to the domestic reality. Based on the lessons learned from Asia and Latin America, U.S-based organizations initially emphasized credit models and set up loan funds to meet microentrepreneurs' capital requirements. One of the attractions of this approach, at least in theory, is that such loan funds would be self-sustaining, as the repayments on existing loans could be used to finance new loans. This would allow organizations to expand their scale rapidly, just as the Grameen Bank and Acción International had done.

It has not worked out that way. While 70 percent of the 280 programs currently active in the United States provide lending services, none has achieved the kind of financial success experienced in the developing world.[8] For some revolving loan funds, demand for capital has fallen short of expectations, while others have experienced higher than anticipated default rates. The Self-Employment Learning Project, a five-year survey of microentrepreneurs carried out by the Aspen Institute, tracked default rates over time and found that they ranged from 2.4 percent to nearly 24 percent.[9] Creating a revolving loan fund that is self-sustaining may never have been a realistic goal for U.S. programs in any case, as the interest rates charged by organizations like Grameen are unacceptably high by U.S. standards. What has become clear is that most low-income entrepreneurs do not need capital as much as they need knowledge—in fact, of the 47,000 individuals served by microenterprise organizations in 1997, 89 percent were nonborrowers.[10] As a result, a large segment of the microenterprise development field in the United States has come to emphasize training and technical assistance over lending.

ISED is at the forefront of these efforts. Its program consists of four basic services: a comprehensive thirteen-session training course, individualized technical assistance, access to capital, and follow-up assistance. These services are designed to provide inexperienced, low-income microentrepreneurs—including a large contingent of welfare recipients—with the skills, knowledge, and support they need to achieve self-sufficiency through business ownership. Participants are recruited in several ways. Some, like Marguerite, hear about the program from their welfare caseworkers. ISED posts fliers at local elementary schools, grocery stores, and self-serve laundries. Community organizations publicize the program. Twice a year, ISED mails information to everyone in the state receiving a cash welfare grant. ISED's business consultants also speak at orientations for welfare recipients.

People who are interested in the program call ISED's office toll-free and register by phone. The sole criterion for participating in the training course is an income eligibility requirement under which trainees may not earn more than 200 percent of the poverty line. (The income cutoff does not apply to special programs for refugees, residents of rural communities, and women business owners who receive training through the Iowa Women's Enterprise Center.) Provided the income requirement is met, people are eligible for ISED's services whether or not they have a high school diploma, work experience, or credit history, and regardless of any problems in their personal lives. ISED calls its program "self-selecting," meaning that clients have the opportunity to go through training and decide whether self-employment is a good choice for them.

ISED is especially adept at serving welfare recipients. When John Else returned from Zimbabwe and set up ISED, one of the first things he discovered was that the State of Iowa had opted into a national program called the Self-Employment Investment Demonstration (SEID). (Iowa was one of six states to participate.) Organized by the nonprofit Corporation for Enterprise Development, a think tank based in Washington, D.C., SEID was designed to test whether self-employment could help welfare recipients achieve economic self-sufficiency. The State of Iowa had put out a request for proposals to find an organization that could train welfare recipients to start their own businesses. Else's brand-new organization, still lacking staff, an office, or a budget, was the only one to apply. ("Apparently I was the only person in Iowa who thought it was possible," Else jokes now.) The training course developed as part of SEID was the first of many instances in which ISED worked closely with the state. SEID also brought ISED into contact with pioneers in the microenterprise development field nationwide. Both the state and ISED were pleased with the results of their first collaboration. When Iowa passed its welfare reform bill in 1993, self-employment was included as an option for welfare recipients and ISED was again enlisted to provide training.

Jason Friedman, ISED's director of special initiatives, notes that Iowa was one of the first states in the nation to acknowledge self-employment as a viable strategy for welfare recipients. Under Iowa's current rules, all welfare recipients must sign the Family Investment Agreement—an outline of the path they will follow to leave welfare within the five-year time limit. Along with looking for a job, going back to school, and entering a job-training program, self-employment training through ISED is considered a full-time approved activity by the State of Iowa's Department of

Human Services (DHS). But in order for welfare recipients to benefit from this option, ISED must ensure that DHS caseworkers understand the goals and capabilities of the program. "As much work as you can put in with your clients, there's as much if not more work you're putting in with the caseworkers around the state," says Friedman. Some caseworkers are skeptical about whether their clients will be able to succeed at self-employment, while others insist that clients make finding a job their top priority. Several of Jane's clients had to struggle to convince their caseworkers to refer them to ISED. In one instance, a caseworker was adamant about his client getting a high school equivalency degree before attending ISED's training course. The client, who had never done well in school, was not enthusiastic about returning. She was, however, eager to learn how to run a business since she and her husband, a mechanic, had the opportunity to buy his employer's shop. Only after Jane intervened, telling the caseworker that the client had never missed a class, always arrived early to work on the computer, and was doing well with drafting her business plan, did he agree to provide the needed referral. At the last session of the training course, the client told Jane that she had changed her mind about earning her high school equivalency degree and felt ready to take on the challenge of going back to school.

ISED's classes are taught by business consultants based in ISED's five branch offices and Iowa City headquarters along with contractors hired by ISED to provide services in rural areas. In addition to the formal thirteen-session course, trainers work one-on-one with individuals who need specialized assistance. All of ISED's trainers have been in business for themselves and know firsthand the challenges of self-employment. Christine Mollenkopf-Pigsley, ISED's director of microenterprise and one of its trainers, draws on her experience of running a combined women's clothing shop, tuxedo shop, and tanning salon while heading the local chamber of commerce and raising two children. The trainers' collective knowledge has gone into a carefully crafted 285-page curriculum that serves as a guide to the course. Sessions are informal, with an emphasis on class participation. Many of those who come to ISED have had negative experiences with traditional classroom learning, and ISED tries to avoid re-creating such an atmosphere. The course requires no special qualifications—just a willingness to think out loud, share ideas, and go through the process laid out in the curriculum. At each meeting, participants undertake small, attainable steps that lead them toward a larger goal: the preparation of a business plan that will serve as a road map for the owner and could be presented to a commercial lender if financing is needed. It is a tall order for the kind of population served by ISED. The fact that so many participants accomplish this larger goal is testament to the quality of the curriculum, the commitment of ISED's trainers, and the motivation of class members.

A Rainy Day in Davenport

It is hard to imagine a bleaker setting than the area just west of downtown Davenport on a wet February morning. Like many towns along this stretch of the Mississippi, Davenport has pinned the revival of its downtown on riverboat gambling, but any renaissance that might be under way has not yet reached this part of town, just a few blocks from the river. Here the gray streets are dotted with pawnshops, empty lots, and shabby store-fronts. The Cottage Family Resource Center sits in the shadow of the massive Kraft Foods plant. Even so, the atmosphere inside is warm and welcoming. The center is part of the John Lewis Coffee Shops (JLCS), a community program named after a homeless man who died in a fire he started to keep warm. JLCS offers an array of programs and services to the area's poor. It also makes this center available for Jane I. Duax to use as one of the locations for her training course.

Jane, who grew up just a few blocks from here, is the ninth of eleven children. Her father was a beekeeper, entrepreneur, and one-time mayor of Davenport. After attending Catholic schools and a local college, Jane taught elementary school for a while, then opened a women's bookstore and art gallery in town. When Jane talks about her bookstore, which she started with $1,500 in savings, she dwells on what she considers her two biggest mistakes: she did not prepare a business plan and she did not set aside any money for advertising. The importance of these measures is pounded home in her classes. Although the business survived, Jane had to supplement her income with private tutoring. After a stint in graduate school and a period spent working for the New York State Assembly, Jane returned to Davenport. At a loss for what to do, she took a job selling power tools at Sears and quickly became a manager, learning firsthand how advertising drove sales. Jane explains that when she saw an ad in the paper for the job of ISED business consultant, "I felt like everything I had done in my whole adult life finally made sense." The teaching degree, owning a business, her community work with women, her public policy experience, and the time spent working for a large corporation had all prepared her for this job.

Jane went to work for ISED in September 1997. Her responsibilities were many and varied: teaching courses, working one-on-one with clients, helping business owners secure financing, providing follow-up advice and assistance, lobbying the city council for money, and doing the extensive paperwork required by the State of Iowa and ISED's own management information system. Like the other trainers, Jane was not shy about using her personal connections to help a client. She spoke to the manager of the Sears store where she used to work about selling the stepping-stones manufactured by one of her clients. She called a bank vice president her father used to coach in basketball to encourage him to move another client's loan through his department quickly. Jane's mission was not just to teach but to serve as her clients' link to the business world, providing information and the kind of networks that can be crucial to business success. One of her greatest frustrations—and one of the reasons she eventually left ISED for a position at the United Way—is that she did not have enough time to give all her clients the personal attention they needed. As the number of people who went through her course grew, it became harder and harder to keep up: "I've got ten people, if I only had an extra hour today, or tomorrow, or last week, or two weeks ago—they needed my help and I didn't have the time to do it."

Jane, a petite woman with shoulder-length brown hair, dressed in slacks and a sweater, arrives for class weighed down with paper. In addition to guiding her students through the ISED curriculum and working with them individually if they need extra help, Jane is a font of information. In just a single session, she will distribute a list of legislators and encourage students to get to know them, bring in speakers from the Community Mediation Center located down the hall to discuss how mediation can be used to resolve business problems, and organize a tour of City Hall so students can learn firsthand where to file forms and get assistance. By the time her clients complete the course, they will have accumulated a wealth of resources. "I have every piece of paper still, downstairs in a box," says Angelina Childers, a massage therapist and single mother of three who was still in touch with Jane more than a year after completing the course. "ISED . . . organized all of my aspirations. That's the only way I can say it," she continues. "I mean, you have thoughts and you think, 'Maybe I can do this,' but I can't. And Jane gives you the information, gives you the resources to do what you want to do, and she's right there behind you."

Eighteen students are present for the third session of the course. Thirty-six attended the first meeting and twenty-five came to the second. Today, school closings due to the dense fog and several cases of the flu have diminished the ranks. But a 40–50 percent drop-off in the first few weeks of class is not unusual. At these early sessions, students are asked to assess their readiness for self-employment and many conclude it is not for them.

Today's group consists of twelve women and six men. Six are African American and one is an immigrant from Nigeria; the rest are Caucasian. This, too, is typical. Of the population ISED serves, almost two-thirds are women and one-fifth minorities. A married couple and a brother and sister are part of the group. Almost everyone has a business idea. Some are already working and have come to ISED to learn how to expand or formalize their businesses, including three women who currently provide day care out of their homes. The Nigerian immigrant has a job as a home health care aide but would like to work for herself. The husband-and-wife team is expanding its magic show into the novel but reportedly profitable area of gospel magic. A young man is certified to do small engine repair but knows little about running a business. Other clients are starting from scratch. One woman would like to run a taxi service in a neighborhood ill served by public transportation. An amateur photographer is wondering how to turn his hobby into a business. Some of the participants are on welfare, others receive food stamps or disability benefits. All earn incomes that place them below 200 percent of the poverty line, or $27,760 for a family of three.

The early sessions of the course are devoted to introducing clients to ISED and microenterprise development. People present their business ideas and Jane helps them think through the risks and rewards of self-employment. They assess the feasibility of their businesses and their own readiness to become business owners. By the third session, most of those who have decided against self-employment or who have not come up with a viable business idea have left the course. The remaining ten weeks or so will focus on the preparation of a business plan. Jane will help participants identify and research the market for their business, develop a marketing strategy, analyze pricing and financial feasibility, draw up a financial plan, settle on the appropriate structure for the business, and assess their need for capital. Among the skills taught along the way are decisionmaking, problem solving, marketing, financial management, and time management. By the conclusion of the course, clients are expected to have prepared at least a rough draft of their business plan and, if financing is needed, begun work on a loan application.

Ten weeks later, seventeen clients finish the program. The Nigerian immigrant is among them, but she struggled to understand some of the concepts introduced in class and admits she is not ready to go out on her own. The photographer completed the class but not his business plan and has not yet figured out how to make the transition from amateur to professional. The magicians wrote part of a business plan, but decided they do not need any new financing at this point. The woman who wants to start a taxi service ran into credit problems, making it unlikely that she will be able to borrow the money she needs to buy a vehicle. The small engine repairman and several other class members are ready to start their businesses and may apply for financing down the road. Of the thirteen welfare recipients who started the class, six completed it.

These numbers are familiar to Jane and the other trainers. Many enter the program; far fewer complete it. Some leave after the initial orientation and assessment. Others drop out during training. Of those who do complete the course, not all will start businesses. And of the businesses that are established, not all will survive. One of the challenges ISED faces is to bring more people into its programs. Another challenge is to reduce drop-out rates, which have risen in recent years. One reason for the higher attrition in the late 1990s was Iowa's booming economy and tight labor market, which made it easier for unskilled workers to find jobs and drove up wages for low-skilled work. (In 1999, one could secure an entry-level job at the local Wal-Mart for a starting salary of $8 an hour plus benefits.) A second reason was welfare reform, which moved more than 30,000 Iowans, or more than one-third of the welfare population, off public assistance between 1996 and 2000.[11] As the rolls fell, those entering ISED's programs were drawn from the harder to serve part of the welfare population. Many of these individuals struggle with problems, such as chronic illness, substance abuse, or domestic violence, that have long kept them out of the work force.

As ISED staff members learn more about the reasons people leave training, they have begun experimenting with ways to reduce attrition.[12] At one site, the training course was restructured into two six-week sessions, allowing clients to complete the first part of the curriculum, then take a break before moving on to the preparation of their business plan. Those already on the way to starting their businesses may attend just the second half of the course. Another initiative was to hire a social worker to assist welfare recipients in overcoming personal barriers that might interfere with their success in the training course. Jane expected this to be a big help. "There's just so many other issues in these folks' lives. I mean, I'm not a therapist." Even so, Jane has developed close, lasting relationships with some of the men and women she has trained, relationships that resemble friendships as much as anything else. Marguerite Sisson is among those clients who call Jane their friend.

River City Cleaning

Marguerite was fortunate. The training class she joined in October 1998 was small to begin with, and other members dropped out early on. Jane was able to give Marguerite all the attention she needed, focusing on those parts of the curriculum that were most relevant to her situation. Jane worked with Marguerite to get her books in order and develop a business plan. And, as promised, she helped her find more clients. "When I met Jane we had talked about marketing skills, how I needed to go out and get my name out there," Marguerite recalls. "I put an ad in the newspaper. I thought of these quotes, like 'Cleaning for you,' and Jane really got me fired up about this business stuff." Marguerite began looking up companies in the phone book and making cold calls. Jane also helped her design a flier to put in mailboxes around town. "The telephone calls just came rolling in," says Marguerite. By December, River City Cleaning had several new accounts and Marguerite had hired her first employees.

Then Jane suggested they write a press release and take it to the local newspaper. Much to Marguerite's surprise, the *Clinton Herald* wrote an article about her business. "I couldn't believe it. The telephone rang and it was the chief of police." He asked whether she had the staff to clean the police department six nights a week. Marguerite said she did, even though she was not sure where she would find the needed workers. She met with the chief at the police department and gave him a bid. He looked at what Marguerite had proposed and told her his budget would not cover it. He wrote a lower figure on a piece of paper and passed it to Marguerite. "I looked at it and I thought, God, this is a great chance to get in and say, 'Look, I work for the police department, so that means I'm an honest person.' And I said OK." The police department let its current cleaning service go, and Marguerite and a newly hired employee went to work. "I changed that place from night to day," she says with pride. "It was filthy."

Like many microentrepreneurs, Marguerite started her business on a shoestring. Her friend the night yardmaster had helped her buy the cleaning supplies she needed to get going. Her caseworker got Marguerite a $500 grant from Promise Jobs that she used to purchase a cleaning cart and fix her car. One of the most valuable resources was the State of Iowa waiver that allowed Marguerite to continue to receive her public assistance benefits even after she had started the business, provided the amount of income she drew for herself each month did not exceed the limitations set for welfare eligibility. With her cash grant still available to support herself and her son, Marguerite could use the money she earned to stabilize and expand her business. (Research shows that launching a business and reaching the point where it provides income is a process that can take months and may involve market risks that are well beyond the control of entrepreneurs. As a result, provisions that allow business owners to retain their welfare benefits for a set period are central to the ability of welfare recipients to succeed at entrepreneurship.)[13]

"It was just like a flight of stairs," Marguerite says in describing the speed at which her business grew. Within a year of starting the business, River City Cleaning had nine employees whom Marguerite paid between $7 and $8 an hour. The company's clients included the police department, a medical complex, the construction company that had been her first commercial client, and the Visiting Nurses Association. Her biggest account, where Marguerite cleaned twice a day, seven days a week, was the Union Pacific Railroad where she used to work. She had just bought a car—a slightly used 1995 Sebring—from a dealership that was also one of her clients and was saving money for a down payment on a house. Marguerite expected her company to gross between $65,000 and $70,000 for the year.

These were the facts that Marguerite reported to the House of Representatives Committee on Banking and Financial Services on May 26, 1999. Also testifying were Senator Edward M. Kennedy, representatives of the U.S. Treasury Department, and leaders of various microenterprise development programs, including Jason Friedman. Marguerite was the only business owner to speak. Presiding over the meeting was Congressman James Leach, the Iowa legislator who chaired the committee and a longtime supporter of ISED. "Senator Kennedy was the first person to speak," Marguerite remembers; "I thought it was awesome how I could be on this list [with him]." Marguerite's testimony was inspiring and she received many compliments. "I know there are a lot of books that you can buy to help write a business plan," Marguerite told the committee. "But what I needed was a coach, a mentor, someone who believed in me and was with me every step of the way. You cannot get that in a book. I had no one to tell me I could make it; no one who understood what I was going through.

That is what these microenterprise programs are all about. They give you the tools and they give you the hope and encouragement. Jane is still there when I need her, and she is my cushion, my comfort, and my friend."[14]

Marguerite would need Jane's help, and more, in the months ahead. "Back in the end of May, things were absolutely fabulous," Marguerite recalls. "My business was taking off; I couldn't believe it because I'd started it the April before. I was invited to go to Washington, D.C. Everything was going great and I had just got this car and, oh, I was on top of the world. . . . And then it seemed to fall apart." In a matter of months, River City Cleaning had lost some of its biggest accounts and its payroll had shrunk to two employees—a woman in her late sixties and Marguerite's fiancé, Terry Meyer. Marguerite was having to work harder than ever just to keep her business afloat.

In explaining what went wrong, Marguerite recounts a series of seemingly unrelated events involving new financial pressures, unreliable employees, and difficult clients. In July 1999, Marguerite's housing benefits ended and the rent on her small house jumped from $120 to $315 a month. "It was scary at first, since I'd never paid my own rent before," she says. Two months later, her cash welfare grant ran out, although she retained the monthly medical card that covered her own health care and that of her son. Marguerite had expected her welfare benefits to end, but she had not bargained for a drop-off in business at the same time. One by one, the company's housecleaning clients began canceling her services. Marguerite could not get a straight answer why until one of her long-time customers finally confided that one of Marguerite's employees was doing a terrible job. "When I found that out I talked to her about it," Marguerite says; "I was very upset, but I didn't scream or anything. I just told her what was happening. And of course she denied it all. . . . Then she didn't show up a couple of times, so I fired her." An employee with whom Marguerite had become friends—a bad idea, she admits now—quit without warning. Her replacement kept missing appointments, and Marguerite had to let her go as well. River City Cleaning beat out its competition and landed a cleaning contract with a large new medical facility, but the size of the building made it difficult for Marguerite to come up with an accurate bid before starting work. The owner agreed that Marguerite could set her fee once she found out how many hours the job took, but when she presented him with the bill he refused to pay the full amount. Eventually she dropped the account. Insurance costs rose: "The more employees, the more wages, the more insurance." Marguerite explains. Other bills mounted—year-end sales tax, withholding tax—and it was a struggle to pay them on time.

Much more than a run of bad luck, Marguerite was experiencing something familiar to many small business owners. As demand for a company's services rises, the owner will do his or her best to expand, but more often than not the systems and infrastructure needed to allow the business to grow smoothly are not in place. In Marguerite's case, many of the problems centered on human resources: how to recruit, interview, and manage employees; how to pay them; how to retain them. Marguerite also acknowledges that she has a hard time planning ahead: "I'm one of these people, everything is an emergency for me. I don't sweat the small stuff, and I should." Anticipating year-end costs, setting aside the money to cover them, preparing for the end of her welfare benefits—such planning measures would have helped Marguerite weather these difficult months. But one of the barriers to this kind of planning is that Marguerite not only owned her company but also did the lion's share of its work. The two roles can be difficult to balance. "When you own a company like this it's all on performance," Marguerite explains, "and sometimes I'm exhausted and it's so hard. You know you have to please them but at the same time you're all worn out."

While the work is hard, finding new accounts has been surprisingly easy. When business slowed in the fall of 1999, Marguerite decided she needed more clients. She and Terry took fliers out to businesses in the community and within three weeks she had added four new accounts. Marguerite knows she could do this again. The problem is that she does not have the employees to support a bigger business. "This might sound strange to some people but I will not hire somebody if they're not gonna do a good job. I'm really scared of it. I'd rather keep my business on a steady, even level and make it, than [say], 'Oh, I'm gonna go out and get twenty accounts and hire anybody off the streets.' That's when your business goes down, that's what the problem is with a lot of my competition."

Marguerite learned two lessons from the rapid rise and fall of her business in its first two years. One is that, as the owner of River City Cleaning, she is the sole person responsible for maintaining its reputation. "My main concern is that you keep your standard up," she says. When she had to fire the employee who was doing a poor job she told her, "'Well, I'm really sorry, but I just can't have this. Your performance reflects on my company.'" It is hard to argue with the high standards Marguerite has set for her company. But the other lesson is one that will need to be discarded if her business is to grow. "You cannot count on anybody but yourself," is the way Marguerite puts it, and there is little mystery about how she reached this conclusion. But her reluctance to hire new employees has meant that, until recently, Marguerite had to do the job of several people.

On Mondays and Tuesdays, her easy days, she would clean the railroad twice—once in the morning and once late at night. In addition to her daily trips to the railroad station, she would visit a surveying company on Wednesday and the construction company on Thursday. Fridays were the toughest—the railroad twice and two other businesses. And on Saturdays and Sundays, she made her usual trips to the railroad and cleaned one bank each day. On easy days Marguerite would work for about six hours, on hard days for as many as twelve or sixteen. "Jane's scared because she wants to keep me going, that's her job, and she worries about that. She don't have anything to worry about. . . . So what? If I have to work these hours, I have to do it. It's not gonna kill me. If anything, it makes me a stronger person. And she should be happy that I'm worried about just hiring anybody off the street."

For several years, the person on whom Marguerite relied most heavily was her fiancé, Terry. "He's such a wonderful help to me. Sometimes I don't know how I'd make it without him, really. I mean, I know I would because I'm a strong person. But he works so hard. . . . We switch on and off trying to give each other a day off. I can remember for months on end we worked seven days a week, it was just part of life, for months straight not a day off. He doesn't really like to take too many days off, maybe once a month or once every other month." A year into their engagement, Marguerite and Terry set a wedding date for June 2000. A honeymoon would be out of the question; there was no one to cover the company's accounts if Marguerite and Terry went away.

While Marguerite resisted hiring new employees—a task admittedly made much harder by Iowa's low unemployment rate—she did come up with other ways to expand her business. Terry had done a lot of outdoor work in the past and, after some research, Marguerite decided to add snow removal and lawn care to the services she provides. "I want to be like the one-stop shopping," says Marguerite. "I can remove your snow, I can have your grass cut for you in the summertime. We will clean for you, we will do your carpets, we will do all your upholstery, we will clean your windows, all that. . . . I've done a lot of my work on the Internet, looking around. Wow, it's a good money-making thing to get into snow removal and lawn care. You can make a lot of money in one day. And Terry loves to do it. He loves to be out there in the cold and do it."

But this new line of work would require new equipment and neither Marguerite nor Terry had the money or credit to pay for it. "I don't know what it is," says Marguerite, "but there's a very high percent of women [who have been on welfare] that will not take out loans once they become self-sufficient. It's really scary and it was for me, too. I was so scared just to get my car loan. You're afraid because you say to yourself, 'But I only lived on $360 a month. How can I possibly buy this thing and afford this $200-a-month car payment or this $160-a-month equipment loan payment? What if things go south in one day?'" Like many of those who complete ISED's training course, Marguerite did not need to go into debt in order to start her business, but she did need to do so in order to expand.

ISED is unusual among microenterprise development organizations in that, for most of its history, it has not operated its own loan fund. When John Else started the organization he fully intended to have one. But Else feared that the small grant ISED had received to start its operations would not cover all of its clients' capital needs. To stretch the money, ISED insisted that each person finishing the training course go to two banks before applying for a loan from ISED. The first client to finish a business plan dutifully took it to the largest bank in Cedar Rapids, expecting to be turned down. Else was surprised to get a call from the loan officer saying, "This is one of the best business plans I've ever seen. I was so thrilled with it that I took it to the president of the bank." As the conversation progressed, the loan officer suggested that the bank set up a $10,000 loan pool set-aside for ISED clients. Else said he thought that was a fine idea, hung up the phone, and promptly called a banker friend to ask, "What's a loan pool set-aside?" His friend explained that banks will occasionally commit funds to be used exclusively by people who meet certain qualifications, in this case the completion of microenterprise training and ISED's endorsement of their business plan. Not only that, but he offered to have his own bank dedicate $25,000 for ISED clients. It proved remarkably easy to convince other local bankers to do the same, and in short order the organization had amassed a large enough pool to serve its clients without having to develop its own financing capacity. Instead, ISED took the money from the original grant and put it into a guarantee fund that could be used to secure up to 50 percent of a bank loan, thereby providing additional assurance to a commercial lender.

Not all of ISED's clients can get commercial financing. Fortunately, other options exist. With poor credit and no collateral, Marguerite was not a candidate for a bank loan, but Jane thought she might qualify for a program administered by Iowa's Department of Economic Development. The Self-Employment Loan Program lends up to $10,000 to low-income individuals who work for themselves; the loans carry an interest rate of 5 percent and a term of five years. Marguerite and Jane had discussed the program shortly after they met but had agreed that it was too risky for Marguerite to take on any debt at that point. The loan process itself—including the thirty-page application—was also a big barrier. But now Marguerite needed some form of financing and Jane believed this was her best chance. Jane helped with the application. "I'll tell you what," says Marguerite, "that lady spent countless numbers of hours after work . . . we were on the phone for hours. She was willing to drive up here just to sign these papers." Marguerite submitted her application in November 1999. The loan, for just over $8,000, was approved quickly, but it took several months for the check to wend its way through the state bureaucracy. In the meantime, Jane helped Marguerite apply for a bridge loan from a commercial bank so she could go ahead and purchase the needed equipment. Marguerite used the proceeds to buy snow removal equipment, a power mower, and a combination floor stripper-waxer-buffer. Payments on the loan began in March 2000. Doing her best to plan ahead, Marguerite arranged to have the paycheck from the banks she was cleaning deposited directly into accounts there—a means of forced savings that ensured she would have the money available for her loan payments. Provided she remains current on the loan, Jane believes that the next time Marguerite needs capital she will qualify for credit from a commercial bank.

Marguerite can envision a great future for her business. She has heard that the Union Pacific Railroad recently talked about hiring a single van company to provide its stations up and down the line with transportation services. She thinks she could do the same thing with River City Cleaning, setting up branches in cities served by the railroad and negotiating contracts city by city as they come up for renewal. "I would want to do it all over the United States," she says. "That is my long-term goal that I don't think about every day, and then I got these little short-term goals that are step by step."

Jane is glad to see Marguerite thinking ambitiously, but she has her concerns. "If she could get the employee thing down on the local level then she could manage that perhaps in the future," she says. Jane is afraid Marguerite will burn out if she does not figure out how to expand. She would like Marguerite to have a buffer in case something goes wrong.

A few weeks after Marguerite received the proceeds of her equipment loan, Terry was diagnosed with malignant melanoma. He underwent surgery and a round of chemotherapy, which his doctors believe were successful in removing the cancer. Terry had no medical insurance and the cost of his treatment strained the couple's already tight finances. The June wedding was postponed. Terry's illness made Marguerite's complicated schedule even more difficult. She spent a great deal of time accompanying him on the seventy-mile trip back and forth between Clinton and Iowa City, where he was treated. After chemotherapy, Terry was able to work only very limited hours, which meant that Marguerite needed to take on extra responsibility. "The thing is," she says, "when you're a businessperson and you own your own business, the people that you're serving—your clients—if something comes up in your life it's not their problem. So you have to do the best. You have to do it anyway."

Learning from Experience

Recent years have seen the publication of extensive evaluation data on the impact of microenterprise development programs. One of the most comprehensive studies is the Aspen Institute's Self-Employment Learning Project, which tracked participants in seven of the nation's leading microenterprise development organizations (including ISED) over a five-year period. Among the key findings of the project were income gains for 72 percent of the poor microentrepreneurs participating in the programs (the average increase in income was $8,484)—gains large enough for more than half of the programs' low-income participants to move out of poverty.[15] Because this was not an experimental design where participants were assigned randomly to a treatment group and a control group, it is impossible to determine what percentage of the income gains were directly attributable to microenterprise training. However, one study that did use an experimental design (an analysis of two sites carried out by the U.S. Department of Labor, the results of which were published in 1994) also found income gains, as have virtually all other studies of microenterprise training.[16] Studies have also yielded evidence that microenterprise training leads to an increase in both assets and net worth.[17]

Another outcome tracked by evaluation studies is the number of businesses started by participants in training programs and the survival rates of these businesses. Here, ISED's scale and effectiveness stand out. Since it was established, ISED has trained more than 6,800 clients and has assisted them in starting or expanding 1,400 businesses. The one-year survival rate for these businesses is 87 percent and the overall survival rate of all assisted businesses since 1988 is 58 percent—impressive numbers, given the odds of small business failure for poor and nonpoor alike.[18] (The seven programs tracked by the Self-Employment Learning Project yielded a five-year survival rate of 49 percent for businesses started by low-income participants.)[19] ISED clients run day care centers, hair salons, consignment shops, appliance repair services, even a goat farm. Many of these businesses have yielded gains in income for their owners, allowing those on public assistance to become self-sufficient. ISED has facilitated access for its clients to $7.76 million in business financing, most of it from the private sector, and has helped business owners expand and hire new workers, contributing to the revitalization of communities across the state.

Microenterprise development training is not a panacea for poverty, and it does not work for everyone. A recent study shows that welfare recipients enrolling in training differ demographically from the general population of those receiving public assistance.[20] Overall, enrollees are older, have higher levels of education (86 percent of enrollees had a high school degree or GED), are more likely to have been married and divorced, and have more employment experience. Moreover, it is clear that not everyone is temperamentally suited to working for him- or herself. But just as a certain proportion of people in the nonpoor population is inclined toward self-employment, so is a certain proportion of the poor. Estimates suggest that more than 2 million low-income people are already working for themselves. Yet microenterprise organizations, taken together, have served only a few hundred thousand people since they were established. One of the challenges facing ISED and the microenterprise field as a whole is how to reach all those in need of assistance.

There are several reasons for the gap between the number of clients served and the potential scope for microenterprise assistance.[21] Existing organizations tend to be small and locally based. Few resources are available for market research to determine the actual demand for services and where expansion should occur. The lack of a reliable income stream also limits the scale of microenterprise services. Initially, it was thought that an ever-expanding pool of entrepreneurs could be supported with revenue from revolving loan funds, as it had been in the developing world. This has turned out not to be the case, and most microenterprise organizations continue to operate on shoestring budgets with funding patched together from foundations and government agencies. Demand for these resources is high, with hundreds of organizations clamoring for money from a handful of sources. Overlap is another problem. In Maine, for example, thirteen organizations provide services to a relatively small population of micro-entrepreneurs. Eight other states have between ten and thirty-three orga-nizations engaged in microenterprise development. With such overlap, economics of scale become difficult to achieve and resources may be wasted. The trade association for microenterprise development organizations, the Association for Enterprise Opportunity, in 1998 announced an ambitious goal for its membership: to help a million low-income individuals in the United States reach self-sufficiency through self-employment by 2008. If this diverse and fragmented field is to meet such a goal, it will need to build on the experience of organizations like ISED that have already achieved a measure of scale.

One reason that ISED has been able to reach a large population is be-cause it does not face the kind of competition for resources described above. ISED is in the enviable position of being the only microenterprise develop-ment organization in the State of Iowa. As such, it is committed to provid-ing comprehensive statewide coverage and has developed a system of branch offices and rural contractors to accomplish this task. The logistics of such a system are complicated. Resources must be devoted to communicating with a geographically dispersed staff and ensuring that policy changes are carried out across the organization. But the advantages are clear when it comes to the question of scale. For Iowans, ISED is quite simply the place to go for microenterprise services. ISED can recruit from Iowa's entire pool of welfare recipients. Its rural consultants offer training in every cor-ner of the state.

A close relationship with the State of Iowa has helped ISED grow and granted it a modicum of financial stability. From its participation in the Self-Employment Investment Demonstration in the late 1980s to its role in shaping Iowa's welfare-to-work legislation in the early 1990s, ISED has collaborated with the state's Department of Human Services. In 2001, this relationship changed when budget cuts led to the end of ISED's long-standing welfare-to-work contract with DHS. (ISED still trains welfare recipients but not on a sole source contract; instead, payment for ISED services must be arranged through individual caseworkers—a more time-consuming and complex process than in the past.) "A lot of other microenterprise organizations are either just now developing those partnerships or are still struggling with the state's perception of the value of self-employment," says Angela Gravely-Smith, ISED's former associate director of field operations. "We've [had] twelve years of funding from DHS to work with welfare recipients. . . . That, I think, is one huge piece that has been a strength for the organization because it gets to the institutionalization of self-employment." ISED also works with Iowa's Department of Economic Development, which helps fund programs in rural communities and administers the loan program that Marguerite turned to for her equipment purchase. Finally, ISED is the state's chief repository of expertise on microenterprise development, which keeps it on the radar screen of policymakers.

ISED's programs are evolving both to meet the changing needs of the state and to more fully achieve its mission strengthening the social and economic well-being of individuals and communities. Mollenkopf-Pigsley explains that the organization's activities are becoming both broader and deeper. ISED is expanding to serve new groups, providing microenterprise training to Spanish-language speakers (the fastest-growing segment of Iowa's population), refugees (another rapidly growing group), and female inmates at the Women's Correctional Facility. (Fifteen percent of the female inmate population in the state is either in training or on a waiting list to be trained.) The organization is also broadening its geographic scope, offering programs in other states and teaching its first seminar overseas (an evaluation techniques session offered in Russia in 1999). In Iowa, ISED is moving beyond microenterprise services, starting a construction trades training program for low-income individuals in Des Moines and working with the state to administer an individual development account (IDA) program for low-income Iowans. (For more on IDAs, see chapter 6.) The program offers a dollar-for-dollar match for savings by people earning below 200 percent of the poverty line, with matching funds provided by the state and federal governments. The savings can be used only for the down payment on a house, tuition for college or vocational training, or capital to start or expand a small business. The program also includes classes in financial literacy. Most recently, ISED received a grant to provide free tax preparation services in the inner city of Des Moines and teach eligible low-income taxpayers how to file for the Earned Income Tax Credit.

"If we're really interested in poverty alleviation," says Jason Friedman, "we have to develop more tools in our toolbox." Microenterprise training helps build a client's ability to run a business, while the IDA program and financial literacy training help people acquire the savings needed to start or expand that business. But ISED's vision goes further, leading the organization to offer a range of services focused on both poverty alleviation and community economic development. Most of ISED's existing programs emphasize the first of these goals—helping individuals escape poverty through self-employment, job training, and asset building. The recent decision to become a community development financial institution (CDFI) will emphasize the second.

CDFIs are specialized financial institutions that work in market niches that have not been adequately served by traditional financial institutions. CDFIs may apply for funding from the CDFI Fund, authorized by Congress and administered by the U.S. Treasury Department—money that must be matched by additional investments from the state government or private sector. As a CDFI, ISED will have access to new pools of capital that will allow it to fulfill more of a traditional community development role, something that virtually no other organization in Iowa is doing. "It's not so much an expansion of our mission as a natural evolution of it," says Friedman. "If our mission is to strengthen the economic and social well-being of individuals and communities, CDFI puts teeth into the communities piece."

In his congressional testimony, Jason Friedman told a House committee, "We have demonstrated that a strong training and technical assistance program, backed by innovative credit enhancements, will encourage banks to do more lending to low-income clients, obviating the need to maintain a loan fund."[22] Still, ISED has found that the demand for capital outstrips the dollars available, especially for its low-income clientele. As a CDFI, ISED will be able to provide small start-up loans to microentrepreneurs through a subsidiary it has established called Iowa Community Capital. Establishing its own loan fund is an important departure for ISED, which made its mark as a training organization. But ISED is confident that more than a decade of experience training low-income individuals will enable it to succeed where other organizations have not. "We have the advantage going in many years later in that there's [been] a tremendous amount of learning," says Friedman. Some organizations started out making loans without ensuring that clients had sufficient knowledge to use the money wisely. Low demand and high default rates were often the result. Friedman believes that ISED's prospects for success are good because it is moving into the lending business as a more mature organization. And ISED's trainers are excited about the prospect of having a micro loan fund at their disposal. All of them have encountered clients who have viable business plans but cannot get financing either because they have poor credit or no collateral. A micro loan from ISED's own fund would allow these clients to get their businesses going while establishing a credit history that would qualify them for commercial financing later on.

ISED's entrance into the lending business is being done cautiously. "We're not going to do anything without the results that prove it can work," says Friedman. One of ISED's hallmarks is this commitment to evaluation. "We've been lucky," he continues. "John, our founder, had two heads"—by which he means that John Else is both a practitioner and an academic. When Else first set up ISED's microenterprise training program, he made sure that its effectiveness would be rigorously assessed along the way. No organization in the field collects as much data as ISED or has as comprehensive a management information system. ISED has also participated in numerous outside evaluations as well as evaluation by its in-house unit.[23] "People are trying lots of new things, but they're not evaluating them," says Friedman. The addition of a social worker to the staff in ISED's Des Moines office is one example of the organization's commitment to outcome-driven results. Other organizations have used social workers to support their welfare clients, and anecdotal evidence suggests that the effort has helped reduce attrition. But there has been no formal evaluation of the impact of such a move. ISED is testing the impact of the new staff person on training program completion rates by comparing a period in which no case management services were offered with a period in which they were. In addition, the case manager has worked with three programs—traditional microenterprise training, bilingual training, and refugee services—allowing for comparison of the impact of her services among these various populations. The findings of the experiment, funded by the Microenterprise Fund for Innovation, Effectiveness, Learning, and Dissemination (FIELD), will enable ISED to decide whether to add similar services in all its offices and will give other microenterprise organizations some hard data on the costs and benefits of this approach.

ISED is also exploring ways to increase business survival rates among its clients. In the early days, the number of clients who required ISED's ongoing assistance was small and the organization's consultants could meet their needs. But as Jane Duax's frustration suggests, one of the consequences of achieving scale is that it is hard to keep up with the growing population of ISED graduates. Most of the funding the organization receives is geared toward getting people through the training program and helping them start their businesses. While follow-up assistance has always been a part of ISED's philosophy, there is little money to support it. Instead, as Friedman says, "Those that scream get the service," leaving those that do not to sink or swim. ISED would like to be able to provide a line of business growth services to clients whose businesses have been up and running for twelve to eighteen months, a point at which many low-income entrepreneurs encounter barriers to consolidation or expansion. In some cases, these barriers are related to technical know-how. For example, an ISED client may be successful at a local level but have no idea how to reach a metropolitan, regional, or national market. In other cases, the barriers to expansion involve human resource issues, as they did for Marguerite. The potential for growth is there; Marguerite even knows what needs to be done. But, working as hard as she can just to keep her company afloat, Marguerite has neither the time nor the skills to recruit, hire, and manage the workers necessary for expansion.

Whether the limits on growth are technical or personal, ISED's clients would surely benefit from hands-on assistance geared specifically toward business survival and expansion. One of Friedman's favorite books these days is Azriela Jaffe's *Starting from "No."*[24] Subtitled "10 Strategies to Overcome Your Fear of Rejection and Succeed in Business," the book, Friedman maintains, was unwittingly written precisely for low-income business owners. "In some ways nothing has changed for these entrepreneurs," he says. "They're doing their business but they're not doing it to their full ability. Part of it just may be that they need help, but part of it also is that the mind-set or the orientation of that person hasn't necessarily changed dramatically as far as barriers, perceived or real: fears of failing, fears of getting too big, fears of not being liked, fears of rejection, separating out the person from the business." Jaffe's book presents strategies for helping people identify these fears and offers practical advice for overcoming them. "We're not doing this for our clients," says Friedman, "and we should."

Finally, ISED is reconsidering the fundamental question of how to measure success. Like most other microenterprise organizations, ISED assesses performance by counting how many people complete its training program, how many start businesses, and for how long those businesses survive. But the organization has found that, especially in a low-unemployment environment, people will sometimes close their businesses and move into jobs where they earn more than when they were self-employed. (A similar phenomenon is evident among small businesses in general; 38 percent of sole proprietorships and 57 percent of small businesses that close are reported to be successful at closure.)[25] In addition, a considerable proportion of those completing the training course never start businesses but instead find wage employment. The focus on business start-ups and survival rates does not account for what would otherwise be considered a positive outcome.

The Will to Succeed

In *Bootstrap Capital*, Lisa Servon concludes that it takes three things to succeed as a low-income microentrepreneur: strong and reliable support networks, experience or training in a line of business, and determination and resourcefulness. Of these, Marguerite thinks the last is by far the most important: "It takes a certain person, it really does. You have to have determination. [You have] to say, 'Hey, this is what I'm gonna do.' You have to dedicate yourself. It takes a lot out of you. You have to be prepared and willing to take a chance, and so many people are afraid of change. I was afraid. I was so afraid of changes."

When it comes to support networks, Marguerite has had a hard time relying on others. She is not particularly close to her brothers or sisters, and while she and her mother are on good terms, her mother does not understand why Marguerite has chosen the life she has. "My mom has no understanding of business or what I'm going through. She's never really said much about it, nobody's ever really said, 'I'm proud of you.' She always tells me to quit and go get a regular job for 6 bucks an hour." So Marguerite has turned to people outside her family. "The strangers are the ones that give me the validation," she says. Larry, her friend from her days at the railroad, is among those who have been a great help, from paying for the supplies Marguerite needed to get started to believing in her future. "He's like a father to me, because I had never had anybody. He'd come over and look in the fridge and it would be bare. He would buy me milk and pop and this and that, anything I needed. . . . He just, like, became my dad. . . . He always tells me, 'You deserve better, you need better.'" When she was planning her wedding, Marguerite asked Larry to walk her down the aisle.

While such personal relationships have helped Marguerite emotionally, Jane's counsel and friendship helped her succeed as an entrepreneur. "She has been a very supportive person and a very important one in my business career. You know, sometimes I just call her and I'm frustrated. I just want somebody to tell my frustrations to. . . . She says, 'Well, have you looked at it this way?' or 'This is all you really need to do.'" Beyond her initial work with Marguerite to strengthen her marketing, Jane was most helpful in connecting Marguerite to resources she would not have known about otherwise. Jane told Marguerite about a workshop offered by the local college on occupational safety and health issues. She encouraged her to apply for the state loan. "She's done a lot of things out of the way that she didn't have to do," says Marguerite. "She's very dedicated. She'll put off things in her life to [help others]. She's very intelligent. She kept saying how proud she was of me . . . and I could never see it."

"She thinks she's dumb," says Jane. "She's smart. She's so, so smart. The things that she's figured out on her own, never mind my help. She figured out how to do all of her own taxes, even payroll taxes." Marguerite is coming to believe what Jane says is true. "Everything I've done, pretty much, I've taught myself. I taught myself how to drive, I taught myself how to use a computer, I taught myself how to hook up electrical equipment and take things apart and change my spark plugs; I went to the library and got a book. I did all that on my own. . . . Jane helps me out with bookkeeping, but the taxes and all that I've learned on my own [by] reading. I always thought I'm terrible at numbers, and I found out I can run a whole entire business. I can walk into somebody's business and do the books if I had to." Marguerite bought herself a computer with the help of a grant from the Trickle Up Foundation, a private group that provides $700 grants to low-income microentrepreneurs. (She found out about the grant through ISED.) Jane showed her the basics of cutting and pasting, but Marguerite taught herself the rest, learning to use a scanner, e-mail, and the Internet. "I'm self-educated, a lot of it. I'm the type of person, I can figure stuff out pretty quick."

Lisa Servon calls self-employment "a survival strategy for many but a secure one for few."[26] When Marguerite first thought of going to work for herself, it was as a joke: "Yeah, right, how could I ever do that?" But after she got fired, the only work she could find was another job on the late shift at a low wage. In this light, the risks of self-employment did not seem so great. Since she started her company, Marguerite's standard of living has undoubtedly improved. "It's nice, you know," she says. "I can go to the grocery store now and buy bread *and* peanut butter, and milk. I can eat steak and roast and chicken and whatever for supper, not hot dogs or macaroni. You know what I'm saying? I'm living a lot better." Even with the drop-off in business, Marguerite's gross earnings for 1999 were $55,000, down only slightly from the projections she had provided in her congressional testimony. "I'm happy and proud," she says, "but there's a lot of bills that go with it. . . . And the more you make, the more you spend." After expenses, Marguerite's net income was $16,000—enough to survive but barely sufficient to lift the family above the official poverty line, let alone provide a buffer in case things go wrong.

Her business has brought other benefits. Marguerite is intensely proud of her new car. "My cars that I always owned back then were junk," she recalls. "There were wires hanging out the doors. There were electric windows that were off the tracks; they would fall down. I once had a fire in the car—two wires touching. That's what kind of cars I drove because I couldn't afford anything else." Marguerite's son talks about the car a lot; it is perhaps the clearest sign to a young boy that his mom is doing better.

Marguerite had long had another major acquisition in mind. Desperate to get out of her dilapidated house on a busy corner just off Clinton's main street, she approached a local bank for preapproval on a home loan. "I want to buy a house really, really bad," she said at the time. "I rent this place now and it's very small, way too small." She was disappointed to discover the bank would lend her only $38,000—not enough to get the kind of house she wanted—so she decided to continue saving until she could qualify for a loan of at least $50,000. For a while, she managed to set aside about $600 a month, although occasionally she had to dip into these funds to pay quarterly taxes and the interest on her equipment loan. The direct deposits from the banks where she cleans helped. Like those in the middle class who put part of their paycheck into a retirement plan each month, Marguerite recognizes that this is a good way of building up her savings: "I will sit here and go without because I forget about that money," she says.

There is another asset Marguerite has acquired since she became a business owner—one harder to quantify than a savings account or newfound computer skills. The literature on microenterprise development points to the creation of new forms of social capital as one of the positive impacts of microenterprise training.[27] One source of social capital is the linking of participants with business development resources such as trainers and consultants, financial institutions, and professional associations. As the owner of River City Cleaning, Marguerite has come into contact with people she would never have met otherwise: business owners in Clinton, journalists who have written stories about her, the chief of police. She has also become a role model to others, something she never thought possible. Just before she left for Washington, Marguerite visited Jane's class to speak about her experience as a business owner. "They were very impressed because at that point I had only been in business a little over a year and I was answering all these business questions. I was explaining [to] them how to do bookkeeping, and I was telling them about business cards, what you need to do to start a business, from A to Z. I had people coming up to me and they were really proud and really excited. I gave them a lot of confidence. I couldn't believe that these people were looking up to me. But when I stood there and talked to them, I knew where they were coming from and they knew where I was coming from, because we had been in the same boat."

The training and support Marguerite received from ISED made it possible for her to start her own business, a change that has brought her new connections, greater self-confidence, a higher standard of living, even her first trip on an airplane. As she told the congressional committee, "I learned more than how to run a business. I learned that I am important. I learned that I am a strong and intelligent person. My son is very proud of me, and tells his teachers that I own a small business. And being a role model to my son is one of the most important achievements, setting aside everything else. I am showing him that anything is possible, and when he grows up, he will understand that hard work can take you any place you want to go."

This sense of pride and optimism is a far cry from Marguerite's state of mind a decade ago, just after Will was born. "I was going through a lot of depression in my life then," she remembers. "I drank a lot. I just didn't think there was anything out there. I watched a lot of friends get married. I was jealous 'cause they were married. A lot of them had things, they had houses and stuff, and I didn't have anything. . . . I always felt, 'Well, I'm going to have to find a man to marry that's gonna take care of me.' But from what I've found now, this many years later, most of the women that were my friends ended up getting a divorce and they're in my old shoes. And I'm now making the money. For everything that needs [to be] paid, I'm paying it. For everything that needs [to get] done, I'm doing it."

Today, River City Cleaning has three employees and is turning a profit. The slowing economy has led to the loss of some contracts, but these have been replaced by new accounts. Marguerite has gotten better at hiring. Previously, she would interview job candidates and hire them, as she puts it, "on a hunch." Now she takes down the name and number of everyone who calls, asks them for references, then follows up on these. As a result, she has found some better-qualified and more reliable employees than in the past. Marguerite has also finally been able to afford to purchase health insurance for herself. Best of all, she is finding that she can now run the business from her home office and leave most of the physical labor to others. At the moment, she works only one small job once every other week. Marguerite has not completely conquered her fear of expansion. She is content for the time being to keep her business at its current size and has abandoned any grand plans for the future. But she is very proud of one achievement—being completely free of the welfare system. "I can't believe it," she says. "Two and a half years, that's all it took, and I'm in a different place."

Marguerite's personal life has also taken a turn for the better. She and Terry were married in the summer of 2001. In a stroke of good fortune long overdue for Marguerite, a close friend came into some money and helped her buy a house in a much nicer neighborhood. Marguerite took out a home equity loan to cover the cost of some improvements. But her spending got out of hand, in part due to the swimming pool she had installed and the purchase of new furniture and a big-screen TV. She has since committed herself to a strict repayment schedule and has begun paying off some of her credit cards. Marguerite is trying to get her finances in order and plan for the future. Next on the agenda is to figure out how to invest her savings; an investment adviser at the investment firm she cleans has already offered to help.

Four years after starting her business, Marguerite is beginning to experience what self-employment has brought millions of other Americans: stability, security, a buffer when things go wrong, a nest egg for the future. After years of struggle, Marguerite is finally doing well. And if things should turn out badly, she is in a much stronger position to weather the change than she has been at any point before. Both the house and business are in her name. She has assets against which she can borrow, a support network on which to rely, and a newfound sense of personal confidence. When the father of her son left many years ago, Marguerite's only options were welfare or low-wage work—alternatives that only intensified the depression born of a troubled personal life. Now, come what may, Marguerite has a business to run and the will to make it a success. As she says, "At first I thought, 'Man, if I don't keep this business I'm gonna let a lot of people down.' I wasn't even thinking of myself. . . . Now I don't think about that. Now I think, if this business goes, I'm gonna let *myself* down."

CHAPTER SIX

Can
the Poor
Save?

In 1997, a group of nonprofit organizations embarked on an initiative to answer the question: Can the poor save?[1] At thirteen sites around the nation, community organizations offered low-income people the opportunity to open an individual development account (IDA)— a dedicated savings account to be used only for asset-building purposes such as home ownership, education, starting a business, or retirement.[2] The incentive to participate was that every dollar saved by an individual in such an account would be matched by another dollar or more contributed by the foundations supporting the program and local funders. Along with the match would come economic literacy training and other services.

Over a four-year period (1997–2001), the Downpayments on the American Dream Demonstration sought to reveal more than whether the poor can save if provided with the opportunities and incentives to do so; it also examined what low-income families would do with their savings and what impact such savings would have on their lives. An extensive evaluation process was built into the program to answer these questions and others. The organizers of the demonstration also hoped to assemble a set of "best practices" that would move the IDA field forward and drive the development of federal and state IDA policies.

As the demonstration entered its final year, a great deal had been learned. Almost 2,400 people, 88 percent of them low income, were participating in the program. Participants' average net deposits were just over $25 a month.[3] The average participant was able to make a deposit to his or her

IDA in seven out of every twelve months. Perhaps surprisingly, the lowest-income families were saving a higher proportion of their income—5.6 percent—than those with the highest incomes, who were saving 1.2 percent. With an average match rate of two-to-one, participants were accumulating about $900 a year in their IDAs. Thirteen percent of participants had withdrawn some of their savings for an approved use—24 percent to purchase a home, 24 percent to invest in their own business, and 21 percent to pursue postsecondary education. Of the more than 2,000 account holders who had not yet withdrawn any money from their IDAs, 57 percent intended to buy a home, 18 percent planned to invest in a business, and 15 percent were saving for postsecondary education. The remaining participants expected to use their IDAs for home repair, retirement, or job training.

These results showed that the poor can indeed save. But they also demonstrated how difficult it is for low-income individuals to accumulate assets, even within the supportive environment of an IDA program. Unmatched withdrawals from balances that qualified for a match were frequent, with about 37 percent of participants withdrawing some money from their IDAs to use for purposes other than those approved by the sponsoring organization. On average, these participants removed $320 from their accounts. Some of these funds were subsequently replaced, but not the full amount. The high rate and size of unmatched withdrawals suggests that, for many participants, the need to cover current expenses outweighed the value of the match money and the possibility of future asset ownership.

Much remains to be learned. Savings rates at the thirteen demonstration sites have varied, and research is just beginning to provide insight into the reasons why. The evaluation component of the demonstration will extend two years beyond the actual savings programs; it is these data that will track the ultimate use of the IDA and the impact saving has had on the families involved. The relationship between the costs of IDA programs and the benefits they bring are still being assessed.[4] And there are questions about the degree to which the saving behavior seen in the demonstration was due to the strong economy of the late 1990s and whether IDAs will remain a viable approach in leaner times.

Nonetheless, the introduction of IDAs has profoundly affected the lives of many program participants and altered the landscape of antipoverty programs at the federal, state, and local levels. The American Dream Demonstration and the many other IDA programs under way provide clear evidence that the poor can and will save under the right circumstances. This finding alone makes IDAs a promising new policy tool for helping people leave poverty behind.

The Genesis of IDAs

Without savings, it is nearly impossible to purchase a home or invest in further education. Without savings, an injury, illness, or divorce can push a family into poverty or homelessness. Without savings, it is difficult to start a business or apply for a bank loan. A recent survey of existing research on the effects of asset holding shows a range of positive results, from greater economic stability and higher property values to lower rates of divorce and a decreased risk that poverty will be transmitted to the next generation.[5] There are also intangible benefits that accrue to those who have money in the bank: greater personal satisfaction, the ability to plan for the future, the freedom to take risks. As Melvin L. Oliver and Thomas M. Shapiro write in *Black Wealth/White Wealth*, "Wealth is a special form of money not used to purchase milk and shoes and other life necessities. More often it is used to create opportunities, secure a desired stature and standard of living, or pass class status along to one's children."[6]

Poverty in the United States has generally been defined in terms of income, and policy has followed suit. Antipoverty measures have focused almost exclusively on providing the poor with regular income support and its equivalent in the form of food stamps or housing vouchers. At the same time, welfare policy discouraged savings, imposing limits on how much money a welfare recipient could hold in a bank account without forfeiting benefits. It is no surprise, then, that the question of whether poor people can save has rarely been asked or answered.

Michael Sherraden was one of the first to confront this question, prompted by two personal experiences.[7] In the mid-1980s, Sherraden held a number of informal conversations with local welfare recipients in his capacity as a professor of social work at Washington University in St. Louis. The families he spoke with relied on public assistance to meet their monthly needs for food and shelter, but they were deeply frustrated with the welfare system. Its meager benefits and strict rules were like a trap, making it hard to break free and even harder to get ahead. Around the same time, Sherraden attended a university meeting at which faculty members were briefed on the investment options for their employer-sponsored 403(b) plans, the nonprofit equivalent of a 401(k). Sherraden noted that the room was full—an unusual occurrence for a faculty gathering. "I thought, 'Wow, what got them in the room?'" Conventional theories of saving suggest that assets accumulate because those doing the saving are thoughtful, prudent, and motivated to plan for the future. Many of Sherraden's colleagues were none of these things, yet there they were. "They didn't think of it, they weren't prudent, they didn't figure it out," says Sherraden. "It was offered to them. . . . The reason they're here is that somebody accumulated this money for them, and then they decided they needed to pay attention to it and figure out where to invest it."

Sherraden recognized that this was a pattern of saving that stood conventional theories on their head. Faculty members' assets were growing because the university contributed money on their behalf while providing them with powerful incentives to save (tax-exempt savings and matching contributions) and an easy way to go about it (automatic payroll deductions). Once the assets grew, those who controlled them *became* thoughtful and prudent. A virtuous circle had been set in motion, with growing savings contributing to an orientation toward the future, and future orientation in turn reinforcing the effort to save.

Similar patterns can be found elsewhere in the economy. Most savings in a typical American household accrue through institutionalized mechanisms—specifically, home ownership and retirement accounts. The deduction for mortgage interest acts as an incentive to buy a home, and for most American households the home is their chief asset. Retirement savings, too, enjoy institutionalized support. Money can be invested in a retirement account or pension plan on a pretax basis, and many employers facilitate retirement savings through automatic deductions and matching contributions. As Sherraden looked around the room, it dawned on him that if someone were working to accumulate resources on behalf of the welfare population while providing them with a strong incentive to save, they too might begin to pay more attention to their options.

To test his idea, Sherraden set about designing a tool that would encourage saving by low-income individuals. He called the tool an individual development account, or IDA, to underscore its parallels with individual retirement accounts (IRAs), an easily accessible vehicle for savings held by many in the middle class. Sherraden's proposal was simple. IDAs would enable low-income individuals to accumulate several thousand dollars in a dedicated account. The savings could be used only for high-return investments such as education or job training, home ownership, or starting a business. Participants would save monthly and their savings would be matched by any one of a number of public or private organizations: state or federal government, foundations, financial institutions, churches, or employers. Community-based organizations would administer the programs, counseling participants, providing training in money management and financial literacy, controlling matching funds, and authorizing participants' withdrawals.

Here was an antipoverty instrument that was concrete and manageable, rooted in a broader theory about why people are poor. IDAs also addressed the catch-22 inherent in the traditional welfare system: Aid to Families with Dependent Children (AFDC) and affiliated programs were designed to lift families out of poverty, but the asset limits imposed on recipients made it impossible for them to save for the future without forfeiting their benefits. Sherraden argued that the welfare population should be able to accumulate resources in an IDA while retaining their benefits. It was a promising idea, and Sherraden was eager to put it to the test.

Connecting to the Policy Arena, 1989–92

The notion that assets can play an important role in the fight against poverty is relatively new. "While income and consumption are obviously important," Sherraden writes, "it is also true that most people cannot spend their way out of poverty. Most people who leave poverty . . . do so because they save and invest in themselves, in their children, in property, in securities, or in enterprise to improve their circumstances."[8]

Sherraden knew that by emphasizing assets as opposed to income he was departing dramatically from the traditional discourse on poverty. He also knew that he wanted to connect his ideas to the policy community. To be effective in this sphere, it would be necessary to talk about small and concrete applications, such as IDAs, rather than the sweeping policy measures that might constitute a more comprehensive asset-building policy. In seeking the attention of the policymakers, Sherraden found the ideal partner in the Corporation for Enterprise Development (CFED), a think tank founded in 1979 by Bob Friedman. Friedman's early experiences in employment policy had taught him an important lesson—that it is not enough simply to have good ideas. "Ideas are cheap; it's practice that's expensive," he says. Friedman came up with the notion of joining policy development to the development of practice, of taking the ideas that were being discussed at CFED and putting them into action through small-scale demonstration projects. The combined emphasis on policy and practice distinguishes CFED from most other Washington-based advocacy organizations and has earned it the label of a "think and do" tank.

Bob Friedman had long been focused on the idea of investing in the poor. He had even written a book about it.[9] "Income maintenance and the social service structure of the twentieth-century welfare state are huge achievements," says Friedman, "but what they don't do very well is help people move toward economic independence. Essentially we withdraw the safety net the moment people move forward." In the mid-1980s, CFED had organized and run a small demonstration project to test whether welfare recipients could succeed at self-employment (see chapter 5). Its results made clear that the existing welfare system posed major barriers for those seeking independence. As soon as a welfare recipient's business began making money, he or she bumped up against the $1,000 asset barrier, facing the loss of public assistance before becoming financially secure enough to weather the transition. The role assets could play in family stability was also underscored by the data, which showed that self-employment led to some improvement in income but a more dramatic accumulation of assets. In addition, evaluators of the demonstration noted the psychological impact of asset ownership, the growing self-confidence not just of program participants but of their children as well.

Friedman was convinced that what was needed was a simple, central building block from which to develop a system of investment in the poor that would go beyond income support. When Michael Sherraden showed up on CFED's doorstep one day with three chapters of his book on IDAs, "that's the building block I was looking for," Friedman recalls. For the next several years, CFED worked to promote Sherraden's ideas among a growing circle of policymakers, community activists, and foundation executives. The results were nothing short of spectacular. Through a combination of policy savvy, good timing, and a generous dose of luck, CFED was able to cut through the gridlock and complexity of federal and state welfare policy to bring the IDA concept into the mainstream.

Good timing was critical in Ray Boshara's entry onto the scene. A soft-spoken and thoughtful man in his late thirties, Boshara emerged as the pivotal figure in bringing IDAs to Capitol Hill. Boshara moved to Washington after a stint as an accountant with Ernst & Whinney, a role as an activist for the American peace movement, and a master's degree from Yale Divinity School. Rather than enter the priesthood or academia, Boshara decided that he wanted to work on poverty. He returned to Washington as an unpaid intern for Congressman Tony Hall (D-Ohio) and two months later was hired into a paid staff position. Happily for Boshara, Hall had just been named chair of the House Select Committee on Hunger and was eager for new ideas. "When I started," Boshara remembers, "Tony Hall sat me down and said 'I want to support food stamps, I want to support WIC. These are important programs. But I really want to make this committee a font of innovation. Go out there, do some reading, talk to people, tell me what's new and interesting.' He gave me a mandate for months to do nothing but that."

Soon after, two reports based on Sherraden's work landed on Boshara's desk. "The first time I read [Sherraden's writing on assets], I said, 'This makes sense.' Maybe it was my accounting background, I don't know, but it just made sense. It was fresh, it was interesting, it had a policy tool to go with it." Boshara invited Sherraden to brief the hunger committee staff and organized a breakfast meeting where Sherraden and Friedman met with Congressman Hall. Hall said, "I want to do this," and the committee set about introducing the idea of IDAs in Congress.

At a hearing organized by Boshara in October 1991, Michael Sherraden and Bob Friedman testified for the first time about IDAs and the notion of asset development. The three also drafted a bill, the Freedom from Want Act, introduced in the House of Representatives by Hall and several of his colleagues, with a companion bill introduced by Senators Bill Bradley (D-N.J.) and Orrin Hatch (R-Utah). The legislation called for raising the asset limit in AFDC from $1,000 to $10,000, and included plans for a $100 million IDA demonstration program. In late 1991, Sherraden's book, *Assets and the Poor,* was published. Reviewed in the *New York Times Book Review* and elsewhere, the book introduced Sherraden's ideas to an even broader audience.

By now, Sherraden had been working on IDAs for close to five years. He had refined the concept, attracted national attention, even seen his policy idea take legislative form. A few grassroots organizations had read about IDAs and started their own programs, but these were small and isolated. There was no systematic evidence that IDAs would work, no proof that low-income people would make the choice to save, no reliable source of matching funds. It did not help that Congress had voted to let the Select Committee on Hunger (along with three other select committees) die in 1993. While interest on Capitol Hill was still strong, the existing IDA legislation stood little chance of passage. And there was nothing on the horizon to suggest this would change.

Moving to Practice, 1992–97

IDAs were at a standstill, and Bob Friedman's motto was proving true: even the most inspired idea would go nowhere unless it could be linked to practice. "It was smoke and mirrors," says Michael Sherraden. "We had to try to move ideas, foundations, policy, without any concrete referent other than this idea, whatever evidence we had, and the occasional anecdotal story." Without compelling evidence that IDAs could be effective, that low-income people could save if provided with the right incentives, there would be no progress on the policy front. And there would be no such evidence unless someone could be found to organize and finance an IDA experiment. Setting aside any legislative endeavors for the time being, the proponents of IDAs turned their attention to the one arena where they might find the needed resources—private foundations.

Unmi Song had come to the Joyce Foundation in 1991. With an MBA from the University of Chicago, she had spent the late 1980s as a banker specializing in mergers and acquisitions and leveraged buyouts. "I went to New York with the rest of my [business school] class at the height of the junk bond era. It was very exciting and a lot of fun, and I learned a tremendous amount, but after a certain point I had gone up the learning curve and started to think, 'OK, what next?'" Deciding that she would like to work on economic development issues, Song began investigating the field. On a visit to Chicago for the wedding of a friend, she stopped in at the Joyce Foundation. "I was looking at foundation jobs and ended up talking to people here at Joyce really as more of an informational interview. At the end of the interview they said, 'Hey, we have an opening coming up.' When I took the job at Joyce, I didn't appreciate how special a place [it] was."

The Joyce Foundation funds programs to improve the quality of life in seven midwestern states. Its staff had worked with CFED before and saw Friedman and his colleagues as an important source of new ideas. Like CFED, Joyce was especially interested in entrepreneurial efforts. It also could move faster than most foundations. "We had a board and staff culture that was open to trying out new ideas and exploring what other people might consider to be high-risk strategies," says Song. Even so, the foundation proceeded carefully. "[CFED] had to talk to us several times about [IDAs]. Initially, it was like 'Hmm, that's kind of interesting, but what is it really about? What do we know about this?'" The first Joyce Foundation grants were made to CFED itself and to the Center for Social

Development, Michael Sherraden's research unit at Washington University, to support their efforts to introduce IDAs to community groups and policymakers. Soon, some of the nonprofit organizations Joyce funded were approaching the foundation to say that they had seen its work on IDAs and were interested in starting a program. In 1994, the foundation funded a small IDA demonstration.

Three organizations were selected to participate: the Women's Self-Employment Project (WSEP) in Chicago, a group that had played a prominent role in the microenterprise movement; Eastside Community Investments in Indianapolis, which ran a home ownership and community development program; and Advocap, an organization dedicated to alleviating poverty in rural Wisconsin. The foundation hoped the last might be especially important; in the mid-1990s, all eyes were trained on Wisconsin's welfare reform experiment, and an IDA program in that state could be expected to receive substantial attention. All three organizations had been in business for some time. Each had either a home ownership or microenterprise program through which it had gained solid experience in providing services to a low-income population. (IDAs and the home ownership and microenterprise programs were expected to complement each other, with prospective home buyers and entrepreneurs using their IDA to accumulate the resources needed for these investments.) In addition, the organizations had strong, experienced staffs that could monitor the quality of services and work successfully with outside evaluators.

Evaluation was an important part of the project; solid evidence was necessary to influence policy. To this end, Joyce funded independent evaluators from academia to track the progress of the three IDA programs. A separate grant was made to Sherraden to ensure that the information collected could be compared and aggregated. Everyone understood that combined data from three very different kinds of programs would make a greater impact on policymakers than evidence from just one site.

The demonstration yielded positive results despite its small size. Here was the first real indication that poor people could save if presented with opportunities and incentives. Song gives much of the credit to the grantees, particularly the Chicago and Indianapolis programs, which she calls, "arguably two of the most sophisticated community groups in the country at the time." Good information was emerging about savings behavior, and program leaders were proving effective in bringing these data to the attention of legislators. "You see a lot of advocacy efforts that just don't have the strength of the data behind them or don't know how to use the data effectively," says Song. These organizations were able to take the lessons of their day-to-day operations and use them to further their policy goals at the state and local levels—a linking of practice to policy that would be applied on a national scale later.

The next step was to put together a nationwide IDA demonstration, but Friedman and Sherraden knew that the large foundations that might fund such a program would first need to see proof of both successful saving and substantial policy interest. Here, CFED's earlier efforts on Capitol Hill paid off. As information began to come out of the Joyce-funded demonstration sites, those members of Congress who had supported IDAs early on began to think again about national legislation. Their level of interest took the funders by surprise. "CFED, Michael [Sherraden], and the advocacy and education efforts of the demo programs really captured the attention of policymakers at many levels in a way that no one could have reasonably predicted," says Song. "From our perspective, if that policy interest wasn't there, even if the demos had been successful, our grant-making strategy would have been different."

In his ongoing effort to introduce the IDA concept to foundations, Sherraden had accepted an invitation to discuss his book with a small group of staff members at the Ford Foundation. Soon after, the foundation agreed to fund a conference that would bring together representatives of community organizations and others interested in the IDA field. At the 1995 conference, CFED presented the first generation of an IDA handbook. To create it, CFED staff members had interviewed the five or so community organizations that had started or were planning IDA programs. They found not only that the programs had little in common, but that they operated in ways that, according to one of the handbook's authors, would horrify today's administrators of IDA programs: "One program didn't even have participants saving in bank accounts," explains Brian Grossman. "Another lacked any mandatory savings period. Little attention was paid by any of these programs to financial education. It became clear to me that instead of being descriptive, the handbook would need to be prescriptive, offering CFED's view of what is essential to a top-quality IDA program." Grossman attributes the consistency in today's IDA field to the almost universal use of the IDA handbook as a planning tool for the design of new IDA programs. And by communicating the new "best practices," successive versions of the handbook helped ensure that each generation of IDA program would be better than the last.

In 1996, the Ford Foundation underwent a reorganization that involved the creation of a new division called Asset-Building and Community Development. The man hired to head the division was Melvin Oliver, an African American professor of sociology at UCLA who had coauthored the just-published *Black Wealth/White Wealth*. Like Sherraden, Oliver traces his interest in assets to a personal experience. "I went off to my first job as a walking advertisement for the American dream," Oliver explains. "I had achieved education, I had a Ph.D., I had competed for a job. I was making presumably the same amount of income as my colleagues, I was on the same job track. Then, over the next few years, I kept seeing divergences in the life chances that were available to me in comparison to those available to my white colleagues—the neighborhoods people could afford to live in, the kinds of schools they could provide for their children, even the kinds of vacations they could give their families that really gave them access to a different kind of social capital than I could for my kids." Like any good social scientist, Oliver began to search for the variables that might explain this divergence. When he decided to buy a home, he stumbled on the answer.

"The housing market in Los Angeles was very difficult to break into," recalls Oliver, "and UCLA was losing faculty members because they couldn't afford to live in L.A. So the university put together a home mortgage program in which they helped people with low-interest loans." Oliver applied, as did a white colleague earning roughly the same income. The colleague was approved for the loan; Oliver was not. The colleague had received an inheritance that was more than adequate to secure his loan, while Oliver, a first-generation member of the middle class, had only limited savings. The different prospects faced by Oliver and his white colleague came down to their wealth.

Oliver began doing research on black wealth, teaming up with a white colleague, Thomas Shapiro of Northeastern University, for a series of journal articles and then their book. At the same time, Oliver was running UCLA's Center for the Study of Urban Poverty, a research unit funded largely by the Ford Foundation. When Oliver visited New York to present some of the center's findings to foundation staff, he took the opportunity to hand a copy of his book to Ford's incoming president, Susan V. Berresford. A month later, Berresford flew to Los Angeles and offered Oliver a position as vice president of the new division. Oliver was reluctant to give up his teaching job and took a leave of absence from UCLA to try out the new position. Six years later, he had resigned from UCLA to preside over the Ford Foundation's largest division, which places asset building at the center of the foundation's work on poverty.

One of the division's first moves was a $3 million grant commitment to CFED to support a nationwide IDA demonstration being planned by Bob Friedman. At a press conference held by Berresford to introduce the foundation's main funding programs for the year, IDAs grabbed the spotlight. "That one idea of matched savings just caught on," says Lisa Mensah, the Ford Foundation deputy director with primary responsibility for IDAs. "It was a simple concept and it stole the show." A journalistic error fueled the fire when the *Washington Post* misrepresented the foundation's contribution of $3 million over a five-year period as $3 million in *each* of the five years, or a total of $15 million—a large amount even by Ford Foundation standards.[10] The error was picked up by other news services, eventually appearing in an article in *Parade* magazine, which is distributed to 37 million homes inside Sunday newspapers. Program officers were flooded with calls and letters of inquiry, some containing checks that people hoped to deposit in their very own IDA. "People thought we were actually running the program ourselves," says Mensah. The outpouring of enthusiasm for IDAs convinced the staff that this was an idea with widespread appeal and catapulted the Ford Foundation into investing heavily in the field.

The American Dream Demonstration, 1997–2001

By mid-1997, other major foundations had come on board and the Downpayments on the American Dream Demonstration was under way. CFED had cast its net widely in identifying organizations that could run IDA programs. "We deliberately designed the process to get the idea out," says Friedman. "We wanted more organizations doing IDAs than we had money to fund." CFED's expectations were met when its call for proposals was heavily oversubscribed: 233 letters of intent and ninety-nine full business plans were submitted, from which thirteen sponsoring organizations were selected. The demonstration sites were diverse, ranging from community development organizations to social service agencies to credit unions. Each would receive matching funds from CFED of up to $500 per account in each year of the demonstration as well as a $25,000 annual grant for program operations. Beyond administering the IDA program, which involved economic literacy training as well as managing the accounts themselves, sponsoring organizations would participate in semiannual meetings of those involved in the demonstration and provide data to program evaluators through a newly devised management information system known as MIS IDA.

While the demonstration sites attracted most of the attention of funders and policymakers, they tell only part of the story of the IDA movement. There has been a virtual explosion of IDAs outside the demonstration. Many of the eighty-six organizations that submitted full business plans to CFED but were not selected to participate in the demonstration went on to start IDA programs anyway. Grossman emphasizes that, throughout the late 1990s, "the locus of activity in the IDA field would not only be in the demonstration, it would also be outside of it." While CFED's first priority was to support the demonstration project, its staff felt an equal responsibility to provide tools to any community organization interested in IDAs and to continue to spread the word about IDAs to the larger community development field. Grossman estimates that he spent fully 50 percent of his time as director of the demonstration on activity beyond the demonstration, including organizing successive national conferences, contributing to subsequent versions of the IDA handbook, editing a newsletter, and developing the IDAnetwork, an Internet site devoted to exchanging information on IDAs.[11]

The demonstration's IDA programs began operating in late 1997 and early 1998. Each site was responsible for determining its own rules and match rates, based in part on the amount of money available locally. All the programs permitted IDAs to be used for home purchase, microenterprise investment, and postsecondary education. Eleven also allowed job training or technical education, nine allowed home repair or remodeling, and four allowed the money to be used for retirement.[12] A few permitted saving for all these purposes. Match rates, too, varied, from one-to-one to seven-to-one, with most opting for a two-to-one match.[13]

Economic literacy training has from the beginning been considered an essential component of any effective IDA program. Brian Grossman explains why: "It became apparent very early on that one of the key pieces to successful IDA programs is combining the financial product with the financial literacy, with the counseling and training. It's the case with 401(k)s, for example, if you don't provide education to people about them, they don't use them. Certainly the way that [people save] in this country, with even very few middle- and upper-income families doing it successfully, low-income families have much less margin for error. And now there are all these traps out there, with predatory lenders, and many, many more people have really bad credit. So if you don't combine the financial product with something to educate people about the financial system, you're just not going to succeed."

It was also clear that the sponsoring organizations had virtually no experience doing this kind of training. "We know financial literacy is important," says Grossman. "Everything tells us that, but what do we do?" CFED concluded that the available financial literacy curricula, developed for other purposes, were not appropriate for IDA training—some are too advanced for a lower-literacy audience and others have no particular focus on building assets. An IDA-related financial literacy program would have to be developed at the program sites. (CFED, in collaboration with the National Endowment for Financial Education and the Fannie Mae Foundation, has since undertaken an IDA financial literacy initiative to help standardize this aspect of IDA programs.)

To understand how an individual development account works in practice and to assess the impact savings has had on the lives of low-income families, it is useful to focus on a single program and some of the individuals it has served. There are lessons to be learned from their stories as well as from the broader policy journey, lessons that will need to be kept in mind if IDAs are to serve as one component of an effective asset-based strategy to alleviate poverty.

Saving in the Heart of America

The IDA program sponsored by Heart of America Family Services is one of the most successful of the programs included in the American Dream Demonstration.[14] The sponsoring organization, established more than 120 years ago to aid the poor, is among Kansas City's largest and best-known nonprofits. In addition to providing counseling and other services at locations around the city, Heart of America Family Services operates the Family Focus Center, which offers parenting classes in English and Spanish, social activities, and other community-building programs to families living on the city's predominantly Latino west side. It is here, in a creaky and outdated elementary school building, that one finds the small staff responsible for running the Family Asset Building program, the IDA initiative sponsored by Heart of America Family Services.

The Family Asset Building program (FAB) provided participants with a two-for-one match, two dollars for every dollar saved. The money for the first match came from foundation funds channeled through the Corporation for Enterprise Development; the second match was contributed by the Ewing Marion Kauffman Foundation, a Kansas City–based not-for-profit. The seventy-five participants enrolled in FAB were required to save between $10 and $30 each month over the four-year program period. Account holders' savings and matching funds were held in separate accounts at another longtime west side institution, the KC Terminal Employees/Guadalupe Center Federal Credit Union. As of October 31, 2001, as the program came to an end, total participant savings stood at $62,445, or an average of $900 per account holder. Match dollars had amounted to $124,117, bringing total IDA accumulation to $186,562, or an average of $2,700 per participant.[15]

When the demonstration began in September 1997, the sponsoring organizations were given considerable autonomy in setting up their own programs. FAB's rules were simple—so simple, in fact, that its staff admits to being embarrassed at meetings with the other sponsoring organizations. (As it turned out, simplicity appears to have been an important factor in the success of the program.) There were only two requirements for admission: individuals needed to have a Social Security card, and they needed to be poor. Most program slots were reserved for those earning less than 150 percent of the federal poverty level, or $19,995 a year for a family of three. (One-quarter of slots could accommodate those with slightly higher incomes of up to 200 percent of the federal poverty level, or $26,660 for a family of three.) "It was amazing to me that these people would even try to save," says Kathy Kane, former director of the Family Asset Building program, "and I've been blown away by what they've managed to accomplish."

Regina Blackmon, the mother of three girls, first heard about the Family Asset Building program at an orientation for her youngest daughter's preschool, located just across the street from the Family Focus Center. When Regina got home from the meeting, she looked through the material she had received and saw the information about FAB. "I thought, 'Wait a minute, matched funds?' They didn't say how much, they only said matched funds. So my mind blew! 'Ooh, I put in a hundred, they give me three hundred, this is unbelievable!' So I called all my sisters and I told them about it and they said, 'Well, that seems too good to be true. You go see about it and come back and let us know.' And I said, 'Well, that's definitely what I'm going to do.' I was the guinea pig. I went to the orientation class and I learned it was like they said. The maximum you could save was $30 a month and it would be a two-to-one match with a $45 match once a year. And you were required to attend a monthly class for information on other ways to save and live economically. That's all you had to do. I thought, 'This is wonderful,' so I went home and I told everyone and, sure enough, some of my sisters joined with me. My niece, a person at work, and someone from church also joined. I couldn't convince everyone. I don't know why some people didn't sign up. It's a personality thing, I guess."

Regina had never saved before, but she needed to now. "When I first got in the FAB program, my husband and I had just separated, and I knew I wouldn't be able to keep this big, old house without some kind of help somewhere. That's why it was a blessing that this program came along." Displacement due to gentrification is becoming an issue in parts of Kansas City. As code enforcement has become tighter, some low-income residents who cannot afford to maintain their property have had to sell their homes and leave their neighborhoods. Regina knew a good deal when she saw one and vowed to save the maximum each month. "In my head I just said, 'I spend that much eating out with my girlfriends, so if I take this $30 out first I won't miss it.'" She listed the purpose of her IDA as home repair and thanked her lucky stars for the matching funds that would allow her and her three daughters to remain in their home.

George Clark, too, had a reason to save. In 1992, his wife of eleven years had died of an aneurysm, leaving George to raise their three children, the youngest only two. Doris's death plunged the family into crisis. Following the initial shock, George found himself alone, depressed, and anxious about his children's future. In trying to make up for being a single parent, he put himself through a grueling routine: "After their mom died, I worked eight hours, went to school, and then I would get four hours of sleep. . . . I went to school three hours a night, four days a week. I would take [the children] with me and they would stay in the library or the lobby and do their homework, then I'd take them home and feed them, put them to bed, then I'd stay up and study, wash, dine, and cook. And I would do that every night." After a year and a half, George was admitted to the hospital suffering from exhaustion, stress, and malnutrition. By the time he was released a month later, his doctors had convinced him he could not continue doing it all, that if he wanted to be there for his children he would need to take better care of himself.

George's children are not his only responsibility. The eldest of eleven siblings, George is the one his mother relies on to help her get around and take care of her home. But the relationship can be a rocky one. Shortly after his hospitalization, as George's neighborhood was becoming more dangerous, he and his children moved in with his mother. Things were fine at first, but when his mother began to criticize how George was raising the children, he knew it was time to go. Then, when George remarried, the tension between his new wife, Rosemary, and his mother flared, just as it had with his first wife years ago. The couple recently moved into a rented townhouse, along with George's daughter Jeanetté, while his two sons stayed with their grandmother to finish the school year. George is eager, as he puts it, to regain control of his family, and owning a home would be a step in this direction. George has the opportunity to buy the townhouse he is living in at a good price if he can save enough money for the down payment.

When George first heard about the Family Asset Building program, he thought it might help him become a homeowner. But his impressions at the orientation were unfavorable: "A lot of people there were Hispanic, and I was thinking, 'OK, this is just gonna be a whole bunch of black and Hispanic people coming together and we're gonna be making a lot of promises and all this stuff, and then it'll go down the tubes.'" (George is African American.) When he learned of the match, he thought, "Yeah, they'll match it for a while but then they'll drop out of the program. So I was kind of skeptical. I mean, I've been involved in so many programs, man, I get fired up about them and then they fall off the wagon . . . [but] I thought, OK, I'll give this one more chance."

As a low-income worker of Mexican origin, Miguel Juarez was precisely the kind of person targeted by the Family Asset Building program. One of the few demonstration sites that aimed to reach Latino participants, Heart of America Family Services initially focused its recruitment efforts on the economically depressed and largely Latino west side. "We were shocked when we first started intake," says Dennis Boody, director of the Family Focus Center. "We were prepared to have our doors knocked down." FAB staff had even set up a lottery system to allocate the seventy-five spots available in the program. But recruitment proceeded slowly, and the lottery was never needed. Boody thinks local residents may have feared the program was a scam; the promise of matching funds struck many as too good to be true. "Maybe it's because this population is so targeted by scam artists that they've become appropriately skeptical," says Boody. As people came to trust the program—a trust facilitated in part by the longtime presence of the Family Focus Center on the west side and the involvement of the widely known and respected Kauffman Foundation—

the available slots were filled. Word of mouth played an important role; Regina alone referred six or seven people to the program. The ethnic makeup of the participants was one of the most diverse among the demonstration sites: 41 percent Latino, 38 percent African American, and 15 percent Caucasian.[16]

Miguel joined at the very beginning, in November 1997. He deposited $30 monthly, always making the annual matched deposit of $45 and sometimes adding a little extra to the pot. By June 2001, his asset account held close to $4,860, or the maximum allowed under program rules. If not for two features of the Family Asset Building program, Miguel Juarez would have seemed like a model saver and nothing more. But the economic literacy classes required as part of FAB and its one-on-one case management approach revealed to staff members that Miguel's story is decidedly more complex—and much less happy.

Some of the demonstration sites opted to treat financial literacy training as a prerequisite to opening an IDA. Heart of America Family Services went about things differently. "The first thing they did was open the account," says Kathy Kane, "and *then* they started coming to classes. I think that helped quite a bit. They all could see their savings immediately. . . . When they see 'I put in $30, the match was $60, I have $90,' when they see how fast it grows, people are very impressed by it."

At FAB, training consisted of monthly classes, each offered at several times during the week to accommodate the schedules of participants. Instructors were experts recruited from the community who volunteered their services. Staff members from a local housing organization led a session on how to buy a home. A representative of a credit counseling agency offered budgeting tips and guidance on how to obtain and read one's credit report. Employees of financial institutions spoke about saving, investments, retirement accounts, insurance, and home mortgages. Educators from local colleges and universities introduced account holders to the postsecondary education opportunities available in the area. In the first year of the program, participants were required to attend all twelve classes; in subsequent years, the attendance requirement was reduced to nine classes, then six.

The monthly meetings supported a second feature of the Family Asset Building program: case management. The ability to provide case management services as part of its IDA program stemmed from a partnership between Heart of America Family Services and the University of Kansas School of Social Welfare. The university plays a two-part role in the IDA program. First, a research team led by Deborah Page-Adams (a former graduate student of Michael Sherraden) and several of her graduate students designed and is carrying out a detailed evaluation of the program. The evaluation, which is supported by the Kauffman Foundation, involves a lengthy interview with participants done annually on the anniversary of their joining the program. Interviews will also be conducted in the two years following the program's completion. A comparison group is being followed as well. The survey has been designed to test Sherraden's hypotheses about the impact of IDAs on family well-being. Much of the evidence in this area will not be available until participants have made use of their savings, but their responses to the surveys thus far make clear that the program has already had an impact. Marcia Shobe, a doctoral student who worked with FAB from the beginning, says that participants told her the same thing in interview after interview: "I actually feel like I have control over my life."

The second contribution of the university partnership to the Heart of America Family Services program is a group of graduate student interns who serve as case managers. The School of Social Welfare has a strong practicum requirement; students go to class only two days a week and spend the remaining hours in internships, some in clinical settings, others with community organizations. Each year, FAB has been assigned one or more interns from the school. They are responsible for getting to know participants and providing support to anyone who needs it. Interns attend the training program, administer the surveys called for by the research team, and check in with account holders whenever there is a glitch in their saving behavior.

At fifty, Casey Eike was one of the oldest students in her class, although her short, spiky hair and abundant jewelry made her seem much younger. Eike has had a checkered career as the founder of a series of start-up companies. She is also an inventor and avid volunteer who works with female prison inmates, goes on a yearly medical mission to Haiti, and provides mentoring and support to twenty-seven children not her own. Pressed for money in the aftermath of a divorce, Eike realized that the one thread tying together her interests was social work and made the decision to return to school. In the first year of the program, she was assigned to an internship with FAB and it is here that she met Miguel.

Miguel is a quiet man, and although he attended the FAB training classes regularly he said little along the way. It was only when Casey Eike sat down with him to administer the research team's annual survey that she had the opportunity to engage him in a lengthy conversation. The Juarezes have a long history with the Family Focus Center. Their youngest daughter, Gladys, attended Project Early for four or five years. The center put Miguel in touch with Westside Housing Organization, which helped him procure a low-income home mortgage. Project Early staff assisted Miguel's wife, Margarita, in finding a job as an outreach worker for a local health clinic. When the FAB program was announced to Project Early participants in the fall of 1997, Miguel had no qualms about joining. He had already come to trust the Family Focus Center and the Kauffman Foundation through their support of Project Early, and he knew they could be counted on to tell the truth.

Miguel and his wife had immigrated to Kansas City from Mexico with one child in 1980. Three more children were born in the United States, and the couple became legal residents, then citizens, as soon as they could. Although low income, they have many of the trappings of middle-class life: a mortgage, a minivan, a new computer for their daughter. Miguel also has an addiction. "Right now I've been having a pretty difficult life," he says. "I've been going to the casinos and I've been spending my savings. My marriage is not very stable right now because of that and because of my work. . . . I had almost $9,000 in savings last year. They're all gone, I don't have nothing." Miguel has also run up thousands of dollars of debt on his credit cards. Riverboat gambling came to Kansas City in the 1990s; Missouri law now allows for casinos, provided they are located on the water. "It's just depressing to go in there," says Kane," because you'll see people who, that's all they do, all day long. And [they're] the people who can least afford to be in the casinos."

Miguel estimates that it will take him several years to get out of debt, provided he can keep his habit in check. In the meantime, he is trying to offset his spending behavior with a variety of savings strategies. Miguel works as a supervisor in a tomato-packing plant, a job he has held for three years. His employer offers a 401(k) plan, to which Miguel contributes the maximum allowed. Miguel also plans to convert his IDA into a Roth IRA to use for retirement now that the FAB program has ended. He had invested some of his savings in certificates of deposit (CDs), thereby placing it off limits to himself for the term of the CD, but he has since needed to use this money to pay bills. Miguel has even tried to trick himself into saving the money he would otherwise spend gambling. "I say, 'I'm gonna act like I went to the casinos and I spent $100, but I didn't go to the casinos. I'm just gonna put $100 aside, like OK, I already went to the casinos and I lose my $100.' And I put it away, then, maybe after one year I go and check and see, 'Oh, I got much money. I already saved this money.'" Sometimes he just forces himself to think about something else when he feels the urge to return to the riverboats.

The financial education Miguel received through FAB and his habit of contributing regularly to an IDA have helped him develop these strategies. But the monthly classes and case management services played an even more important role. It was these regular opportunities for contact that made it possible for Miguel to confide in Eike and seek help for his underlying problems. Without this relationship, Miguel would have been just another account holder, one with an excellent track record and by all apparent measures a success.

Whether Miguel is able to resolve the contradictions between his disciplined saving and compulsive gambling is up to him, but FAB staff has done what it can to help. Eike put Miguel in touch with Gamblers Anonymous and worked with him to consolidate his credit card debt. She gave him her home and cell phone numbers and told Miguel he could call at any time. While she could not ensure he would follow through, she could offer resources, connections, and support. It took time to build a relationship of trust. "I think that he needed to feel comfortable enough with the program and with me," says Eike. "I think he was just ready to get it out of him and ask for help."

Regina Blackmon does not face the same kind of challenges as Miguel, but the FAB program has changed her life nonetheless. Because Regina intended to use her IDA for home repair, these were the training sessions she most looked forward to when the program began. But it was a different session that made the greatest impact on Regina's thinking. Since before FAB began, Regina had been decorating and filling candy jars as gifts for friends and family. The jars have a doll's face and hair made from candy, and come costumed for holidays or special events. Regina began to receive requests for the jars from people who had seen them. Because Regina has a full-time job, she worked on weekends and in the evenings to fill these orders and, although she did not have a good sense of her expenses or a steady supply of materials, expanded to the point that she gave her company a name—"Oooh! That's So Cute!" Candy Jars—and printed up brochures and business cards.

One of the sessions included in FAB's first-year training program was Successful Small Business, taught by a graduate of a Kauffman-funded microenterprise development program operated by the First Step Fund.

"At that time, whatever the classes were about, you had to go," recalls Regina. "Thank goodness!" The name of the speaker was Chestia Dial. "She had her own business, and she had such a wonderful presentation that I sat there and I thought, 'What? You mean this craft can be a business?' 'Yes, it can,' she said. 'You can make good money from this and sell them to more and more people in more and more places.' She gave me her number so I could call her later. When Mrs. Dial told the class about First Step, stars started coming to my eyes and I thought, 'This is really a way out here.'" Regina applied for and was accepted into the six-week entrepreneur training program. "They were really impressed that I was so far into doing this myself. I was thinking in this direction but really not focused. That's what they gave me; they put me in the right direction. I had to pull all these ideas together and put them in a business plan, and I was able to do that with their help."

As a result of her business plan, Regina made some changes. To strengthen her marketing, she began paying her sister-in-law a commission on each of the candy jars she sells. Valentine's Day and Christmas are Regina's strongest seasons, but she has added candy jars with a June graduation theme and is working on marketing ideas for the rest of the year. She also tightened up on the range of choices offered her customers. "At one time I was giving them whatever candy they wanted on the inside. That was costing me too much money. They wanted Tootsie Roll hair, but they wanted something else on the inside. And I ended up with a bag of their something else. No, no, we don't do that anymore."

There have been miscalculations along the way. The year 2000 turned out to be a bust for the business. Just before Valentine's Day, the supplier of Regina's doll heads ran out and she had to stop production. It was October by the time they came back into stock, and by then Regina had lost almost a full year of sales. For 2001 she planned ahead, making withdrawals from her IDA to buy all the supplies she would need for the coming season. Regina expected to make and sell as many as 200 jars for Valentine's Day, netting $2,400 after expenses. As the holiday approached, she said, "I hope that this week is the beginning of a real year that I can sit down and say this is how much I spent and this is how much I made, and this was profit and this is how it's done."

George Clark's experience with FAB may be more typical than either Regina's or Miguel's. Unlike Regina, George seems always to have been outspoken and self-assured. Neither must he confront the pressing financial problems of Miguel. But there are other challenges, and the FAB program has been helpful in addressing these. Like Regina, George went through First Step's entrepreneur training program. George's first love is preschool education (he worked at a preschool for several years), and his initial business idea was to open a child care center for parents who work nights. But as he researched this option, he discovered that the licensing, insurance, and facilities costs would be prohibitive. Instead, he put together a plan for a home repair business. After working on his own for two years, George "got scared" (in his words) and took a job at a manufacturing company. But he soon decided that he "wasn't cut out for this time clock thing." Instead, he became a union painter while continuing to do home repair on the side. He would like to expand his business to a level where he will not need the union job, a goal that his IDA savings could help him meet.

Like Miguel, George has amassed the maximum allowed in his IDA account. But it is what he learned through FAB, not what he saved, that George values most highly. More than a decade ago, saddled with $10,000 in credit card debt, George made an economic mistake he regrets to this day. Following the advice of a poorly informed lawyer, he declared bankruptcy. ("The worst thing I've ever done," he says.) It took George ten years to repair his credit standing. He knows now that there was no need for such a drastic move. He could have consolidated his debt, worked out a payment plan with his creditors, and avoided the long-term costs and stigma of bankruptcy.

Even though the FAB classes have come to an end, George continues to educate himself. "They teach you that even if you have some idea of financial stability you can always learn something new every day," he says. "Knowledge is wealth and you can't get wealthy without knowledge." George is researching options for low-cost mortgages. He is gathering information on mutual funds so he will know how to invest wisely. And he has learned a lot about running his own business from people he meets who are self-employed or who work in finance, real estate, or other fields. "Many of them are willing to share information," he says, and George, acknowledging his gift of gab, makes maximum use of these connections.

In the third year of the American Dream Demonstration, the Center for Social Development evaluation team asked over 300 account holders about the effects of their IDAs on their lives. The results echoed the experiences of Regina, Miguel, and George. Eighty-five percent of current participants said that their IDA classes had helped them save. Respondents were also overwhelmingly positive about the institutional attributes of IDAs—they liked the match rates, their accounts seemed secure, they felt the rules regarding withdrawals were fair. It was clear that the positive effects of IDAs had extended beyond savings, with account holders saying that they feel more confident about the future (93 percent of those surveyed), more secure economically (84 percent), and more in control of their lives (85 percent).[17] Future evaluations will look at whether these positive effects endure beyond the end of the demonstration. In the meantime, advocates are focusing on the next big step: how to make IDAs available to millions of poor Americans.

Scaling Up, 1998–Present

With the American Dream Demonstration beginning to yield results, CFED turned once again to the legislative arena. Ray Boshara had been out of the picture for several years, having left Washington in 1993 to accompany his wife to a job posting in Italy. Before he moved, Boshara wrote a paper for CFED's staff advising them on how to move IDAs forward in Congress. The paper had little influence since the political landscape soon changed dramatically, with the Republican Party assuming control of Congress in 1994. But it did set a course for Boshara upon his return.

When Boshara moved back to the United States in 1995, he went first to Harvard University's Kennedy School for a master's degree in public policy. "I knew I wanted to keep working on asset development and this was a way for me to reconnect with the latest thinking about poverty, about economics, about asset building," says Boshara. After graduation, he returned to Washington and interviewed with several organizations, eventually alighting at CFED. "I had had my eye on them for a long time," he says. "I liked Bob [Friedman], I liked the people. Here was this opportunity to work full-time on assets policy . . . and, professionally, no one was doing this work. It was wide open."

CFED's goal at the time was to build legislative support for a federally funded IDA demonstration program. The hope was that passage of a federal act would not only validate the notion that IDAs are a good use of federal funds but also leverage other policies, such as state-level IDA plans. Boshara was CFED's chief strategist. Crucial to his approach was the systematic linking of practice and policy that had been seen earlier in the Joyce-funded IDA programs. By 1997, IDA programs were operating in about ten states, with more in the pipeline. (IDAs had been given a boost when, in the context of welfare reform, states began lifting the limits on savings for welfare recipients and added provisions in their welfare laws to exclude money in IDAs when determining eligibility for public assistance.) Just by chance, some of the most successful programs were located in states or districts whose representatives could be influential in moving legislation forward. "People would hear about these IDAs and say, 'Why isn't there one in my district or my state?'" Boshara remembers. CFED sent legislators to visit their local IDA programs, introduced them to leading IDA practitioners based in their districts, beefed up lobbying efforts, and arranged for IDA proponents to testify before Congress. Throughout the process, Boshara and his colleagues made sure to line up Democrats and Republicans who were willing to work together on the issue.

By 1998, the bipartisan consensus in favor of IDAs was strong enough that Congress authorized and funded the Assets for Independence Act (AFIA), a five-year demonstration program to support the establishment of IDAs on a national scale. "It was really remarkable because we had members of Congress who were categorically opposed to new federal spending—and, in particular, new federal spending on poor people's programs—who nonetheless authorized this program," says Boshara. While many attribute the achievement to Boshara's hard work and skill on Capitol Hill, he gives credit to the power of the idea itself: "My job is a lot easier because we're dealing with an idea that naturally crosses bipartisan lines. It's interesting, it has a whole theoretical framework to support it, all wrapped up in a single tool. The packaging was really important."

AFIA was essentially an updated version of the bill drafted by Boshara, Friedman, and Sherraden in 1991. The act authorized $125 million in federal funds over five years to support the creation of 30,000–40,000 new IDAs. Grants are made to nonprofit organizations, provided that an equal amount of money has been raised from other sources (such as a state government or foundation). Those who qualify for Temporary Assistance for Needy Families or the Earned Income Tax Credit or whose income is less than 200 percent of the poverty line are eligible to participate in the program. The maximum federal match to a single IDA account is $2,000. The matched savings in IDAs may be used for three purposes: the purchase or building of a first home, the capitalization of a business, or the costs of postsecondary education. Although $25 million has been authorized for each year of the program, in its first two years Congress appropriated only $10 million. In the third year of the demonstration (2000), the full $25 million was appropriated.

The availability of federal matching funds under AFIA served as the catalyst for new IDA programs to form and allowed existing programs to expand. Heart of America Family Services, for example, received AFIA funding to support a second IDA program geared toward youth at one of Kansas City's poorest high schools. The Wyandotte Individual Development Account program, funded by the federal government and the Kauffman Foundation, supports a total of 250 IDA accounts, including 75 for high school students. (It has proven extremely difficult to fill the youth holder slots, and Heart of America Family Services has revised program rules and expanded beyond the original focus on Wyandotte High School to other high schools in Kansas City, Kansas, in an effort to increase enrollment.) A second AFIA grant was received for a program that will serve 500 account holders on both sides of the Kansas-Missouri state line. The focus of the initiative, which will run from 2002 to 2006, is for participants to accumulate enough savings for the down payment on a home.

The passage of the act also helped clarify the legal and regulatory status of programs and their providers.[18] Among the key rulings are Internal Revenue Service decisions that account holders who receive matching IDA funds under AFIA will not be taxed on those funds and that contributions made to IDA initiatives funded under AFIA are tax deductible. Another important ruling is a U.S. Treasury Department decision that investments made by financial institutions in IDAs count toward Community Reinvestment Act requirements for service to low-income communities. These rulings and others like them have facilitated the continued expansion of the IDA field.

More than 10,000 Americans are currently saving in IDAs offered by at least 350 programs nationwide. Twenty-nine states and the District of Columbia have passed some form of IDA legislation, and thirty-two states have included IDAs in their welfare reform plans.[19] Expanded AFIA funding in the third year of the demonstration made it possible for these organizations to serve new account holders numbering in the thousands. But IDA advocates want more. "Where we are now is on the verge of going to scale," says Bob Friedman. "What I mean by that is millions of accounts, billions of dollars, and a multisector marketplace."

CFED believes that the best way to get to scale is through the tax code, where the United States subsidizes asset building for the nonpoor. The current vehicle is the Savings for Working Families Act of 2002, which creates a tax credit for financial institutions for supporting and matching the savings of up to 900,000 low-income families. Similar bills were introduced in 2000 and 2001, but did not make it through Congress. A new version of the bill, sponsored by Senators Joe Lieberman (D-Conn.) and Rick Santorum (R-Pa.) and Representatives Joe Pitts (R-Pa.) and Charlie Stenholm (D-Tex.), was included in a broad charitable giving bill and highlighted by President George W. Bush at a White House event in February 2002. The fact that President Bush endorsed the concept of IDAs while on the campaign trail (as did Vice President Al Gore and President Bill Clinton before him) and included funding for an IDA tax credit in his proposed budget has contributed to a sense of optimism about such a bill's eventual passage.

In its current form, the act would make IDAs available to citizens or legal residents of the United States between the ages of eighteen and sixty whose incomes fall below a certain level.[20] (The income guidelines are based on an adjusted gross income of up to $20,000 for a single filer, $30,000 for a head of household, or $40,000 for a married couple.) Savings would be matched on a one-to-one basis, with a $500 cap per person per year. Matched savings could be used for the purchase of a first home, postsecondary education and training, or small business development. Under the bill, any qualified financial institution becomes eligible for a tax credit for the aggregate amount of matching funds provided (up to the $500 cap), plus an annual $50 credit per account holder to maintain the account and provide financial education. Individual deposits, matching funds, and all accrued interest would be disregarded in determining eligibility for other means-tested federal programs. The act would provide funding through 2009 for accounts opened between 2003 and 2007. The cap on the number of accounts means that the total cost of the bill would be $1.7 billion (the amount included in President Bush's budget). Because this funding will not cover everyone eligible for an IDA under the proposed rules, the 900,000 accounts would be allocated by the Secretary of the Treasury among qualified IDA programs.

The proposed legislation would make it more affordable for financial institutions to offer IDAs, but it does not mean that they will find it profitable to do so, at least in the early years. Neither is the $50 annual credit sufficient to cover the costs of the educational component of an IDA program, not to mention the one-on-one case management that seems necessary for a number of participants to save successfully. Yet the opportunity to offer IDAs does hold some attraction for banks and other eligible financial institutions. It is not just that they will have use of individuals' savings for three or four years, along with any matching funds. Much more important is that IDA providers have the opportunity to establish relationships with a large number of people who have never before used any kind of financial institution. Estimates place the "unbanked" population—those who have no bank account of any sort—at between 10 percent and 20 percent of American households, with much higher rates for low-income and racial and ethnic minority groups (one study shows 45 percent of African American households without any kind of bank account).[21] These are the people who rely on check-cashing stores and payday lenders for their financial needs, and they represent a huge, untapped market for mainstream financial institutions. Research has shown that once a low-income person acquires a single banking product, he or she is likely to acquire other products down the road. Some of the participants in the American Dream Demonstration have already followed up on their IDAs by buying life insurance, opening a retirement savings account, or starting savings accounts for their children. They also have turned to the financial institution where they keep their IDA when they need a home mortgage or business loan.

This is not to say that the IDA business is about to become a profitable sector of the banking industry. "We've realized that you can't develop a multibillion dollar IDA market without providing more services to that market," says Boshara. That is why CFED has created an intermediary to provide certification, training, and marketing materials to IDA programs, thereby reducing transaction costs for financial institutions. The intermediary is currently located within CFED, but there are plans to spin it off into a separate organization. Once large-scale IDA legislation passes Congress, CFED hopes to use the intermediary to pull matching funds from nonfederal sources.

Preliminary calculations suggest that as many as 40 million families could be eligible to open IDAs under the terms of the Savings for Working Families Act. Even the 900,000 accounts provided for in the current legislation represent a huge increase of scale from current efforts. "Talking about scalability, you can look at the tax code," says Grossman, "and it's very easy to imagine how we get to where there are millions of IDA accounts. What's a little more difficult is figuring out how you scale up on the financial literacy piece."

It is clear that community-based organizations will play a different role in the large-scale IDA world of tomorrow than they do today. Current IDA programs are labor-intensive and have high administrative costs. Community organizations will certainly retain a role—for one thing, without their advocacy it is unlikely that financial institutions will offer IDAs on their own initiative. Many envision some kind of partnership between community organizations and financial institutions, with the former involved in recruitment, education, and one-on-one assistance where necessary, and the latter handling the accounts themselves and providing the matching funds.

Another approach for delivering IDAs is being explored by Peter Tufano, a professor of finance at the Harvard Business School. "Rather than rely on banks and their expensive bricks and mortar, we are designing a feasible way to give low-income families access to excellent investment products at a low cost," says Tufano. "They can gain this access by joining together as a pool. Our dream will combine local access—points at which savers can put their money into the system—with a very high-tech system that will pool together the assets of millions of savers to allow them to enjoy excellent returns."[22] Boshara says of Tufano's efforts: "You've got some of the best minds in the country, in the world, thinking about this as a business product and telling us how we need to think about both developing the field as well as the legislation to make this market work." Bob Friedman stresses that a system of IDAs that reaches millions of families will require many players fulfilling different roles: "When I first thought of going to scale, I thought it was just legislation. But it's really bigger and more complicated than that. IDAs will work only if there's public participation, private corporate [financial institution] participation, nonprofit participation, a stream of funding, and philanthropic resources."

From the beginning, CFED's policy vision has extended beyond the promotion of IDAs. "We have this thoroughgoing set of tax-based asset policies for the nonpoor that amount to nearly $300 billion a year," says Friedman, "so even if you could make a marginal change you're talking about delivering billions of dollars to millions of people. And this is not income redistribution, but wealth creation, 'investment' in the sense of galvanizing a productive value-added process and generating returns." Sherraden, too, has long been interested in asset-based policy more generally: "I've never just thought of this as doing IDAs. We've always been laying the groundwork for a larger policy." To move this broader discussion forward, CFED and the Center for Social Development (CSD) have convened the Growing Wealth Working Group, a kind of brain trust of individuals committed to the idea of expanding and institutionalizing asset-based policies for the poor. The mission statement adopted by the nonpartisan group reads as follows: "We seek an asset-building policy that is inclusive, progressive, simple, participant-centered and enduring." IDAs are one of the building blocks of such a policy, but the larger goal is to extend the reach of the asset-building system already in place for the taxpaying nonpoor to encompass the poor as well.

Regina Blackmon made and sold 150 Candy Jars for Valentine's Day. With her profits, she bought a car for her family—the first dependable one they have ever owned. (Because automobiles are an asset that tends to depreciate, rather than appreciate, their purchase is not an approved use for IDAs in either the American Dream Demonstration or under the Assets for Independence Act. Yet for many low-income people, having a decent car is a crucial step on the road to self-sufficiency, and some IDA programs do permit the purchase of vehicles. Whether this is a good idea remains a point of debate within the IDA community.) Sales were disappointing the rest of the year. Regina had some health problems, but the more important reason for the slow sales is that her business has turned out to be highly seasonal. Until she can focus seriously on marketing her candy jars, she is unlikely to expand beyond the occasional individual order and a busy period around Valentine's Day.

Despite her slowing business, Regina is in a better place than she has been for a long time—a change she attributes in part to the people at FAB. For seventeen years, Regina had worked as a receptionist for a state agency in a job she calls "mentally abusive." "I've always hated it," she says, "but being a single parent for so long it was a stable job. And having a sick child, I could attend to her and still get a paycheck and not worry about losing my job." (One of Regina's daughters has sickle-cell anemia.) The staff of the FAB program had long encouraged her to look for a new job, but Regina was resistant. Finally, at the urging of Aishah Jackson (a VISTA volunteer who was hired by FAB to run its Wyandotte IDA program), Regina put together a rudimentary résumé. Aishah reviewed it and sent it back with some corrections and suggestions. "She was so great," says Regina; "I valued her opinion since she was just freshly out of college." Regina had attended a FAB session where a representative of the Women's Employment Network had spoken about changing professions. With Aishah's encouragement, Regina sent her new résumé in to the network. "I didn't think anything of it," she recounts, "[but] people started calling me for jobs. . . . It just made me think, 'Wait a minute, I *do* have skills people want.'" Soon after, Regina celebrated her fortieth birthday, a milestone that prompted her to reevaluate her work situation. "I went out and put my application in at the Board of Education and was hired at the first interview," she relates. "I haven't enjoyed getting up and going to work for a long time. [Now] I have a lot more responsibilities, a lot of people depend on me, and I'm not being abused anymore. The people there [at FAB] are still affecting me, my life, and my children, still affecting the decisions I make. They helped me with so much more than just savings."

Regina was sad to see FAB end, and not just because it meant an end to a match for her savings. "This has been an active part of my life for the last three years," she said. "I call these people here, at home even. I know these people well. I'm going to really, really miss this. But also I have this drive, not only for me and my girls, but I want *them*, the administrators and staff at the FAB program, to know, 'Look what you guys did for me, look how your work amounted to this.' I'm still doing well, and I have the drive now to keep on going even after they're gone." Regina may not have to say goodbye. She is planning to enroll in the new IDA program starting up in 2002, assuming she qualifies. Although the emphasis of the program is on home ownership, saving for other purposes is allowed, and Regina would like to be able to help her middle daughter, now eighteen, pay for college. When FAB announced that it was forming an advisory board for its new program made up of graduates of the first program, Regina volunteered.

Miguel continues to struggle to control his gambling, but says he is doing better. He is working as much overtime as possible—sixty to seventy hours a week on average. His job keeps him busy Mondays through Saturdays. Sometimes he even goes in on Sundays to take inventory or receive deliveries. He is happy about the extra hours, since he earns one-and-a-half times his salary for overtime hours, but the schedule is draining. Miguel has not been able to find the time to get to a meeting of Gamblers Anonymous. He also stopped attending the sessions offered by FAB and did not attend the recent graduation ceremony: once Casey Eike moved on and Miguel reached the maximum savings allowed under the program, his connection with FAB seemed to weaken. Like Regina, he hopes to participate in Heart of America Family Services' upcoming IDA program, but is afraid that with his overtime hours he will exceed the income cutoff. He continues to invest in his 401(k) plan, but at the moment his chief saving strategy is to roll over his credit card balances to new cards that charge lower interest rates. "I haven't saved so much this year," Miguel says, "because there are too many bills." On a brighter note, relations with his wife have improved. "We have more communication now; we're closer."

George also intends to enroll in the successor to FAB and, like Regina, has joined its advisory board. Last summer, he accompanied Julie Riddle (Heart of America Family Services' new IDA program director), the Kauffman Foundation's Andrés Dominguez, and Javier Silva of CFED to a conference in Connecticut where he spoke about his experience as an IDA saver. "We wanted people to know they can empower themselves by saving money," he explains. George still must decide how best to use his $4,860 in savings. "There's a lot of hard work and effort in there," he says, "so you don't want to just blow it out." In the meantime, his sons have moved back home and his mother recently initiated a reconciliation with her son. It seems that George's hope of regaining control of his family is within his grasp.

Lessons from Practice

The outcomes of the American Dream Demonstration in savings performance and family well-being will not be known at least until the evaluation component of the demonstration is complete in 2003. But with a wealth of experience accumulated within and outside of the demonstration, it is possible at this stage to identify some of the key ingredients of a successful IDA program.

—*Trust.* IDA programs that are part of large, stable umbrella organizations appear to do a particularly good job of recruiting account holders and encouraging them to save. There are several reasons why this is the case. The staff is likely to have the skills, experience, and community connections necessary to get an effective program up and running quickly. Recruitment is easier if the organization already has close ties with potential IDA savers through other programs it offers. And the organization itself may enjoy the trust and confidence of program participants because of its reputation or presence in the community.

The FAB program has enjoyed all these advantages. There was remarkable continuity in staffing, with the two lead individuals present for most of the duration of the program. FAB was able to recruit members through the other programs of the Family Focus Center and build on its physical presence on the west side. (Julie Riddle believes that one reason the organization is having trouble signing up youth savers for its high school IDA program is precisely because it does not have a prior relationship with the target population.) The program staff has made a concerted effort to be responsive to the community, offering classes in both English and Spanish, translating surveys into Spanish, and providing on-site child care. FAB's partnerships with well-established local entities, including the University of Kansas, the Kauffman Foundation, and the KC Terminal Employees/ Guadalupe Center Federal Credit Union further strengthened its reputation and helped it overcome any initial skepticism that might have greeted the offer of matching funds.

—*Relationships*. The relationships forged between program staff and IDA account holders can help keep savings on track and provide an early warning system for participants who may be on the brink of crisis. At FAB, both the monthly training classes and ongoing case management services afforded the opportunity for one-on-one contact. As was the case for Miguel Juarez, account holders are likely to ask for help only if they have a relationship with the organization and its personnel. The relationships with other participants can also be important. For many, the classes and occasional social events offer a rare opportunity to socialize with other adults. "There's a lot of support here," says Marcia Shobe. "If someone can't save one month, their friend will help them out." The personal touch, too, is highly motivating: "We do little things," says Kane, "like every month when we send those statements out we write a little note on them— 'You're doing a great job,' 'You've passed the $1,000 mark'—and that seems to make a difference. It's just a way of showing we do care."

—*Simplicity*. Simplicity of account design is another advantage. FAB staff members quickly got over their embarrassment when it became clear that their straightforward rules regarding participation had helped get their program up and running smoothly. Recruitment turned out to be difficult enough without a complicated set of requirements to be met; other programs with tougher requirements had an even harder time filling the available slots. "We figured if people are saving, that's what we want to have happen in the program," says Kane. "We don't want to bog them down with a million rules." The quick start to the program, with savings beginning immediately, also allowed participants to see results that motivated them to continue to save. (Staff members point to the parental release forms and other paperwork required as part of their youth program as one of the reasons enrollment has been disappointing in this second initiative.) An even more important finding is that, even with simple rules, deposits tended to be irregular from month to month in the FAB program as well as at the other demonstration sites. (Even the model savers profiled here often had to make up a missed deposit in a subsequent month.) IDA programs will have a greater impact if deposits can be made via automatic electronic deductions from paychecks (as 401(k) deposits are made), rather than requiring participants to physically deposit money at a credit union or bank. This would be an especially important feature of a large-scale IDA program, where many of the supportive features of the demonstration, such as the building of one-on-one relationships, will be lacking. The fear of some IDA advocates is that a large-scale program may generate only very low levels of deposits—a danger that automatic electronic payroll deductions could help allay.

—*Human and social capital*. The building of human and social capital—knowledge, resources, connections—appears to be at least as important to the well-being of account holders as the accumulation of financial capital. Information about how to manage one's assets, connections to other asset-building organizations, an understanding of the importance of credit ratings, cautionary words about predatory lending—all these are nonfinancial assets created by the FAB program, and they may represent its most lasting contribution. It is a good thing that Regina Blackmon now has savings to draw on to keep her home in good repair, but it is even better that she learned about running her own business and gained the confidence to leave a job she hated. George Clark will never again make the mistake of declaring bankruptcy if faced with mounting credit card debt. And Miguel Juarez has acquired not just some savings to help him offset his gambling debts but also strategies to help him overcome his addiction. (The phone number of Gamblers Anonymous may be the most important piece of information Miguel has received, but FAB staff cannot ensure that he will use it—a profound illustration of the limits of IDA programs in addressing the deep-seated issues that hinder some people in their efforts to leave poverty behind.)

IDAs have their limits. Not every low-income person will benefit from the opportunity to open an IDA. Early research on the FAB program has found that women are more likely to join the program than men and that people who already have some assets are more likely to participate than those who have none.[23] The fact that the Family Asset Building program and other demonstration sites have struggled to fill available slots suggests that there is a proportion of the eligible population for whom IDAs hold little appeal or who do not fully trust the offer of matching funds. "While savings and asset accumulation are good ideas for everyone, the truth is that some people simply aren't ready—or aren't willing—to accept the discipline required by IDAs," writes Tom Riley.[24] Or, as Regina said in explaining why some of her sisters joined FAB while the others did

not, "It's a personality thing." As Riley points out, "By requiring participants to make a very real (if short-term) sacrifice, and by insisting upon
the financial education component, IDAs can, by design, sort out the people
that they can help from those that they can't." Contextual factors, such as
illness, family commitments, and the overall economy, can also interfere,
not just with one's propensity to save but with one's ability to avoid making unmatched withdrawals. Above all, successful saving requires an understanding of the trade-off between present and future consumption. This
is a difficult trade-off even for the average American, as high credit card
balances and low U.S. savings rates attest. It is even more challenging for
a population that has pressing current needs and little experience in saving. The institutional support and matching funds provided by IDA programs go a long way toward enabling a low-income population to make
the trade-off, but they do not work for everyone.

Those designing IDAs for the masses have tried to incorporate the lessons learned from the IDA programs already under way. They understand
the importance of keeping it simple. And one of the underlying goals of
the proposed tax credit to financial institutions is the building of trust
between mainstream financial institutions and low-income households.
But some of the factors that are correlated with successful IDA programs
will be lost in the scaled-up world of millions of accounts. Certainly, there
will be less room for one-to-one relationships once IDAs are offered chiefly
through financial institutions, and casework may fall by the wayside. But
it is crucial that, whatever the design of the system, it include provisions
for building not just the financial but also the human capital of account
holders. While some low-income individuals already have the skills and
information they need to become successful savers, many do not. Lacking
the critical component of economic literacy training, IDAs will fall short
of their promise of asset building for the poor. This conclusion echoes the
theme of preceding chapters—that it is knowledge above all that enables
people to fully realize the value of the assets they hold.

Lessons from Policy

The second set of lessons about IDAs relates to the broader policy story.
Why have IDAs captured the imagination of policymakers and the public?
What is it about the idea that draws bipartisan support at a time of sharp
political polarization? To what extent can IDAs serve as an effective tool
in the fight against poverty?

Critical to the success of the IDA movement is the power of the concept itself. IDAs are a simple tool that can be explained in a sentence or two, yet they have the power to change the behavior and outlook of thousands, perhaps millions, of people. The concept is also familiar. Most Americans have some experience with tax-deferred savings, such as IRAs or 401(k)s, even if they do not fully understand the public subsidies inherent in these investments. IDAs sound like a natural extension of this system, analogous to what the government already does for the middle class. According to Melvin Oliver, this is part of their appeal: "IDAs are seen as a legitimate way—in line with the way we have provided incentives and financial resources for the middle and upper class—to provide some of those same kinds of resources for folks that are less advantaged." This is an argument frequently used by those selling IDAs to a tight-fisted Congress. As Ray Boshara testified before a congressional subcommittee, "Asset building has a long tradition in the U.S., and reinforces basic American values of work, saving, and responsibility. We're not asking Congress do something for the working poor that's not already being done for the middle class."[25]

The idea of IDAs appeals across the political spectrum. People are drawn to IDAs for different reasons. Michael Sherraden explains: "The part that appeals to people with free market and entrepreneurial interests is the importance of building assets, controlling your life, becoming an economic actor. The part that appeals to people with social justice interests is that IDAs are progressive. Somebody saves and then it gets matched." IDAs also appeal to the poor themselves. "For the poor," says Oliver, "the attraction is about dignity. Waiting for a handout or waiting for a check that you didn't earn has a certain negative value to it. . . . [T]he fact that this money represents not a check but something that matches their own effort, that matches their own impetus, is really a life-changing event. So I think poor people are saying, 'This is something that I work for, this is something that I deserve.' It doesn't have the kind of negative implications that traditional support does."

If anything, suspicion of IDAs has been voiced by the Left, not the Right. Oliver admits there's a problem: "IDAs have a laissez-faire, individualistic attraction about them. People who are not committed to the social safety net see the policy as a sort of alternative. That's a dangerous ally that says, 'See? We don't need this safety net stuff. We just need to get people the right kind of resources so they can control their lives.'" IDA advocates have emphasized that asset building should be seen as a complement to, not a replacement for, income support. "We're not out to destroy the safety net," says Oliver. "We're really trying to expand it."

Despite these suspicions, IDAs enjoy one huge advantage in the marketplace of ideas: they do not fit neatly into either a liberal or a conservative worldview. As a result, public discussion of matched savings tends to avoid these categories and thus is less politicized than that regarding almost any other antipoverty program. The bottom line, according to Bob Friedman, is "Does this work? Once something can be shown to work, ideology is a lot less important."

The IDA movement has benefited from its fit with larger economic and social trends. Sherraden speculates that there is a certain sense in which the time is right for this kind of idea. "We were maybe a little early, and people were just starting to figure it out," he says, but the path of public policy is clearly going in the direction of asset-based policies. IDAs also received a boost from the rethinking of the existing welfare system in the mid-1990s, which created a receptive environment for new ideas. "In terms of policy ideas, IDAs have burst on the scene," says Oliver, voicing some concern. "Policy ideas usually take a lot longer. This has captured so many different constituencies' imagination that it has taken off, in a way, before we're ready for it to take off. We're excited about it, but we're troubled about it because you don't want to have a big failure that turns you off the idea before you really know how to do it."

There is more to the IDA story than the strength of the idea and good timing. Specific organizations and individuals played a crucial role in bringing the concept of IDAs into the policy mainstream. Michael Sherraden, with whom the idea originated, combines his academic research with creativity and a high degree of policy savvy. And the connection with CFED proved crucial. "They are the best," says Sherraden. "There is no organization that I've seen that can move an idea as they can." Bob Friedman's gift for policy innovation and Ray Boshara's skill on Capitol Hill contributed to CFED's ability to act as a true policy entrepreneur when it came to IDAs. At the same time, the work of Melvin Oliver and Susan Berresford in reorienting the priorities of the Ford Foundation helped leverage the large-scale resources needed to move the field forward.

Community-based organizations, philanthropic foundations, banks, and credit unions have all played important roles in the complex process that brought IDAs to public attention. Throughout, CFED and CSD worked systematically to link policy to practice and policymakers to practitioners. Bob Friedman reminds people that when Sherraden first brought up the

idea of IDAs, no one knew anything about match rates, account struc-
tures, banking relationships, or what kind of organizations should run
IDA programs. "It was the old lesson, that it's the stories," he says. "We
needed stories to show it works, then we iterated that with policy, doing
smoke and mirrors, saying to the Feds, 'You ought to do this because
there's local demand,' saying to local folks, 'You ought to do this because
there's federal money available.'" It was essential for there to be good
information coming out of the various IDA programs, and it was also
essential that the organizations involved were able to get this information
in front of policymakers. "A little bit of hard evidence can leverage a lot of
policy," says Boshara.

The legislative process was also furthered by elected officials who ad-
vocated IDAs in Congress. In March 2001, CFED presented its Champion
Awards to a group of legislators to thank them for their work on IDAs.[26]
Those honored ranged from liberals like Senator Tom Harkin (D-Iowa)
and Representative Nancy Pelosi (D-Calif.) to conservatives like Senator
Rick Santorum (R-Pa.) and Representative Judd Gregg (R-N.H.). Earlier
support from Representative Tony Hall (D-Ohio) and former senator Dan
Coats (R-Ind.), the principal Republican behind the Assets for Independence Act, was also crucial. The national policy agenda remains unfinished, but the commitment of key policymakers to make IDAs available to
all who qualify is the surest guarantee that broad IDA legislation will
ultimately be passed.

A final and essential word of credit is due the account holders in the
many IDA programs that exist around the nation. One of the realities of
IDAs is that low-income people must invest in themselves before any other
investment can be leveraged. The evidence that has moved the policy process forward emerged from the decisions and actions of thousands of low-
income individuals who succeeded in making the trade-off between current
consumption and future saving, who put off purchases or stretched their
tight budgets even further to make their monthly deposit. Their actions
give credence to Sherraden's chief contention, that the poor can indeed
save if they are provided with the incentives and opportunities to do so.

Over 800 attended CFED's annual IDA conference in Washington, D.C.,
in March 2001. (The number of attendees, up from 300 only three years
earlier, is another testament to the rapid growth of the field.) Bob Friedman summed up for the crowd what he had learned from account holders:
"Poor people—even very poor people—do save, not because it is easy or
they have extra income, but because saving is the price of stability, hope,

progress. IDAs are earned, not given: account holders work, save, learn, and invest. The impact of IDAs comes earlier and more profoundly than we expected, appearing after a few months of savings when account holders realize that although their asset goal may be months or years away, they can exert a measure of control over their economic lives."

Our individual savers in Kansas City, Missouri, have found that added measure of control. Regina Blackmon, armed with a savings account and a new set of connections, was able to expand her business, make needed repairs to her home, and find a better job. George Clark is on his way to buying a home and perhaps becoming self-employed full-time. Even Miguel Juarez, who expects to be paying off his debts for the next few years, has found new ways to save and taken steps to address his addiction.

Not every story has a happy ending. Some participants in IDA programs have dropped out or failed to meet their goals. For others, having an IDA makes only a small dent in the array of problems they face. But IDAs have encouraged and enabled many low-income Americans to build assets, both tangible and intangible. The IDA field is on the brink of bringing that hope to millions of Americans. "That's the goal, that's the prize," says Ray Boshara, "to get significant funding for asset policies. We do it for the nonpoor, and it's good policy, so we should do it for the poor." With savings, a low-income family can purchase a home or send a child to college. With savings, an injury, illness, or divorce will not necessarily push a family into poverty. With savings, one can start a business or apply for a bank loan. In this sense, IDAs can act as a central building block in public efforts to help the poor gain greater stability and a brighter future.

Epilogue

What do the stories recounted in this volume tell us about asset building as an antipoverty strategy? As Michael Sherraden has pointed out, not many people manage to spend their way out of poverty. Economically, it is saving and the accumulation of assets that are the keys to development for poor households. Investments in other kinds of assets provide similar benefits. Education and training represent forms of human capital that provide workers with higher incomes, greater job security, and more options in a rapidly changing economy. The networks of connections, trust, and reciprocity that constitute social capital offer people support in troubled times and strengthen the ability of poor communities to develop economically. And investments in natural assets can help resource-dependent communities achieve sustainable livelihoods and enhance the quality of life in rural and urban settings alike.

Several themes emerge from the stories told in these pages. Some concern individuals, others are related to institutions, and still others involve the broader economic and political context. An understanding of the potential and limitations of the asset-building approach requires attention to all three dimensions.

The Impact of Asset Building on Individuals

Different kinds of assets are interconnected and acquiring one makes possible the acquisition of others. Most people in the middle class or better off possess an array of assets that underpin their well-being and provide security to their families. They are likely to own their homes and have some retirement savings. They have probably attended college or received specialized job training. They live in neighborhoods with good schools, parks, and residents who work together to keep the community clean and safe. Individuals who are poor, on the other hand, may lack all of these assets. Little or no savings, limited job skills, and deteriorated or dangerous neighborhoods make day-to-day survival hard and long-term planning almost impossible.

The stories told here suggest that the odds of overcoming poverty improve when even one kind of asset is acquired and that each helps in the acquisition of others. The IDA movement is premised on the idea that acquiring even a small amount of savings makes possible other asset-building opportunities. Regina Blackmon, for example, used the money in her IDA to maintain the value of her home and expand her business, while George Clark plans to use his to purchase his first home. Financial resources also make it possible to get an education, which in turn leads to higher pay and the potential for greater savings. The investments made in training Sandra Bradford and Marguerite Sisson enabled both women to achieve higher standards of living as well as other benefits. Owning a home increases one's involvement in the community, as Denise Washington's experience bears out. And where networks of relationships are strong, people are able to work together to improve the material and social conditions of their lives, as in Hayfork where the efforts of residents leveraged a substantial investment in their community. Human and social capital play an especially critical role in changing the opportunities of low-income people. Perhaps the most valuable gains of those who have participated in the programs profiled here are the knowledge and networks they have acquired—resources that are often as important as their more tangible acquisitions. Effective asset-building organizations understand the connections among different kinds of assets and work to help those they serve acquire the range of resources needed for greater self-sufficiency and an improved standard of living.

The asset-building process almost always involves a mix of progress and setbacks as individuals and communities face issues both within and beyond their control. "The path out of poverty is not drawn by a smooth, clear line from hardship to plenty," write Peggy Clark and Amy Kays in an Aspen Institute study of microenterprise development. "It is a course of small steps forward and back, leaps ahead and hard falls."[1] The stories related here show both gains and reversals, some due to individual actions and others to larger forces over which people have little control. Sandra Bradford lost a good job both because her performance at work had suffered and because of a downturn in the economy. She is especially unfortunate in trying to find a new position in an industry suffering from recession and the trauma of the September 11, 2001, terrorist attacks. Marguerite Sisson's business grew, then all but collapsed, then revived due to her talents and weaknesses as an entrepreneur. Her story also suggests that luck, both good and bad, can play an important role in shaping one's future. Marguerite had no control over the troubled family into which she was born, but chance also played a role in her acquiring a new house thanks to the generosity of a friend—an acquisition that contributes greatly to the better quality of life Marguerite and her family now enjoy. The residents of Hayfork have had mixed results in their quest to renew their community. One reason is that they face an especially difficult complex of forces beyond their control: the fact that the land on which they depend is subject to decisions made at a far remove, changes in Forest Service personnel and policy that have reduced the opportunity for productive work in the forests, and the mill closure that cost many residents their jobs and increased poverty throughout the community. Rather than measuring success in terms of linear progress, asset-building efforts should be evaluated based on whether they have increased the capacity of low-income people to weather the ups and downs they will inevitably experience.

Asset building takes time. The cases discussed in the book underscore the fact that asset building is a slow process. While various initiatives may show positive results in the short term, reversals are not just possible but likely. The real results of asset building may best be seen over a much longer time frame, in the impact not just on today's poor but on subsequent generations. Denise Washington will leave her home to her children. Sandra Bradford's daughters have witnessed an alternative to welfare. Marguerite Sisson's son is beginning to enjoy a standard of living his mother never experienced as a child. The stories of many Americans bear out the importance of assets in shaping the prospects of their children and grandchildren. As a young professor, Melvin Oliver's status as a first-generation member of the middle class and consequent lack of assets put him at a disadvantage in the Los Angeles housing market. Happily, his children will not suffer the same fate. Research shows that a significant proportion of wealth— probably one-half and possibly more—first reaches its owners by way of intergenerational transfer.[2] The offspring of the poor are better served by a social welfare system that helps low-income people build assets than by one that focuses on income maintenance alone.

Asset building leaves many issues untouched. Most low-income people confront issues that have little to do with assets but that make the journey out of poverty substantially more difficult. Family demands, health problems, or other personal barriers may interfere with the abilities of poor individuals to participate in and benefit from asset-building programs. Even those who do participate may find their progress derailed by challenges in their lives that are not directly related to a lack of assets. Three of the women profiled in this book have family responsibilities that place an added burden on their quest for self-sufficiency. Although only in their forties, they are already grandmothers, their daughters having become pregnant in their late teens and, for the most part, outside of marriage. Two of the three are also grappling with the fear of their sons turning to violence. Denise's son has been in and out of foster care because of her concerns about his conduct at home and in school. The energy that has gone into helping him resolve his problems has infringed on Denise's ability to focus on work, school, or her community connections. Sandra felt the need to send her son to live with his father in another state to curtail his growing gang involvement and truancy.

Health problems, depression, and substance abuse are often cited by the leaders of asset-building programs as reasons why participants drop out or fail to meet their obligations. Miguel's compulsive gambling is a clear example of how an addiction can interfere with otherwise responsible behavior. Denise and Marguerite have both struggled with depression, due in large part to the economic strain under which they lived for many years. Drug abuse is a common feature of the landscape in Hayfork, where the lack of employment and economic vitality leaves many at loose ends. The asset-building strategies described in the previous chapters do not address these issues directly, but they often help people feel more competent and empowered in at least one sphere of their lives. The greater self-esteem acquired in the process of building assets makes the other challenges faced by many low-income people easier to handle.

Institutional Issues

Most asset-building organizations face operational challenges related to insecure funding and limited organizational capacity. This book has profiled five organizations at the forefront of building assets for the poor.

These organizations were selected because their approaches are innovative and successful, they can be replicated on a wider scale, and they enjoy broad support across the political spectrum. In short, they represent a sampling of what can be considered the state of the art in the asset-building field. Even so, most of these organizations face challenges of insufficient funding, demands that exceed resources, and personnel and leadership turnover. Neighborhoods Incorporated, generally considered one of the most effective members of the NeighborWorks network, must confine itself to working in a few targeted areas of Battle Creek because of limited financial and staff resources. Another issue that has affected the organization is personnel turnover, with three executive directors heading the group in as many years and staff positions going unfilled, particularly in the critical outreach area.

The Watershed Research and Training Center has enjoyed stable leadership, with its founder still in charge of the organization almost a decade after it was established. The center's focus on local problems and Lynn Jungwirth's local roots have contributed to this comparatively enduring relationship, while the lack of alternative employment in Hayfork means that people stay with the organization as long as they can. Still, center staff must invest a great deal of time in raising funds for its operations, and a shortage of resources makes programs vulnerable when the person responsible for them—perhaps a graduate student or someone in a grant-funded position—is ready to move on.

The IDA program run by Heart of America Financial Services illustrates another kind of organizational challenge. Although the umbrella organization is one of the oldest and largest nonprofits in Kansas City, its IDA program is operated quite independently. As a result, it must rely on foundation or public funding, most of it for limited-duration demonstration projects, and can function only as long as money is available or new grants can be found. The generally low salaries found in the nonprofit sector, demand for services that exceeds an organization's capacity to deliver, and the constant grind of raising money constrain the effectiveness and stability of most organizations working to build assets on behalf of the poor, with the efforts profiled here no exception.

Asset-building organizations will be most successful when relationships with funders and other supporters are institutionalized. One of the factors contributing to the relative stability of asset-building organizations is the degree to which their relationships with the larger entities that provide them with support are institutionalized. Does support rest on the decisions of specific individuals or is there a more established connection that transcends changes in personnel? Must an organization secure resources on a project-by-project basis or is a more predictable funding stream in place? How much of an organization's energy must go into building and maintaining relationships?

The Watershed Center's experience with the U.S. Forest Service provides an illustration of the kind of ad hoc relationship that can hinder organizational effectiveness. When individuals within the Forest Service who had supported the center's work were promoted or transferred, the center found itself hindered when seeking permission to undertake stewardship projects on Forest Service land. A considerable amount of energy had to go into building relationships with new personnel, acquainting them with the mission of the center, and developing the level of trust needed for their support. (This is an especially difficult issue for small organizations—in this case, the Watershed Center needed the Forest Service much more than the Forest Service needed the Watershed Center, meaning that the burden of maintaining the relationship fell on the center alone.)

An example of a more institutionalized connection can be found in Wildcat Service Corporation's multiyear contracts with the City of New York and New York State to train and place welfare recipients in jobs, and in the relationships with employers developed over the years by the Private Industry Partnership. Although Barbara Silvan's support for the partnership was a critical factor in its initial success, five years of collaboration meant that when Silvan left Salomon Smith Barney, the relationship with Wildcat remained in place.

Institutionalized relationships also exist between some of the organizations profiled here and philanthropic foundations. Neighborhoods Incorporated benefits tremendously from the presence in Battle Creek of the W. K. Kellogg Foundation. The Kellogg Foundation devotes a portion of its funding each year to local activities, and Neighborhoods Incorporated's programs regularly receive some of these resources. Neighborhoods Incorporated also enjoys an ongoing relationship with the City of Battle Creek and local financial institutions, in part because civic leaders appreciate the contribution the group has made to their own goals of community revitalization. These connections have endured despite the turnover in leadership. The presence on Neighborhoods Incorporated's board of representatives of foundations, the city, and local banks has further cemented these links.

A lucky confluence of interests enabled Heart of America Family Services to draw on the resources of the Ewing Marion Kauffman Foundation when its IDA program was established. The Kauffman Foundation's interest in asset building and entrepreneurship, along with its focus on local programs, made it a logical place to turn when the Family Asset Building program was seeking a source of matching IDA funds. Relationships, even those that are institutionalized, require maintenance. But the deeper and more regularized the connections between asset-building organizations and the larger entities on which they depend, the more effective the organization will be in serving its primary clientele.

The overriding challenge for antipoverty advocates is how to expand the scope of asset-building activities to serve a larger population. Among the criteria for selecting the organizations profiled in this book was whether their activities are replicable and whether the principles on which they rely make sense outside their original setting. In general, some aspects of an organization's work are bound by a specific context while others are applicable more widely. The challenge is to take the universal elements of successful programs and devise ways to deliver them on a larger scale.

At least four routes to this end are suggested by the cases examined here. The first is geographic expansion. ISED, for example, initially expanded to provide microenterprise training throughout Iowa and now offers its services in several other states. The Private Industry Partnership replicated its New York City–based program at another site and is advising the British government on how to set up a similar program in London. Jeffrey Jablow, one of the individuals involved in creating the Private Industry Partnership, has founded a new organization to provide career development services to low-income individuals at multiple sites nationwide. By aggregating demand for entry-level workers in a given field (in this case information technology) among employers located in several cities and then supplying their needs through existing public funding streams and local work force training programs, Origin, Inc. is extending the principles of the Private Industry Partnership beyond their original focus on a single geographic market.

A second route to expansion is to use an existing network to disseminate the core elements of an asset-building program. Neighborhoods Incorporated, for example, has served as a model for organizations that are part of the NeighborWorks network; staff members speak at conferences, host visits by representatives of other neighborhood housing organizations, and train their counterparts in how to use the Community Builders curriculum. The relationship with the W. K. Kellogg Foundation has also been useful in this regard. The foundation has both a special connection with Neighborhoods Incorporated and a national focus in its grant making, providing a way for lessons learned locally to be disseminated to a much broader audience.

A third avenue for moving to scale is the creation of new networks for the sharing of information and the expansion of these networks to include new participants. One example is the field-building role played by the Corporation for Enterprise Development in the IDA movement. Through initiatives like the annual IDA conference, the IDA handbook, and the Internet-based IDAnetwork, CFED has helped disseminate the latest knowledge about IDAs to a growing number of community organizations interested in starting their own programs. These efforts have imposed a level of standardization on the field that some find overly centralized but most view as helpful in expanding and unifying the IDA movement. It is not always necessary for a network to be created by a central institution like CFED, but it may be the most efficient way for a field to develop.

The microenterprise movement is often contrasted with the IDA movement in that the former lacked any centralization and subsequently developed in a more diverse and less cohesive manner. Recently, microenterprise organizations have coalesced around some centralizing institutions, including their trade association, the Association for Enterprise Opportunity, and the grant-funded Fund for Innovation, Effectiveness, Learning, and Development (FIELD). These institutions contribute to the sharing of information among organizations and enable new entrants into the microenterprise business to benefit from what more established groups have already learned.

A smaller and less formal set of networks plays a role in the community-based forestry movement. That movement is young relative to both the microenterprise and IDA fields, and consequently networks are less well developed. But the Watershed Center has benefited from participating in a variety of groups that constitute a nascent community-based forestry network, from the Healthy Forests Healthy Communities marketing initiative to collaborative efforts like the National Network of Forest Practitioners to ongoing interaction among nonprofits supported by the Ford Foundation's community-based forestry initiative. Networks make it possible for new organizations to get up to speed more quickly, benefit from knowledge acquired by their peers, find solutions to common problems, and avoid "reinventing the wheel" when confronted with new challenges.

A fourth way to increase the scale of operations is to collaborate with large public sector entities or to enshrine asset-building mechanisms in state or federal law. Wildcat's relationship with the City of New York and New York State and ISED's collaboration with the State of Iowa have granted these organizations greater stability, predictability, and expanded scope. Such relationships are still vulnerable, as contracts require periodic negotiation and budgetary cutbacks can reduce the amount of state money available to pay for services. A more secure strategy is to embed asset-building provisions in law, as the current Savings for Working Families Act proposes to do for IDAs. Even this effort may be limited in duration and subject to budgetary cutbacks down the road, but locating asset-building opportunities in the tax code, where similar provisions benefiting the middle class are already found, is the most reliable means to substantially expand scale.

The Economic and Political Context

A slowing economy has created a new set of challenges for asset-building organizations. Asset-building strategies for fighting poverty emerged in the early 1990s and received growing attention throughout the decade. It is no coincidence that the excitement generated by the idea of asset building coincided with an unprecedented period of growth in the U.S. economy. As the stock market rose and millions of middle-class Americans became investors, the notion that the poor, too, should be able to acquire assets had broad resonance. In addition, the strong economy saw a continued appreciation in housing prices, growing demand for workers, and healthy markets for newly minted entrepreneurs—all factors that contributed to asset acquisition among the poor. The success of welfare reform in putting people to work was also facilitated by the economic boom.

Slower growth has affected both the public and private sectors and has implications for any organization that depends on them. Falling tax revenues have led to budget cutting in Iowa, as in other states; one result has been an end to the contract under which ISED was guaranteed a certain number of slots for training welfare recipients. ISED still receives state money for its microenterprise development programs, but the arrangements under which payment is made are more ad hoc and subject to the discretion of individual caseworkers. Consequently, ISED must expend greater energy in maintaining these relationships and negotiating the terms under which it serves those on public assistance. In New York, the financial services industry suffered a major decline made worse by the events of September 11, 2001. Demand for workers has fallen, requiring the Private

Industry Partnership to invest in developing new employer relationships in sectors less affected by cutbacks.

The slowing economy poses special challenges for organizations that serve welfare recipients. The end of 2001 saw the first wave of recipients reaching the end of their time limit for benefits. For the previous five years, the welfare system had acted as a safety net when asset-building efforts did not pan out. Sandra Bradford returned to welfare when she lost her job; Marguerite Sisson was able to retain her rental assistance and health benefits while she built her business. As recipients of public assistance reach the end of the five-year limit, there will be less margin for error and a greater urgency to ensure that people are gainfully employed. This is likely to mean a return to the "work first" ethos that characterized the early days of welfare reform. In such an environment, organizations will find themselves constrained in their ability to engage in longer-term asset-building efforts on behalf of low-income people, even at a time when investments in economic, human, and social assets are more essential than ever.

A supportive policy environment and dedicated public funding is the ultimate prize for asset-building organizations. The asset-building efforts profiled in this book all began as local, community-based efforts. Some have succeeded in developing institutionalized relationships with public or private sector entities, relationships that provide them with reliable funding streams and ongoing support for their work. Others operate more informally, securing grant funding where possible and building relationships one at a time. Public policy must play an essential role if asset-building organizations are to achieve scale—meaning that they reach a large proportion of those eligible for their services through some kind of institutionalized mechanism. The IDA movement is the best example of the contribution public policy can make. If national IDA legislation is passed, close to a million Americans will become eligible for matched savings to be used for asset-building purposes—a huge increase in scale from the 10,000 low-income people who currently hold IDAs. If IDA contributions can be made through automatic payroll deduction, even greater scope can be achieved.

The ten-year campaign for IDA legislation illustrates the mix of costs and benefits that go along with policy support. The benefits are obvious: if the Savings for Working Families Act is passed, an asset-building opportunity currently available to 10,000 Americans will have the potential to reach one hundred times that many. Matched savings for the poor will be enshrined in the tax code, where similar provisions that benefit the middle class and wealthy are already found. Funding will no longer be subject to the time limits of demonstration projects or the availability of grants. Asset-building efforts for the poor will gain greater legitimacy, with the legislation providing a platform for the expansion of such efforts. This is the much sought-after prize cited by IDA advocates.

Less recognized are the costs of public support. Legislative success inevitably requires compromise, and the current legislation is no exception. Provisions of the Savings for Working Families Act have been altered in the political process to secure the support necessary for passage. The most obvious recent change is that instead of leaving open the number of families that can receive matched funding based on their eligibility (a number that could total 40 million), the current legislation caps the number of accounts at 900,000 and provides funding only at this level. Another cost of moving to scale is the diminution of the role of community-based organizations and a likely decline in the availability of one-on-one counseling and in-depth literacy training. Securing federal funding for IDAs and embedding them in the tax code means that matched savings opportunities will be open to many more individuals but will almost certainly be less effective in helping those at the margins who require greater personal attention or education.

It should also be kept in mind that national legislation is not the way to get to scale for every asset-building instrument. For some of the strategies discussed in this book, a focus at the state or local level is more likely to yield results. One could envision, for example, microenterprise training programs that provide coverage in each state along the model developed by ISED or demand-driven job-training initiatives like PIP that serve the welfare population in every major city. Because welfare rules vary from state to state, programs that focus on welfare recipients must work closely with state agencies if they intend to serve this population. For other strategies, a particular federal agency is the appropriate focus of attention. The success and scope of the community-based forestry movement in helping revitalize natural resource–based communities, for example, depends less on national legislation than on policy decisions made by the U.S. Forest Service, both in Washington and in its regional offices.

Probably the key strength of the asset-building approach is its political appeal. As J. Larry Brown and Larry W. Beeferman have written, "Asset development combines the liberal objective of poverty reduction with the conservative dream of individual wealth building to achieve the shared goal of economic opportunity. And it uses a collective institution—government—on behalf of individual self-sufficiency."[3] The experience of the IDA movement bears out the ability of asset-building policies to attract support across the political spectrum. The involvement of the Private Industry Partnership and ISED in training welfare recipients suggests the role asset-building organizations can play in helping to meet previously established policy goals. Increasing home ownership rates among the poor is another asset-based strategy that has long enjoyed bipartisan support. There are three reasons why asset-building approaches are able to transcend the long-standing political divisions that have hindered the development of effective antipoverty policies. First, they are not exclusively government programs but represent collaboration among public, private, and nonprofit entities—hence, they tend to be immune to the charges of "big government" that have often derailed other policy initiatives on behalf of the poor. Second, the approaches they take embody a combination of empowerment and responsibility for individuals and communities—the idea of a "hand up" rather than a "handout"—that resonates with much of the American public. (The social contracts entered into with participants by organizations like Neighborhoods Incorporated and the Private Industry Partnership are examples of this dual emphasis.) Third, the parallels between asset-building policies that help the poor and those already in place for the middle class mean that such policies fit comfortably with widespread beliefs in a level playing field and equal opportunity.

The political appeal of asset-building strategies raises a critical question: Do they constitute a genuinely new approach to fighting poverty or are they just the equivalent of old wine in a new bottle—a way of presenting the discredited antipoverty policies of the past in a more politically acceptable manner? Admittedly, there is a marked degree of continuity between the emphases of today's programs and those of the past. Housing, job training, and community development have been staples of the fight against poverty since the 1960s. But there are also some marked departures. Neighborhood housing organizations are paying greater attention to the value of the homes owned by the poor as well as their customers' degree of economic literacy and capacity to maintain their property. Some, like Neighborhoods Incorporated, are even intervening in the market to raise property values for the mostly low-income residents of their target neighborhoods, a break with past policies of benign neglect that left subsidized housing tracts to sink into disrepair and the homes within them to decline in value. Jobs programs no longer prepare their clients to be generically "work-ready"; they are tailoring their training to match employer needs and forging systemic connections with companies to identify high-quality jobs and achieve labor market attachment for their low-income clientele. Community revitalization, as in the case of Hayfork, depends less on public sector investment and more on the initiative of local residents in identifying economic opportunities and bringing new players, both public and private, into the community. Attention to the creation of new assets and to the sustainability and value of those already owned is a key departure from past antipoverty policies and a critical selling point for asset-based strategies.

An even more basic question is whether such strategies can succeed in alleviating poverty. Clearly, they have helped the individuals written about in these pages to achieve personal transformations—as past policies did not. These are only a few of the thousands of people who have been helped by asset-building programs. Such programs depart both philosophically and practically from past policies: they invest in the assets of low-income individuals and communities. As Ray Boshara testified before Congress in support of IDA funding, "Ever since the New Deal, America's public and private sectors have spent billions on the poor in the form of income support, safety nets, rental assistance and transitional aid, but these sectors have rarely invested adequately in the poor, empowered them with assets, enabled them to build wealth. Thus, while the U.S. has succeeded in preventing the vast majority of poor families from falling through the bottom, it has failed in offering the asset-building tools necessary to let those families move from the bottom to the middle or top."[4]

We as a nation have a historic commitment to equal opportunity. The individuals, communities, and organizations encountered in this book embody this ideal, suggesting that what matters most in changing the prospects of the poor is not whether they have enough income to make it from month to month, but whether they have a stock of assets that allows them to invest in their future. It is hoped that these stories offer a promising direction for those seeking to extend the asset-building approach to cover all who remain in need.

Notes

Chapter One

1. See Bureau of the Census, *Poverty in the United States: 2000* (Dept. of Commerce, 2001). Some analyses dispute the Census Bureau's assertion of the narrowing income gap. See, for example, the Center on Budget and Policy Priorities (CBPP), "Poverty Rates Fell in 2000 as Unemployment Reached 31-Year Low," news release, September 26, 2001. The CBPP analysis relies on after-tax income figures from the Congressional Budget Office rather than on Census Bureau data. For a comparison of the two methods, see CBPP, "Recent Census Data Significantly Understate the Increase in Income Disparities," September 20, 2001.

2. Family wealth (or net worth) is defined here as the current value of all marketable or fungible assets less the current value of debts. The value of a home is included in this measure. For details, see Edward N. Wolff, "Recent Trends in Wealth Ownership, from 1983 to 1998," in Thomas M. Shapiro and Edward N. Wolff, eds., *Assets for the Poor: The Benefits of Spreading Asset Ownership*, Ford Foundation Series on Asset Building (Russell Sage Foundation, 2001).

3. Excluding home ownership, wealth is even more highly concentrated, with the richest 1 percent owning 47 percent of the total financial wealth in 1998 and the top 20 percent owning 91 percent. In 1998, the financial wealth of the bottom 40 percent of families was actually negative, meaning that the liabilities of these households exceeded their assets. See Wolff, "Recent Trends in Wealth Ownership," table 2.2.

4. Ray Boshara, Edward Scanlon, and Deborah Page-Adams, *Building Assets for Stronger Families, Better Neighborhoods, and Realizing the American Dream* (Washington: Corporation for Enterprise Development, 1998), p. 13.

5. Poverty rates cited in this paragraph come from Bureau of the Census, *Poverty in the United States, 2000,* and are based on the March 2001 supplement to the bureau's Current Population Survey (CPS), the source of official poverty estimates. Poverty thresholds for the calendar year 2000 were $13,738 for a family of three and $17,603 for a family of four.

6. Quoted in Louis Uchitelle, "How to Define Poverty? Let Us Count the Ways," *New York Times,* May 26, 2001.

7. See CBPP, "Poverty Rates Fell in 2000."

8. Stacy Zolt, "Hunger Experts Call for Broadened Food Stamp Use," *Scripps Howard News Service,* September 11, 2000.

9. Michael Sherraden, *Assets and the Poor: A New American Welfare Policy* (Armonk, N.Y.: M. E. Sharpe, 1991).

10. Melvin L. Oliver and Thomas M. Shapiro, *Black Wealth/White Wealth: A New Perspective on Racial Inequality* (Routledge, 1995).

11. Ibid., p. 7.

12. Ibid., p. 9.

13. Wolff, "Recent Trends in Wealth Ownership," p. 5.

14. See, for example, Edward N. Wolff, *Top Heavy: The Increasing Inequality of Wealth in America and What Can Be Done about It,* rev. ed. (New Press, 1995); "The Rich Get Richer: And Why the Poor Don't," *American Prospect,* vol. 12 (February 12, 2001); and "Recent Trends in Wealth Ownership."

15. See Robert Haveman, *Starting Even: An Equal Opportunity Program to Combat the Nation's New Poverty* (Simon & Schuster, 1988).

16. Robert Haveman and Edward N. Wolff, "Who Are the Asset Poor: Levels, Trends, and Composition, 1983–1998" (paper presented at the Inclusion in Asset Building: Research and Policy Symposium, Center for Social Development, Washington University, St. Louis, September 21–23, 2000).

17. Lisa M. Lynch, "Trends in and Consequences of Investments in Children," in Sheldon Danziger and Jane Waldfogel, eds, *Securing the Future: Investing in Children from Birth to College,* Ford Foundation Series on Asset Building (Russell Sage Foundation, 2000).

18. On the importance of investing in the human capital of children, see Lynn A. Karoly and others, *Investing in Our Children: What We Know and Don't Know about the Costs and Benefits of Early Childhood Interventions* (RAND, 1998); as well as chapters 1–4 in Danziger and Waldfogel, *Securing the Future.*

19. Danziger and Waldfogel, *Securing the Future,* p. 12.

20. Robert D. Putnam, *Bowling Alone: The Collapse and Revival of American Community* (Simon & Schuster, 2000), p. 19.

21. Putnam surveys findings on the relationship between social capital and health in *Bowling Alone,* ch. 20.

22. Jane Jacobs, *The Death and Life of Great American Cities* (Random House, 1961).

23. On the relationship between social capital and education, see Putnam, *Bowling Alone*, ch. 17. See also Pedro A. Noguera, "Transforming Urban Schools through Investments in the Social Capital of Parents," in Susan Saegert, J. Phillip Thompson, and Mark R. Warren, eds., *Social Capital and Poor Communities*, Ford Foundation Series on Asset Building (Russell Sage Foundation, 2001).

24. Sociologist Robert J. Sampson has written extensively on the connection between crime rates and the extent of social ties. See, for example, Sampson, "Crime and Public Safety: Insights from Community-Level Perspectives on Social Capital," in Saegert, Thompson, and Warren, *Social Capital and Poor Communities*. See also Putnam, *Bowling Alone*, ch. 18.

25. William Julius Wilson explores this trend and its implications in his classic work, *The Truly Disadvantaged* (University of Chicago Press, 1987).

26. Putnam, *Bowling Alone*, p. 317.

27. James K. Boyce and Manuel Pastor, *Building Natural Assets: New Strategies for Poverty Reduction and Environmental Protection* (Amherst, Mass.: Political Economy Research Institute, 2001), p. 5.

28. H. Patricia Hynes, *A Patch of Eden: America's Inner-City Gardeners* (White River Junction, Vt.: Chelsea Green, 1996).

29. For more on natural assets, see James K. Boyce and Barry Shelley, eds., "Natural Assets: Democratizing Environmental Ownership," Ford Foundation Series on Asset Building (unpublished manuscript).

30. Christopher Howard, *The Hidden Welfare State: Tax Expenditures and Social Policy in the United States* (Princeton University Press, 1997).

31. These figures come from Michael Sherraden, "Asset Building Policy and Programs for the Poor," in Shapiro and Wolff, *Assets for the Poor*.

32. Howard, *The Hidden Welfare State*, p. 97.

33. Sherraden, "Asset Building Policy and Programs for the Poor," pp. 303–4.

34. Peter Orszag and Robert Greenstein, "Toward Progressive Pensions: A Summary of the U.S. Pension System and Proposals for Reform" (paper presented at the Inclusion in Asset Building: Research and Policy Symposium, Center for Social Development, Washington University, St. Louis, September 21–23, 2000). Their estimates are based on U.S. Treasury data from 1999.

35. U.S. Department of Health and Human Services, Administration for Children and Families (ACF), "Percent Change in AFDC/TANF Families and Recipients" (www.acf.dhhs.gov/news/stats/afdc.htm [February 2002]).

36. Jason DeParle, "Bold Effort Leaves Much Unchanged for the Poor," *New York Times*, December 31, 1999.

37. See Karen Edwards and Carl Rist, *IDA State Policy Guide: Advancing Public Policies in Support of Individual Development Accounts* (Washington: Corporation for Enterprise Development, 2001).

38. Michael Sherraden, "From Research to Policy: Lessons from Individual Development Accounts," *Journal of Consumer Affairs*, vol. 34, no. 2 (2000), pp. 159–81.

39. Sherraden, "Asset Building Policy and Programs for the Poor," p. 305.

40. First Nations Development Institute, Native Assets Research Center (www.firstnations.org/main/ [December 2001]).

41. Robert Friedman, comments presented to the Ford Foundation conference "Benefits and Mechanisms for Spreading Asset Ownership in the United States," New York University, December 1998.

Chapter Two

1. Fannie Mae, *National Housing Survey 1996* (Washington, 1996), p. 5.

2. Ibid., p. 5.

3. On these initiatives, see Associated Press, "Fannie Mae, NAACP Form Partnership," January 22, 1999; "The American Dream Gets Bigger," *Ford Foundation Report* (fall 1998); and Associated Press, "Nation's Biggest Bank to Lend $3 Billion," August 10, 1999.

4. With two exceptions, home ownership rates in this paragraph come from the Joint Center for Housing Studies of Harvard University, *The State of the Nation's Housing, 2001* (Cambridge, Mass.: Joint Center for Housing Studies, 2001). Rates for female-headed households and households headed by married couples are from 1998 and come from Wolff, "Recent Trends in Wealth Ownership," table 2.11.

5. For information about the home-building activities of C. W. Post, see Larry B. Massie and Peter J. Schmitt, *Battle Creek, the Place behind the Products: An Illustrated History* (Woodland Hills, Calif.: Windsor, 1984).

6. Al Jones, "Battle Creek on the Rise," *Kalamazoo Gazette*, September 20, 1992, p. E1. On Battle Creek's decline and subsequent revival, see Haya El Nasser, "Battle Creek Snap-Crackle-Pops Back to Life," *USA Today*, January 3, 1997.

7. David Rusk, interviewed in *Back from the Brink: The Economic Renaissance of Battle Creek, Michigan*, a William Jamerson production (Marquette, Mich.: Forgotten Films & Video, 1999).

8. *Battle Creek Enquirer*, May 31, 1978, p. 1.

9. *Battle Creek Enquirer*, August 12, 1987, p. A-1.

10. *Battle Creek Enquirer*, March 3, 1989, p. 3.

11. *Battle Creek Enquirer*, August 31, 1991, p. A-2.

12. Personal communication from Greenwood Avenue residents and Neighborhoods Incorporated outreach staff, March 19, 1999, and April 20, 1999.

13. Neighborhood Reinvestment Corporation (NRC) is a national nonprofit organization chartered by Congress in 1978. NRC's goal is to revitalize America's older, distressed communities, which it does by creating and supporting local nonprofit organizations around the country.

14. Figures provided by Pat Massey, CEO, Neighborhoods Incorporated.

15. Figures on the percentage of Battle Creek children eligible for free or re-duced-price school lunches come from Neighborhoods Incorporated. The 2000 census shows the poverty rate for Calhoun County, where Battle Creek is located, exceeding the state average by 13.4 percent to 11.4 percent, while the poverty rate for children in Calhoun County is 19.9 percent versus 16.8 percent statewide. See Associated Press, "Poverty Rate for Michigan Counties," December 19, 2001.

16. According to Neighborhoods Incorporated, for the year ending December 31, 2000, 41 percent of all loans were to low-income customers (personal com-munication, December 13, 2001).

17. Figures from Neighborhoods Incorporated (personal communication, De-cember 13, 2001).

18. Forty percent of operations are funded by loan fees, interest, and revenue; 30 percent by community fund-raising; 20 percent by local and national grants; 7 percent by the City of Battle Creek; and 3 percent by government contracts. See Neighborhoods Incorporated, "Strengthening Neighborhoods through Commu-nity Investment" (2001).

19. On the leading the market strategy, see David Boehlke, "Leveraging Home-Ownership Promotion as a Tool for Neighborhood Revitalization," and Michael Schubert, "Asset Building and Neighborhood Revitalization through Home Own-ership: Lessons from Battle Creek, Michigan," in Warren Craig, ed., *When a House Is More Than Home: Home Ownership as an Asset-Building Tool for Families and Communities* (Washington: Neighborhood Reinvestment Corporation, 1997). See also Neighborhoods Incorporated, "Healthy Neighborhoods: A Neighbor-hoods Inc. Model."

20. Jenna Tomalka, quoted in *Battle Creek Enquirer*, October 13, 1997, p. 6A.

21. Bill Jones of the Fund for Community Development and Revitalization, comment at a meeting at Neighborhoods Incorporated, April 20, 1999.

22. Schubert, "Asset Building and Neighborhood Revitalization through Home Ownership."

23. Michael Schubert, "Re-building Healthy Neighborhoods: An Evaluation of the Impact of Neighborhoods Inc. of Battle Creek on the Quality of Life in Neighborhoods" (Chicago: Community Development Strategies, November 1998), table 5.1, p. 35.

24. Neighborhoods Incorporated, "Fast Facts" (January 1992–September 1999).

25. "B.C. Area Welcomes Growth: Census Shows Steady Increases in Hous-ing," *Battle Creek Enquirer*, May 27, 2001.

26. Perspectives Consulting Group, City of Battle Creek, Citizen Survey (1998); available from City of Battle Creek, city manager's office.

27. David Rusk, *Inside Game, Outside Game: Winning Strategies for Saving Urban America* (Brookings, 1999), p. 61; and personal communication from David Rusk, February 16, 1999.

28. *Battle Creek Enquirer*, October 15, 1997.

29. Putnam, *Bowling Alone*, p. 323.

Chapter Three

1. James K. Boyce, "Introduction: From Natural Resources to Natural Assets," in Boyce and Shelley, *Natural Assets*. The collected essays in the Boyce-Shelley volume make clear that natural assets exist not only in rural settings but in urban areas where residents are striving to realize their value by developing vacant lots, cleaning up waterfronts, and converting brownfields to productive use.

2. The discussion of routes to natural asset building draws on Boyce and Pastor, *Building Natural Assets*.

3. Henry Carey, quoted in Jane Braxton Little, "The Woods: Reclaiming the Neighborhoods," *American Forests*, vol. 103 (winter 1998), p. 13.

4. Gerry Gray and Jonathan Kusel, "Changing the Rules," *American Forests*, vol. 103 (winter 1998), p. 30. Gray is vice president for forest policy at American Forests, the nation's oldest nonprofit citizens' conservation organization. Kusel is director of Forest Community Research, a consulting firm located in Taylorsville, California.

5. Figure reported in Cecilia Marie Danks, "Community Participation in National Forest Management: The Role of Social Capital and Organizational Capacity in Collaborative Efforts in Trinity County, California" (Ph.D. diss., University of California, Berkeley, 2000), p. 94.

6. County of Trinity, "Hayfork Downtown Revitalization Master Plan" (USDA Forest Service, Northwest Economic Adjustment Initiative, December 1998), p. 2; available from Planning Department, Trinity County, Weaverville, California.

7. *Trinity County Economic and Demographic Profile 2000* (Center for Economic Development, California State University, Chico, 2000), p. 33.

8. Danks, "Community Participation in National Forest Management," pp. 74–76.

9. State of California, Employment Development Department, Labor Market Information Division, "Annual Average Labor Force Data for Counties, Year 2000," in *Counties Report 400C* (Sacramento, Calif., 2002).

10. County of Trinity, "Hayfork Downtown Revitalization Master Plan," p. 2.

11. "Industry Finding Owls Wherever It Searches," *Redding Sentinel*, July 30, 1989.

12. Quoted in Ted Gup, "Owl vs. Man," *Time*, June 25, 1990, p. 60.

13. Ibid., p. 61.

14. Representatives of the logging industry are not alone in calling for dramatic reform or even the abolition of the Forest Service. Robert H. Nelson, a

professor of environmental policy at the University of Maryland, makes such a case in his book, *A Burning Issue* (Lanham, Md.: Rowman & Littlefield, 2000).

15. See Gerald J. Gray, Maia J. Enzer, and Jonathan Kusel, eds., *Understanding Community-Based Forest Ecosystem Management* (Binghamton, N.Y.: Food Products, 2001).

16. Cecilia Danks and Lynn Jungwirth, "Community-Based Socioeconomic Assessment and Monitoring of Activities Related to National Forest Management," Working Paper (Watershed Research and Training Center, rev. July 1998, charts updated August 1999), fig. 3B.

17. Cecilia Danks, "Community-Based Stewardship: A Way to Reinvest in Forests and Forest Communities," in Boyce and Shelley, *Natural Assets.*

18. Danks and Jungwirth, "Community-Based Socioeconomic Assessment," pp. 3–4, fig. 10.

19. Quoted in Mieke H. Bomann, "Turning Lumbermen into Stewards of Forest," *American News Service*, article no. 1297 (2000).

20. Douglas Jehl, "U.S. Weighs Plan to Limit Spread of Forest Fires," *New York Times*, August 22, 2000, p. A1.

21. Timothy Egan, "Why Foresters Prefer to Fight Fire with Fire," *New York Times*, August 20, 2000; and Denny Truesdale, fire specialist, United States Forest Service, on *Talk of the Nation*, National Public Radio, August 14, 2000.

22. Watershed Center, "A Brief Overview of the Watershed Research and Training Center and Its Relationship with the USFS, RCA, and NFS" (July 11, 1994), p. 3.

23. Danks, "Community-Based Stewardship. "

Chapter Four

1. Pamela Loprest, "How Families That Left Welfare Are Doing: A National Picture" (Washington: Urban Institute, August 1999); and Pamela Loprest, "How Are Families That Left Welfare Doing? A Comparison of Early and Recent Welfare Leavers" (Washington: Urban Institute, April 2001). Loprest's data show that 29.1 percent of those who left welfare between 1995 and 1997 and 21.9 of those who left between 1997 and 1999 have returned.

2. On the mismatch between the skills of welfare recipients and projected job growth in the economy, see Anthony P. Carnevale and Donna M. Desrochers, "Getting Down to Business: Matching Welfare Recipients' Skills to Jobs That Train" (Princeton, N.J.: Educational Testing Service, 1999).

3. For a brief history of job-training strategies and how they fell short of meeting the needs of the disadvantaged, see Hillard Pouncy, "New Directions in Job Training Strategies for the Disadvantaged," in Danziger and Waldfogel, *Securing the Future.*

4. The Center for Employment Training (CET), based in San Jose, California, is one of the organizations that pioneered such an approach. Since its establishment in 1967, CET has emphasized close ties with local labor markets and training in job-specific skills. For details, see Edwin Melendez, *Working on Jobs: The Center for Employment Training* (Boston: Mauricio Gaston Institute, 1996).

5. Many states have since amended the "work first" emphasis in recognition of some of its shortcomings. In 1998, the federal government enacted the Workforce Investment Act to provide additional services and support for unemployed individuals who are not succeeding under the new work rules. For more information, see Steve Savner, "Key Implementation Decisions Affecting Low-Income Adults under the Workforce Investment Act" (Washington: Center for Law and Social Policy, August 1999); and U.S. General Accounting Office, *Welfare Reform: Moving Hard-to-Employ Recipients into the Workforce* (2001).

6. Wildcat Service Corporation, "History of the Organization" (www.wildcat-at-work.org/History/history.html [December 2001]).

7. Recent demonstration projects and related research also emphasize the importance of addressing the demand side of the job-training equation (the needs of employers), as well as the supply side (the needs of trainees). See, for example, Annie E. Casey Foundation, "Stronger Links: New Ways to Connect Low-Skilled Workers to Better Jobs" (Baltimore: Annie E. Casey Foundation, 2000).

8. Jeffrey Jablow was with the organization from 1994 to 2000, during which time the research for this chapter was carried out. He now heads Origin, Inc., a nonprofit organization that provides career advancement services to the unemployed and working poor.

9. A survey carried out by the Economic and Social Research Institute supports the view that employers are willing, and in many cases eager, to hire people leaving public assistance provided they present the positive personal characteristics that companies value highly. See Marsha Regenstein, Jack A. Meyer, and Jennifer Dickemper Hicks, "Job Prospects for Welfare Recipients: Employers Speak Out," in *New Federalism: Issues and Options for States,* no. A-25 (Washington: Urban Institute, August 1998).

10. For example, the employers surveyed by the Economic and Social Research Institute (see ibid.) listed "positive attitude," "reliability," "strong work ethic," and "punctuality" as the most important qualities in a job candidate.

11. Wildcat Service Corporation, "Private Industry Partnership: An Employer-Based Initiative for Welfare Reform and Career Opportunities" (March 1998), p. 14; more recent figures garnered from author interviews.

12. The options are made available to employees at a 25 percent discount to the market price. Twenty percent of the options are vested each year, meaning that if an employee receives 100 shares in one year, 20 of them can be exercised at market value one year later. After five years, the employee is fully vested and can exercise the full amount of stock at the market price. Active employees can exercise their stock options until expiration, which occurs after ten years.

13. On the difficulties and importance of employee retention for former welfare recipients, see the National Governors Association Center for Best Practices, Employment and Social Services Policy Studies Division, *Working Out of Poverty: Employment Retention and Career Advancement for Welfare Recipients* (Department of Health and Human Services, 1998). See also Annie E. Casey Foundation, "Stronger Links," pp. 26–28.

14. See Annie E. Casey Foundation, "Stronger Links," pp. 23–25.

15. Mark Granovetter, *Getting a Job: A Study in Contacts and Careers* (University of Chicago Press, 1995), p. 16. On the importance of informal recruitment channels, see Harry J. Holzer, *What Employers Want: Job Prospects for Less-Educated Workers* (Russell Sage Foundation, 1996).

16. William Julius Wilson documented this phenomenon in *When Work Disappears: The World of the New Urban Poor* (Knopf, 1996).

17. For more information, see the website of the Welfare to Work Partnership (www.welfaretowork.org/ [December 2001]).

Chapter Five

1. See Lynch, "Trends in and Consequences of Investments in Children," pp. 19–20.

2. U.S. Small Business Administration Office of Advocacy, *Small Business Economic Indicators, 2000* (Washington, 2001), table 3.

3. Peggy Clark and Amy Kays, *Microenterprise and the Poor: Findings from the Self-Employment Learning Project Five-Year Survey of Microentrepreneurs* (Washington: Aspen Institute, 1999), p. 4.

4. See "Microenterprise Development in the United States: An Overview," Microenterprise Fact Sheet Series (fall 2000), Association for Enterprise Opportunity (AEO), Arlington, Va.

5. On the origins of the microenterprise movement in the United States, see John Else with Janice Gallagher, "An Overview of the Microenterprise Development Field in the U.S." (Geneva: International Labour Office, April 2000), pp. 4–7; and Lisa J. Servon, *Bootstrap Capital: Microenterprises and the American Poor* (Brookings, 1999), ch. 2.

6. See Historical Data Series, Statement of Grameen Bank, 1994–96, 1995–97 (www.grameen.org).

7. Acción website, press room, media kit (www.accion.org/press/main.asp [December 2001]).

8. On the number of microenterprise programs, see Microenterprise Fund for Innovation, Effectiveness, Learning and Dissemination (FIELD), *1999 Directory of U.S. Microenterprise Programs* (Washington: Aspen Institute, 1999), p. xv. On the failure to match developing world successes, see Nitin Bhatt, Gary Painter, and Shui-Yan Tang, "Can Microcredit Work in the United States?" *Harvard Business Review* (November–December 1999), pp. 26–27.

9. See Else and Gallagher, "An Overview of the Microenterprise Development Field in the U.S.," p. 46.

10. FIELD, "Assessing the Effectiveness of Training and Technical Assistance," *FIELD Forum,* no. 1 (October 1999).

11. AFC, "Percent Change in AFDC/TANF Families and Recipients."

12. ISED is one of ten microenterprise organizations serving welfare recipients to receive funding from the Charles Stewart Mott Foundation under its Welfare-to-Work grant-making program. The purpose of the program is to explore how microenterprise organizations might better serve the welfare population. For more information, see FIELD, "Designing Microenterprise Programs for Welfare Recipients," *FIELD Forum,* no. 3 (November 1999).

13. Amy Kays Blair and Joyce Klein, *Microenterprise as a Welfare to Work Strategy: Client Characteristics,* report prepared for the Microenterprise Fund for Innovation, Effectiveness, Learning and Dissemination (FIELD) (Washington: Aspen Institute, July 2001).

14. Testimony of Marguerite Sisson, owner, River City Cleaning, Clinton, Iowa, to the House Committee on Banking and Financial Services on the Program for Investments in Microentrepreneurs (PRIME) Act (May 26, 1999).

15. See Clark and Kays, *Microenterprise and the Poor.*

16. U.S. Department of Labor (DOL) Employment and Training Administration, *Self-Employment as a Reemployment Option: Demonstration Results and National Legislation* (1994). The DOL study found income gains of, on average, $14,859 at one site and $1,093 at the other.

17. For a summary of the outcomes produced by various microenterprise development programs, see Else and Gallagher, "An Overview of the Microenterprise Development Field in the U.S.," pp. 41–53.

18. Figures from "Microenterprise Development: Facts, Figures, and Outcomes"(www.ised.org/EconomicDevelopment/factsnfigures.asp [December 2001]).

19. Clark and Kays, *Microenterprise and the Poor,* p. viii.

20. See Blair and Klein, *Microenterprise as a Welfare to Work Strategy.*

21. The following discussion draws on FIELD, "Achieving Scale: Request for Applications" (Washington: Aspen Institute, 1999), pp. 2–3.

22. Testimony of Jason J. Friedman, vice president, Institute for Social and Economic Development, Iowa City, Iowa, to the House Committee on Banking and Financial Services on the Program for Investments in Microentrepreneurs (PRIME) Act (May 26, 1999).

23. Among the most important outside evaluations was the Self-Employment Learning Project, a five-year study funded by the Ford Foundation and the Charles Stewart Mott Foundation. For more information on the study and its findings, see Elaine Edgcomb, Joyce Klein, and Peggy Clark, *The Practice of Microenterprise*

in the U.S. (Washington: Aspen Institute, 1996); and Clark and Kays, *Microenterprise and the Poor.*

24. Azriela Jaffe, *Starting from "No": 10 Strategies to Overcome Your Fear of Rejection and Succeed in Business* (Chicago: Dearborn, 1999).

25. U.S. Small Business Administration Office of Advocacy, "Small Business Frequently Asked Questions."

26. Servon, *Bootstrap Capital*, p. 92.

27. On the forms of social capital created by microenterprise development programs, see Denise Lynne Anthony, "Investing in Trust: Building Cooperation and Social Capital in Micro-Credit Borrowing Groups" (Ph. D. diss., University of Connecticut, Storrs, 1997); and Servon, *Bootstrap Capital.*

Chapter Six

1. Eleven foundations provided financial support for the demonstration: Ford Foundation, Charles Stewart Mott Foundation, Joyce Foundation, F. B. Heron Foundation, John D. and Catherine T. MacArthur Foundation, Citigroup Foundation, Fannie Mae Foundation, Levi Strauss Foundation, Ewing Marion Kauffman Foundation, Rockefeller Foundation, and the Moriah Fund. Local partners, including churches, corporations, and banks, also provided support. The demonstration is led by the Washington-based Corporation for Enterprise Development. Evaluation is being conducted by the Center for Social Development at Washington University in St. Louis.

2. While the demonstration project involves thirteen sponsoring organizations, one of these organizations operates two programs, bringing the total number of programs to fourteen.

3. This is the average monthly net deposit figure, defined as net deposits (after withdrawals) divided by months of participation. Figures in this and the next paragraph come from Mark Schreiner and others, "Savings and Asset Accumulation in Individual Development Accounts" (St. Louis: Center for Social Development, Washington University, February 2001), pp. v–6.

4. See Mark Schreiner, "Resources Used to Produce Individual Development Accounts in the First Two Years of the Experimental Program of the American Dream Demonstration at the Community Action Project of Tulsa County" (St. Louis: Center for Social Development, Washington University, 2000). See also Michael Sherraden, "On Costs and the Future of Individual Development Accounts" (St. Louis: Center for Social Development, Washington University, October 2000).

5. See Edward Scanlon and Deborah Page-Adams, "Effects of Asset Holding on Neighborhoods, Families, and Children: A Review of Research," in CFED,

"Building Assets: A Report on the Asset Development and IDA Field" (Washington: Corporation for Enterprise Development, September 2001).

6. Oliver and Shapiro, *Black Wealth/White Wealth*, p. 2.

7. Sherraden recounts these events in "From Research to Policy."

8. Ibid., p. 4.

9. Robert E. Friedman, *The Safety Net as Ladder: Transfer Payments and Economic Development* (Washington: Council of State Policy and Planning Agencies, 1988).

10. "Interest Grows in Assisted Savings Plans; Popular Anti-Poverty Tool Gets $15 Million Ford Foundation Boost," *Washington Post*, April 25, 1997.

11. www.idanetwork.org.

12. More information about the demonstration can be found in Michael Sherraden and others, "Savings Patterns in IDA Programs" (St. Louis: Center for Social Development, Washington University, January 2000).

13. For details on the rules of the individual programs, see Schreiner and others, "Savings and Asset Accumulation in Individual Development Accounts," app. C.

14. According to unpublished evaluation data compiled by the Center for Social Development, the Heart of America Family Services program ranked among the top three of the thirteen demonstration sites in terms of savings levels during the first year of the American Dream Demonstration.

15. Figures from Heart of America Family Services, "Total IDA Accumulation Summary," MIS IDA.

16. Sherraden and others, "Savings Patterns in IDA Programs," app. A, p. 109.

17. See Amanda Moore and others, "Saving, IDA Programs, and Effects of IDAs: A Survey of Participants" (St. Louis: Center for Social Development, Washington University, January 2001).

18. For details, see Karen Edwards and Carl Rist, "IDA State Policy Guide: Advancing Public Policies in Support of Individual Development Accounts" (Washington: Corporation for Enterprise Development, 2001).

19. Ibid., p. 3.

20. Details on the Savings for Working Families Act of 2001 are current as of February 2002.

21. The lower estimate and rate for African American households come from Jean Hogarth and J. Lee, "Banking Relationships of Low to Moderate-Income Households: Evidence from the 1995 and 1998 Surveys of Consumer Finances" (paper presented at the Inclusion in Asset Building: Research and Policy Symposium, Center for Social Development, Washington University, St. Louis, September 21–23, 2000). The higher estimate comes from Stacie Carney and William G. Gale, "Asset Accumulation among Low-Income Households," in Shapiro and Wolff, *Assets for the Poor*.

22. Peter Tufano, remarks at the National IDA Conference, Washington, March 8, 2001.

23. Unpublished research on the Family Asset Building program provided by Marcia Schobe.

24. Tom Riley, "Individual Development Accounts: Downpayments on the American Dream," *Philanthropy* (January–February 1999).

25. Testimony of Ray Boshara, policy director, Corporation for Enterprise Development, to the Subcommittee on Select Revenue Measures and Human Resources, Committee on Ways and Means, hearing on H.R. 7, the Community Solutions Act (June 14, 2001).

26. The 2001 IDA Champion Award recipients were Senator Joseph Lieberman (D-Conn.), Senator Rick Santorum (R-Pa.), Representative Joseph Pitts (R-Pa.), Representative Charlie Stenholm (D-Tex.), Senator Mary Landrieu (D-La.), Senator Charles Grassley (R-Iowa), Senator Tom Harkin (D-Iowa), Senator Judd Gregg (R-N.H.), Representative Nancy Pelosi (D-Calif.), and Representative Rosa L. DeLaura (D-Conn.).

Epilogue

1. Clark and Kays, *Microenterprise and the Poor*, p. ix.

2. Mark O. Wilhelm, "The Role of Intergenerational Transfers in Spreading Asset Ownership," in Shapiro and Wolff, *Assets for the Poor*.

3. J. Larry Brown and Larry W. Beeferman, "From New Deal to New Opportunity," *American Prospect,* vol. 12 (February 12, 2001).

4. Testimony of Ray Boshara.

Index